Connected Medical Devices: Integrating Patient Care Data in Healthcare Systems

John Zaleski, PhD, CPHIMS

HIMSS Mission
To globally lead endeavors optimizing health engagements and care outcomes through information technology.

© 2015 by the Healthcare Information and Management Systems Society (HIMSS).

Printed in the U.S.A. 5 4 3 2 1

Requests for permission to reproduce any part of this work should be sent to:
Permissions Editor
HIMSS
33. W. Monroe St., Ste. 1700
Chicago, IL 60603
nancy.vitucci@himssmedia.com

ISBN: 978-1-938904-78-3

For more information about HIMSS, please visit www.himss.org.

About the Author

John Zaleski, PhD, CPHIMS, brings more than 25 years of experience in researching and ushering to market devices and products to improve healthcare. Dr. Zaleski received his PhD from the University of Pennsylvania, with a dissertation that describes a novel approach for modeling and prediction of post-operative respiratory behavior in post-surgical cardiac patients. Dr. Zaleski has a particular expertise in designing, developing, and implementing clinical and non-clinical point-of-care applications for hospital enterprises. Dr. Zaleski is the named inventor or co-inventor on seven issued patents related to medical device interoperability. He is the author of numerous peer-reviewed articles on clinical use of medical device data, information technology and medical devices and wrote two seminal books on integrating medical device data into electronic health records and the use of medical device data for clinical decision making.

Acknowledgements

The author thanks Mr. Kenneth Fuchs, M.Eng, MBA, a friend and colleague of many years, for his review and insight of topics presented in Chapter 4. As of this writing, Ken's current position is Executive Vice President, Interoperability R&D at the Center for Medical Interoperability (http://www.medicalinteroperability.org).

Contents

List of Figures

List Of Tables

Table No.	Caption	Page No.
Table 7-1	Hazard Severity versus Probability of Occurrence. Hazard = Severity x Probability of Occurrence.	162
Table 7-2	Listing of 80001-related Documents.	164
Table A1-1	Example MDI Solution Provider Costing and Quantity Planning Tool.	169
Table A3-1	simMain User Interface Features.	176
Table A3-2	Definitions of *simMain* Parameter Display Fields.	177
Table A3-3	Example HL7 Output from Simulator.	178
Table A3-4	Saved Preferences File ("patient_profile.txt") Containing Simulated Patient Demographic Data and Parameter Settings Data.	179

Acronyms Used in This Book

Acronym	Term
A/C or AC	Assist/Control
AAMI	Association for the Advancement of Medical Instrumentation
ABP	Arterial blood pressure
ACK	Acknowledgement
ACM	Alert Communication Management
ADT	Admission-Discharge-Transfer
AIMS	Anesthesia Information Management System
AL-VNT	Alveolar Ventilation
AOBP	Aortic Blood Pressure
API	Application Programming Interface
APN	Apnea
APN-T	Apnea Time
APRV	Airway Pressure Release Ventilation
ASB	Assisted Spontaneous Breath
ASCII	American Standard Code for Information Interchange
AWP	Airway Pressure
BIPAP	Biphasic Positive Airway Pressure
BIS	Bi-spectral Index
BME	Biomedical Engineering / Biomedical Engineer
BSA	Body Surface Area
BS-FLW	Base Flow
CABG	Coronary Artery Bypass Grafting
CAP	College of American Pathologists
CCI	Continuous Cardiac Index
CCO	Continuous Cardiac Output
CCU	Cardiac Care Unit
C-DYN	Dynamic Compliance
CE	Clinical Engineering/Clinical Engineer
CI	Cardiac Index
CIS	Clinical Information System

Acronym	Term
CMD	Connected Medical Device
CMS	Central Monitoring Station
CMV	Continuous Mandatory Ventilation
CO	Cardiac Output
COMP	Compliance
COW	Computer On Wheels (see WOW)
CPOE	Computerized Provider Order Entry
CPP	Cerebral Perfusion Pressure
CPPV	Continuous Positive Pressure Ventilation
CRNA	Certified Registered Nurse Anesthetist
C-STAT	Static Compliance
CT	Consistent Time or Computed Tomography
CVP	Central Venous Pressure
DCA	Data Collection Appliance
DEC	Device Enterprise Communication
DHCP	Dynamic Host Configuration Protocol
DICOM	Digital Imaging and Communications in Medicine
DOC	Device Observation Consumer
DOR	Device Observation Reporter
D-RAW	Dynamic Resistance (see RAW)
eAGNT	Expired Agent
ECG / EKG	Electrocardiogram / Electrocardiography
ECRI	Emergency Care Research Institute
ED	Emergency Department
eDES	Expired Desflurane
EEG	Electroencephalogram
eENF	Expired Enflurane
EFLW	End Flow
eHAL	Expired Halothane
eHE	Expired Helium
EHR	Electronic Health Record
eISO	Expired Isoflurane
EMIT	Enterprise MDI Integration Team
ETCO2	End-tidal CO_2
ETT	Endotracheal Tube
EXP-T	Expiratory Time
FDA	U.S. Food and Drug Administration

Acronym	Term
FEM	Femoral Artery Pressure
FGF	Fresh Gas Flow
FHIR®	Fast Healthcare Interoperability Resources
FICO2	Fractional Concentration of Inspired CO2
FIO2	Fractional Concentration of Inspired Oxygen
FLW	Flow
FLW-RT	Flow Rate
FRC	Functional Residual Capacity
GE	General Electric
GMP	Good Manufacturing Processes / Good Manufacturing Practice
HAI	Hospital Acquired Infection
HFO	High Frequency Oscillation
HF-PP	High Frequency Peak-to-Peak Pressure
HFV	High Frequency Ventilation
HIMSS	Healthcare Information and Management Systems Society
HIPAA	Health Insurance Portability and Accountability Act
HIT	Health Information Technology
HL7	Health Level Seven®
HP	Hewlett Packard
HR	Heart Rate or Pulse
Ht	Height
I:E or IE	Inspiratory : Expiratory Ratio
IABP	Intra-Aortic Balloon Pump
iAGNT	Inspired Agent
ICE	Integrated Clinical Environment
ICP	Intracranial Pressure
ICU	Intensive Care Unit
IDCO	Implantable Device – Cardiac Observation
iDES	Inspired Desflurane
IEC	International Electrotechnical Commission
IEE or IE-E or I:E-E	Expiratory Component of IE Ratio
IEEE	Institute for Electrical and Electronics Engineers
IEI or IE-I or I:E-I	Inspiratory Component of IE Ratio
iENF	Inspired Enflurane
iHAL	Inspired Halothane
IHE	Integrating the Healthcare Enterprise®
iHE	Inspired Helium

Acronym	Term
IHTSDO	International Health Terminology Standards Development Organization
IIC	Intellivue Information Center
iISO	Inspired Isoflurane
ILV	Independent Lung Ventilation
IMDIS	Interoperable Medical Devices Interface Standards
IN-HLD or INSP-HLD or INSP-HOLD	Inspiratory Hold
INSP-T	Inspiratory Time
IP	Inspiratory Pressure
IPEC	Infusion Pump Event Communication
I-PEEP	Intrinsic Peep
I-PEEPT	Intrinsic PEEP Time
IPPV	Intermittent Positive Pressure Ventilation
IRV	Inversed Ratio Ventilation
ISO	International Organization for Standardization
IT	Information Technology
Kg	Kilogram
L&D	Labor and Delivery
LAN	Local Area Network
LAP	Left Atrial Pressure
LONS	Late Onset Neonatal Sepsis
LVP	Left Ventricular Pressure
LVSW	Left Ventricular Stroke Work
LVSWI	Left Ventricular Stroke Work Index
MAC	Mean Alveolar Concentration
MAWP	Mean Airway Pressure
MCP	Maximum Circuit Pressure
MDC	Medical Device Connectivity
MDD	Medical Device Data
MDDS	Medical Device Data System
MDI	Medical Device Integration / Medical Device Intermediary / Medical Device Interoperability
MDICC	Medical Device Interoperability Coordinating Council
MDS	Medical Device System
MFLW	Maximum Inspiratory Flow
MIB	Medical Information Bus
MICU	Medical Intensive Care Unit

Acronym	Term
MMV	Mandatory Minute Volume
MPAP	Mean Pulmonary Artery (Wedge) Pressure
MSA	HL7 Message Acknowledgement
MSH	HL7 Message Header Segment
MU	Meaningful Use
MV	Minute Volume (or Minute Ventilation)
MVe or MV-EXP	Expired or Exhaled Minute Volume
MVi or MV-IN	Inspired or Inhaled Component of Minute Volume
MVm or MMV	Mandatory Minute Volume
MVsp or SPO-MV	Spontaneous Minute Volume
MVt or MV-TOT	Total Minute Volume
N2O	Nitrous Oxide
NACK	Negative Acknowledgement
NBP or NiBP	Non-invasive Blood Pressure / Non-Invasive Blood Pressure
NEMA	National Electrical Manufacturers Association
NICU	Neonatal Intensive Care Unit
NIP	Negative Inspiratory Pressure
NIST	National Institute of Standards and Technology
NIV	Non-Invasive Ventilation
NLM	National Library of Medicine
NTP	Network Time Protocol
O2	Oxygen
OBR	HL7 Observation Request Segment
OBX	HL7 Observation / Result Segment
OCL-AWP	Airway Occlusion Pressure
OR	Operating Room
ORF	HL7 Observational Report Response
ORU	HL7 Unsolicited Observation Result
OTS	Off-the-shelf (computing hardware)
PA	Proportional Assist
PaCO2	Partial Pressure of Carbon Dioxide in Artrial Blood
PACU	Post Anesthesia Care Unit
PAOP	Pulmonary Artery Occlusion Pressure
PAP	Pulmonary Artery Pressure
PAWP	Pulmonary Artery Wedge Pressure
PB	Puritan Bennett™
PC	Pressure Control

Acronym	Term
PCD	Patient Care Device
PCD-TF	Patient Care Device-Technical Framework
PCHA	Personal Connected Health Alliance
PDI	Parameter Data Interface
PEEP	Positive End-Expiratory Pressure
PEF	Peak Expiratory Flow
PHD	Personal Health Device
PICU	Pediatric Intensive Care Unit
PID	Patient Identifier
PIF	Peak Inspiratory Flow
PIIC	Philips Intellivue Information Center (see IIC)
PIP	Peak Inspiratory Pressure
PIV	Point-of-care Infusion Verification
PLV	Pressure-Limited Ventilation
POC	Point of care
PP/ACA	Patient Protection and Affordable Care Act
PPLAT or PLAT	Plateau Pressure
PPS	Proportional Pressure Support
PSENS	Pressure Sensitivity
PSUP	Support Pressure
PSV	Pressure Support Ventilation
PV1	HL7 Patient Visit Segment # 1
PVC	Premature Ventricular Contraction
PVR	Pulmonary Vascular Resistance
PVRI	Pulmonary Vascular Resistance Index
QRD	HL7 Query Definition
QRF	HL7 Query Filter
QRY	HL7 Query Message
QSR	Quality System Regulations
RAP	Right Atrial Pressure
RAW	Airway Resistance
REST	Representational State Transfer
RFC	Request For Change
RFI	Request for Information
RFID	Radio Frequency Identification
RFP	Request for Proposal
RJ	Registered Jack

Acronym	Term
RR	Respiratory Rate
RRm	Mandatory, or Mechanical Ventilator Setting Component, of Respiratory Rate
RR-SET	Respiratory Rate Setting
RRsp or SPO-RR	Spontaneous, or Patient Component, of Respiratory Rate
RRt or TOT-RR	Total Respiratory Rate
RTM	Requirements Traceability Matrix
RTSB	Transcutaneous Bilirubinometry
RVSW	Right Ventricular Stroke Work
RVSWI	Right Ventricular Stroke Work Index
SB	Spontaneous Breathing
SDK	Software Development Kit
SDLC	Software Development Life Cycle
SDO	Standards Developing Organization
SICU	Surgical Intensive Care Unit
SIMV	Synchronous Intermittent Mandatory Ventilation
SNOMED CT	Systematized Nomenclature of Medicine – Clinical Terms
SPN	Spontaneous/Assisted
SPONT	Spontaneous
SQI	Signal Quality Index
SV	Stroke Volume
SVI	Stroke Volume Index
SVMAX	Maximum Stroke Volume
SVMEAN	Mean Stroke Volume
SVMIN	Minimum Stroke Volume
SVR	Systemic Vascular Resistance
SVRI	Systemic Vascular Resistance Index
SVV	Stroke Volume Variation
TACFR	Tachypnea Frequency
TC	Tube Compensated
TCP/IP	Transmission Control Protocol / Internet Protocol
tcpCO2	Transcutaneous CO_2 Pressure
TIR	Technical Information Report
TRG	Trigger
TV	Tidal Volume
TVe or Vt-e	Expired or Exhaled Component of Tidal Volume
TVi or Vt-i	Inspired or Inhaled Component of Tidal Volume
TVm or Vt-m	Mandatory Tidal Volume

Acronym	Term
TVsp or SPO-TV or Vt-sp	Spontaneous Tidal Volume
UACP	Umbilical Arterial Catheter Pressure
UCUM	Unified Code for Units of Measure
UDI	Universal Device Identifier
UDP	User Datagram Protocol
UL	Underwriters Laboratories
UOM	Unit of Measure
UPC	Universal Product Code
USB	Universal Serial Bus
UTC	Universal Coordinated Time
UVCP	Umbilical Venous Catheter Pressure
VAP	Ventilator Acquired Pneumonia/Ventilator Associated Pneumonia
VC	Volume Control Ventilation Mode (also stands for Vital Capacity)
VD/VT	Ratio of Dead Space to Tidal Volume
VDS	Dead Space Volume
VMD	Virtual Medical Device
VNT-LEAK	Ventilator Leakage
WAN	Wide Area Network
WHO	World Health Organization
WOB	Work of Breathing
WOW	Workstation On Wheels

Introduction

OVERVIEW OF MEDICAL DEVICE INTEROPERABILITY (MDI) AND THE CURRENT STATE OF THE MDI INDUSTRY

WHAT IS MDI AND WHY IS IT NEEDED?

Integrating medical device data (MDD) into health information technology (health IT) systems was at one time an esoteric need, of primary interest only to those conducting research in the healthcare environment. Over the course of the past decade, and in part due to the focus on patient safety and Meaningful Use (MU) guidelines, Medical Device Interoperability/Integration (MDI) has become a significant part of mainstream health IT system deployment and a key requirement:

> "The 2012 U.S. Medical Device Integration (MDI) Study, involving insight from >300 hospitals and vendors, indicates that >54% of U.S. hospitals plan to purchase new Medical Device Integration (MDI) solutions and 40% cite quality improvement as the primary investment driver."[1,2]

Furthermore, studies[3] have estimated that:

> "Each Connected Medical Device (CMD) saves from 4 to 36 minutes of nursing time and prevents up to 24 data errors daily. CMDs can save over 100 hours of nursing time per day in a typical hospital..."

The time required to manually collect and chart data derived from medical devices is not insignificant, with the passage of minutes per measurement not uncommon in the enterprise high-acuity settings of critical care, anesthesia, and other areas—areas in which regular charting of findings derived from medical devices is required per the plan of care and practice of medicine.[4] Hence, the value of connecting medical devices to the IT infrastructure is being recognized institutionally.

This book is intended to be a practical treatment of the process of implementing an MDI solution within a healthcare enterprise. In the context discussed here, MDI refers to the communication of data from connected medical devices to end-point recipients such as electronic health record systems (EHRs), data warehouses, standalone clinical information systems (CISs) and related health IT systems. The most general term for each health IT system will be used throughout this text.

The interoperability of medical devices refers to the ability of these devices to interact with one another to achieve some clinical purpose or use case. The Association for the Advancement of Medical Instrumentation (AAMI) offers the following definition of interoperability in the context of medical devices:[5]

> "...[the] ability of medical devices, clinical systems, or their components to communicate in order to safely fulfill an intended purpose."

In the context presented here, the terms interoperability and integration will be used synonymously. The integration of connected medical device data will refer, for the purpose of this text, to the extraction, translation, conditioning and communication of medical device data for use within a health IT system.

While creation and implementation of software and hardware to achieve MDI is an essential element, this text is not focused on the writing of software—such as medical device drivers, which enable the communication of medical device data through their proprietary language mechanisms. Creation of medical device drivers is outside the scope of this text. One source that provides some detail (including software) as examples of such has been developed by the author and is included as a reference.[6]

While the usual purpose of MDI is to communicate discrete data from medical devices normally employed as part of the workflow at the point of care (POC) to the health IT system, this use is not the only one, or not even the most interesting use of data from medical devices at the POC. MDI helps to remove the manual and error-prone aspects of the recording MDD: introduction of error due to misinterpretation, errors due to transcription, and errors due to associating information from one patient with that of another. So, from the patient safety perspective, MDI aids in ensuring that data are collected regularly and more accurately on any given patient and that they are communicated reliably to the end-point health IT system. Hence, the availability of rich and timely data derived from medical devices helps to improve the knowledge of patient state, thereby facilitating better clinical decision making.

This statement seems to be logical. But what evidence exists to sustain the assertion that MDI benefits patient care?

The Medical Device Interoperability Coordinating Council (MDICC) and the Westhealth™ Institute published an assessment in March 2013 ("The Value of Medical Device Interoperability") in which they asserted that the intrinsic value in MDI can liberate $30B+ in annual healthcare savings, principally drawn from improvements in patient safety.[7]

In addition, a recent InformationWeek Healthcare article asserted:[8]

> "...44% of the nearly 300 responding hospitals said they had purchased an MDI application in recent years. The majority of those purchases were made in 2011 and 2012."

Furthermore,

> "...the adoption of MDI solutions [is expected] to continue to accelerate over the next two years as more than half of U.S. hospitals plan to purchase new MDI solutions."[9]

The value of MDI has received more publicity and a higher profile in recent years. In 2012, the U.S. Food and Drug Administration (FDA) and AAMI convened a joint summit focused on seeking industry input as part of a "multidisciplinary 'learning event'" aimed at identifying and prioritizing issues in MDI.[10] One of the key questions asked was "why interoperability? Why now?"

> *"The advancement and availability of new technologies, coupled with a growing number of serious public health concerns and adverse patient events in which interoperability issues have been [at] root cause... Many events, publications, and conversations have focused on the information side of what technology can do. Little attention to date has been focused on the device side of that connectivity, especially as it relates to patient safety."[11]*

Other uses for data derived through MDI are related to clinical decision making:

> *"[d]ata need to support clinical decision-making, patient safety, and patient care:*
>
> - *Rich, timely data for patient care management;*
> - *Temporally and semantically synchronized data to ensure accuracy in patient management; and*
> - *Secure, ubiquitous access to ensure availability to data for patient care management."[12]*

Distilling the key reasons to the following, MDI supports very pragmatic and real needs to improve patient care and patient safety, including

- reducing clinical documentation transcription errors
- improving data accuracy and density within the clinical records
- ensuring the complete capture of patient care data

Those individuals tasked with implementing MDI within the hospital inpatient setting may have not been previously exposed to the process, technologies or implementation details and, so, are looking at ways to "bootstrap" the process or, at least for a starting or jumping off point for the process. The objective in the pages that follow is to provide constructive guidance toward this end.

CONTENT OVERVIEW

We begin by providing an overview of the chapters to follow, their content, and what will be presented.

Introduction

- The Mechanics of MDI
- Medical Device Driver Software
- The MDI Intermediary between the Medical Device and the Health IT System
- Major MDI Solution Providers
- Vendor Agnostic Representation of MDI Solutions
- Some Tips on Selecting an MDI Solution

Chapter 4: Standards Surrounding Medical Device Integration to Health IT Systems

- Medical Device Standards Specific to Medical Device Integration
- Health Level Seven (HL7) Standards Developing Organization
- IEEE 11073 Medical/Personal Health Device
- Health Level Seven (HL7) Observation Reporting
- Conditioning and Translating Connected Medical Device Data for IT System Consumption
- Patient Administration
- A Few Words About HL7 Fast Health Interoperable Resources
- Integrating the Healthcare Enterprise® (IHE)
- Other Medical Device Integration-Related Standards

Chapter 5: Notification, Alerts & Clinical Uses of Medical Device Data

- Interface Health and Status Notification and Technical Alerts
- Clinical Alerts and Notifications
- Aperiodic versus Periodic Data Collection
- Clinical Uses of Medical Device Data

Chapter 6: Patient Identification and Medical Device Association

- Methods for Patient Identification
- Barcode and RFID
- Medical Device Association Workflows

Chapter 7: Regulatory and Security Considerations of MDI

- Medical Device Data Systems (MDDS)
- Regulatory Classification and Identification of Risk
- Medical Device Security
- IEC 80001
- Software Development Methodologies and Testing

Appendix

- Appendix 1: Medical Device Quantity Planning Table
- Appendix 2: Testing Tools
- Appendix 3: HL7 Testing Simulator

THE MECHANICS OF MDI

The physical and logical connectivity and communication from medical devices in general is still a long way from adhering to an off-the-shelf standard. Some medical devices communicate over local area networks (LANs), either through hardwiring or through wireless communication (i.e., via 802.11 a/b/g, or n protocols). Other medical devices only communicate over serial ports. Whether communicating over LAN or serial port, there currently is no manufacturing mandate that dictates to which specific physical and logical communications protocols medical devices must adhere.

However, there are published standards, such as the Institute for Electrical and Electronics Engineering (IEEE) 11073™ standards, Health Level Seven® (HL7) standards, Integrating the Healthcare Enterprise® (IHE) Patient Care Device (PCD) domain implementation profiles and related standards and profiles. These can guide manufacturers as to how a medical device should or must communicate to achieve more seamless interoperability with health IT systems. More details regarding these specific standards will be discussed in Chapter 4.

The aforementioned industry organizations are attempting to guide more standardized data communication (e.g., IHE, HL7, AAMI, Continua et al.) among medical device equipment, sometimes referred to as patient care devices (PCDs).

Ultimately, the mechanics of MDI is very much a manufacturer decision. More and more manufacturers have recognized the business reasons for enabling and providing more standardized data communications from their medical devices. While many manufacturers are evolving toward more standardized modes of medical device data communication, there is no specific or singular method or industry conformance requirement that is mandated as part of a general manufacturing standard for communication. Ergo, some manufacturers have employed their own proprietary mechanisms for medical device data export.

Because the mechanics of data export communication can vary (i.e., LAN versus serial port), MDI intermediaries that can translate and transform data from their more vendor-proprietary and specific formats and data communications export mechanisms into more traditionally acceptable media and formats have emerged. Companies that provide this intermediary type of function have arisen over the years. These companies, or MDI solution providers, offer hardware and software that may be placed between the medical device and the end-point health IT system. The MDI solutions are usually referred to as medical device middleware within these environments.

The traditional approach of the MDI solution provider is to employ both hardware and software to assist in the medical device communication by providing the translation mechanism from the vendor-specific, proprietary communication formats (i.e., both physical mechanism and data or semantic communication) into more usable formats consistent with the needs of end-point data capture systems. The MDI solution providers typically offer these intermediaries as POC hardware and software, sometimes using physical appliances at the POC, to perform this data translation and communication function. These hardware and software appliances serve in the role of querying for data from the medical devices by connecting with them using the proprietary mechanism required for the particular medical device (e.g., serial port). They then communicate the received data through a more standardized physical connection (e.g., LAN) on the enterprise network. In addition, data are translated from their (usually) unformatted text-based or binary formats into standardized messaging formats (e.g., HL7) that can be received through normally accepted application layer communication means by the health IT system. The hardware appliances that communicate with the medical devices could be a computer that provides serial port communication (or through a universal serial bus interconnection) or a proprietary, vendor-specific appliance or device used for this dedicated purpose. The approaches are unique to the MDI solution provider.

As it is assumed that this book's target audience has minimal knowledge of the MDI process, a basic overview of the physics of data communication is included. The reader who is more versed in this subject matter may skim over this material as a review.

Some medical devices will provide a data export communication mechanism via a serial port, usually located in the back of the medical device. In such cases, the medical device will usually provide a serial port in one of several form factors (e.g., 9-pin, 15-pin, 25-pin) to which a standard serial adapter may be attached. In other cases, the medical device will provide a universal serial bus (USB) port for data communication and will promote data communication access either through a serial-to-USB translation adapter or through a proprietary USB communication protocol that may be accessed via custom software coding specified through a software development kit (SDK) offered by the medical device manufacturer.

Some of these serial adapters allow for use of an RJ45 networking cable to provide a pin-out translation from the standard RS232 class serial adapter to an RJ45 networking cable. An example of the use of an RS232 serial port adapter that employs a networking cable is illustrated in the photographs of the Datascope Passport® V monitor shown in Figure 1.

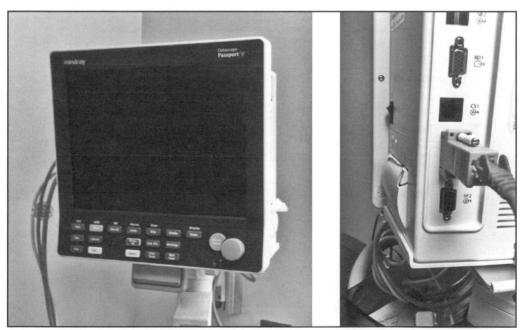

Figure 1: Medical Device (Datascope Passport® V) Serial Port Communication Port Using a Serial Adapter with an RJ45 Cat5e Network Cable.

(Photo by Author)

The physical pin-outs of the RS232 adapters can vary by medical device but more often than not are of either the serial or null modem variety. Figure 2 illustrates the pin-out associated with a serial adapter attached to a Fresenius dialysis machine.

Figure 2: Fresenius Dialysis Machine with Serial Port Adapter Opened to Show Example RS232 9-pin Adapter Configuration.

(Photo by Author)

The difference between standard serial and null modem adapters is in the wiring of the send and receive pins on the RS232 adapter: straight through or transmit and receive crossed. An example of the pin-out difference is illustrated in Figure 3, which depicts the 9-pin RS232 adapter null modem and serial configurations. In many of these serial port implementations, simple Transmit-Receive-Ground pin-outs are all that are required and can be accomplished using serial or null-modem adapter implementations.

The medical device manufacturer will typically provide its particular serial port communication specification upon request or as part of its service documentation.

In addition to the physical communication characteristics, the connection speed of the medical device together with instructions on how to configure the medical device will typically be provided by the medical device manufacturer. Some medical device manufacturers will equip their medical devices with RJ45 (i.e., registered jack) ports, over which serial data communication is provided. In these situations, the medical device communicates using a serial protocol but with the physical form factor of an RJ45 adapter, similar to those used for LAN communication. Other form factors may be offered (e.g., RJ12) as well, while still adhering to serial port communication protocols.

Examples of the speed and serial protocol specifications are the following:
- 9600-N-8-1 (i.e., 9600 bits-per-second – no parity - 8 bits – 1 stop bit)
- 19200-E-8-1 (i.e., 19200 bits-per-second – even parity – 8 bits – 1 stop bit)
- 115200-O-8-1 (i.e., 115200 bits-per-second – odd parity – 8 bits – 1 stop bit)

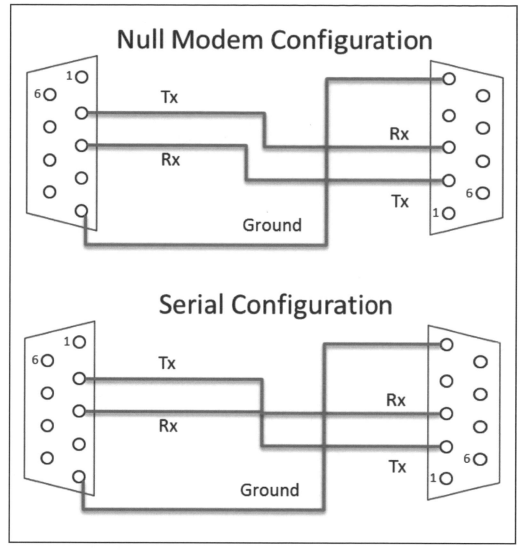

Figure 3: Null Modem versus Straight Pin Configuration (9-pin RS232 adapters).

Some medical devices, such as the Philips Intellivue MP5 and MP30 physiologic monitors shown in Figure 4 communicate using an RJ45 form-factor serial cable on the serial port and can also communicate using a network cable via the LAN port. The LAN port of many physiologic monitors is provided so that they can communicate on high-speed proprietary networks to central monitoring stations (CMS). Hence, these ports are usually reserved for that communication, although access to discrete vital signs data can be received via manufacturer gateway software that can translate these data to more standardized formats on the enterprise network. A discussion of these gateways is provided in Chapter 1.

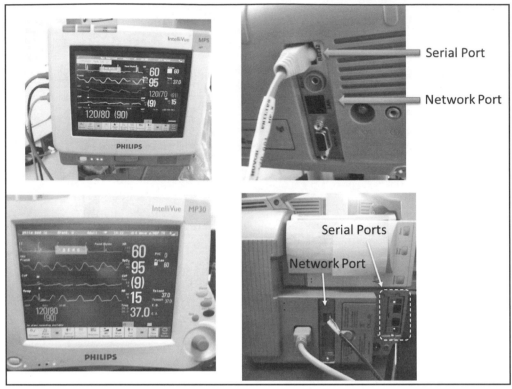

Figure 4: Philips MP5 Intellivue (Upper) and MP30 Physiologic Monitor Serial and Local Area Network Communication Ports.
(Photo by Author)

In cases such as these where physical ports are provided for data access, many medical devices can be queried either over the serial or the LAN port. These ports may be reserved for certain applications. For instance, the LAN port may be reserved for CMS use and telemetry monitoring.

Thus, when considering data communication for health IT system consumption, care should be taken to verify that the available data ports through which medical devices communicate are available for this purpose and not otherwise allocated for other objectives.

As a final note on the topic of physical connectors or adapters, Figure 5 illustrates a selection of serial port adapters for various medical devices. These RS232 adapters range from 25-, 15-, to 9-pin male and female types.

MEDICAL DEVICE DRIVER SOFTWARE

The MDI solution communicates with the medical device using a language or via queries that are tailored to the specifics of the particular medical device, described by the manufacturer's specifications. These queries are normally instantiated in the form of software that can operate on either standalone POC appliances or on multi-purpose computing hardware that is collocated with the medical devices. The queries from the MDI solution POC appliance and the medical device are relayed to the medical device using medical device driver software ("device drivers") that automatically query the particular medical device. The correct communication protocols must be established between the device driver software physical appliance and the medical device so that communication can be initiated. This implies the correct baud rate, parity, stop bits (assuming serial), and the appropriate networking protocols (e.g., TCP/IP, UDP, Multicast) with correct IP addressing and networking communication ports.

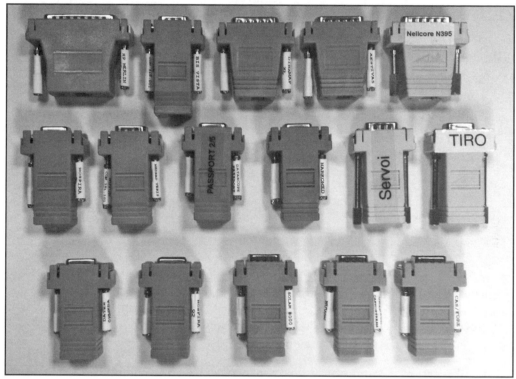

Figure 5: Various Serial Port Adapters for Communication with Medical Devices.

Top row: HP Merlin Physiologic Monitor; Covidien BIS Vista™; GE Dinamap XL Monitor; GE Aestiva/5 Anesthesia Machine; Nellcor N-395 Monitor; *Middle row:* Hospira Q2™ Plus CCO/SO2 Monitor (also shown bottom row, 2nd from left); Medrad® Veris® MRI Monitor; Datascope Passport® II & Passport® V Monitor; Narkomed GS Anesthesia Machine; Siemens (later Maquet) Servo-i® Mechanical Ventilator; Draeger Fabius® Tiro® Anesthesia Machine; *Bottom row:* Datex Ohmeda Anesthesia Machine; GE Solar™ 8000M/I Monitor (third from left); Covidien Capnostream® 20; Casmed Fore-Sight® Cerebral Tissue Oxygenation Saturation Monitor. (Photo by Author)

The query responses are then translated (possibly by the device drivers) into the more commonly accepted and readable syntax for the health IT system, or into a text-based output that can then be further parsed and conditioned for the health IT system or other recipient health IT systems.

Medical device drivers are peculiar to the medical device under inquiry. Hence, the need for medical device drivers for each type or class of medical device are required to accomplish data communication from the medical devices within a healthcare enterprise and the receiving health IT system. MDI solution providers usually maintain libraries of these medical device drivers, and these drivers require maintenance to accommodate updates in medical device firmware and general corrections associated with software defects and bugs. Medical device drivers are, of course, software and, hence, are subject to the same bugs and defects as any other software. MDI solution providers perform a process of unit, system and regression testing to ensure that the device drivers themselves are as error free as they can be determined to be before implementation within a healthcare enterprise. Furthermore, as most MDI solutions must adhere to FDA quality system development standards, they should be developed, managed, and updated in accordance with FDA quality system regulations (QSR).[13]

MDI INTERMEDIARY BETWEEN THE MEDICAL DEVICE AND THE HEALTH IT SYSTEM

At its most basic level, MDI involves translating data from medical devices at the POC to health IT systems. This is illustrated in Figure 6.

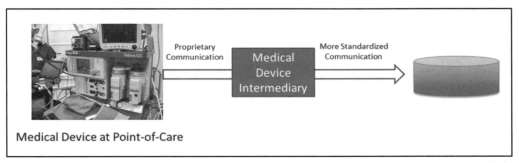

Figure 6: Basic Topology of Communicating Medical Device Data from the POC to an EHR or Health IT System Using a Medical Device Intermediary that Bridges the Proprietary Interface to a More Standardized Interface Readily Acceptable to the Receiving System.

The illustration shows the basic components involved in communication from the medical device (in this case, the example medical device is an anesthesia machine— Dräger Fabius® GS Premium) to the health IT system or Data Warehouse. The "black box" between the medical device is termed the Medical Device Intermediary—the translation technology that takes the data from the medical device in its rather proprietary form and translates into a more standardized form—usually HL7 unsolicited or solicited observation results. These can be received through an appropriately provisioned inbound networking port by the health IT system.

The Medical Device Intermediary comprises the functional hardware and software that provides the physical, data, and semantic linkage from the medical device to the system intended to receive the data. Because many of the medical devices that are used at the POC provide for rather limited or non-scalable data communication (i.e., RS-232 serial point-to-point communication), to share data across the care continuum, the data must be made publishable and interpretable by these end-point systems.

This process of data and information communication must take advantage of the available health enterprise communication mechanisms (e.g., enterprise networking) to be scalable across the entire healthcare enterprise. Ergo, proprietary or "one-off" methods and physical communication mechanisms for communicating from medical devices to health IT systems are non-starters for practical data communication. As many medical devices do not provide for common data standards for communication, the MDI becomes a necessity in either hardware, or software, or combination form as that scalable mechanism.

There are some types of medical devices that provide for their own MDIs: that is, the proprietary data communication directed from the medical device itself is translated into a more common format (e.g., HL7) that is then published through a single interface (usually, network-based Transmission Control Protocol/Internet Protocol [TCP/IP] over Ethernet). In such cases, the medical devices themselves communicate via their vendor-specific proprietary data formats to their own data concentrator or gateway. Many critical care and high acuity physiologic monitors communicate in this way through their own physiologic monitoring gateways. Then, data are translated into the more common format appropriate for receipt by the end-user system and transmitted at some pre-defined interval. The actual data communications from the monitoring gateways to the health IT system take advantage of the enterprise network using standardized communication protocols.

While many of these medical devices (e.g., anesthesia machines, mechanical ventilators, specialty equipment such as capnography monitors, etc.) will communicate via serial port, physiologic monitors generally will have the capability to communicate both via serial ports and over LANs. In the case of LAN-based communication, physiologic monitors will communicate with their own concentrator or gateway that provides for aggregation of raw data into more standardized formats for communication to health IT systems. Both serial-port-based communication and LAN-based communication can coexist as MDI approaches within the same environment. The MDI solution providers, through their product offerings, should be able to field both types of medical device drivers and support multiple types of MDI physical communication topologies.

MAJOR MDI SOLUTION PROVIDERS

There are many MDI solutions and solution providers available today. It is not the objective of this text to dissect and discuss comparatively the benefits of individual MDI solution provider offerings. For a relative comparison among various vendors, KLAS[14] has created a series of reports that provide vendor comparisons in a number of categories. Beginning in 2011, KLAS started reporting on MDI solution provider performance for all vendors with six or more deployed and live clients. As a matter of policy and/or practice, healthcare enterprises may already consult or have consulted with KLAS for other health IT applications and so may be familiar with the process. The addition of MDI to the KLAS evaluation portfolio provides some perspective by ensuring that independent observations from deployed clients are taken into account and reported such that new healthcare enterprises considering MDI rollouts can benefit. Healthcare enterprises can gain access to these reports and are encouraged to review them for the various market segments of interest as a prerequisite to MDI solution provider selection.

The principal MDI solution providers are identified through their solution offerings in Table 1. As stated previously, comparative assessments between various MDI solution providers are available through KLAS Research.[15] In addition, a comparison of MDI solutions has been developed by The ECRI Institute.[16]

Table 1: Principle MDI Solution Providers and their Solution Offerings.

Company	Product(s)	Web Page
Capsule Technologie	Neuron, Data Captor Software, SmartLinx™	http://www.capsuletech.com/
CareTrends	careTrends® Software Platform	http://caretrendshealth.com
Cardio-pulmonary Corporation	Bernoulli® Enterprise Software Platform, single- and multi-port bridges	http://www.cardiopulmonarycorp.com/
Cerner	CareAware iBus™	http://www.cerner.com/solutions/Medical_Devices/Device_Connectivity/
Iatric Systems	Accelero Connect®	http://www.iatric.com/MedicalDeviceIntegration
iSirona (acquired by NantHealth)	DeviceConX	http://www.isirona.com
Nuvon	VEGA™ Server Software, Intelligent Device Managers, NVCS™	http://www.nuvon.com

The current list of MDI solution providers represents but a subset of the offerings on the market today. Many of these solution providers employ similar approaches to data collection and communication, with a POC component (for direct data communication from medical devices) and a server- or network-based component (for communicating from existing physiologic or infusion monitoring concentrators or gateways).

VENDOR AGNOSTIC REPRESENTATION OF MDI SOLUTIONS

Rather than focus on the implementation characteristics of particular vendor-based solutions, the objective is to walk through the process of implementing and fielding an MDI solution from the perspective of the healthcare enterprise and ensuring that the implementation goals are met. To accomplish this, the vendor-specific solutions will be modeled as black boxes. The mechanics and logistics of MDI will be the focus to provide an understanding of what medical device integration means and to provide those selecting an MDI solution provider with knowledge to make the best decision. Clearly, there are vendor-specific aspects of MDI implementation, no question. Nonetheless, the object is to lay out the integration process in terms of the medical device driver requirements (i.e., which devices require communication appliances), the data integration requirements (i.e., translating data from proprietary formats into formats required by the health IT system), and to identify aspects of integration that are independent of the particular MDI solution provider offering. Moreover, identifying the basic integration requirements, and the workflow, security, redundancy and scalability requirements, serves to raise the level of awareness as part of the overall implementation. Thus, regardless of particular MDI solution provider, the team charged with implementing an MDI solution (e.g., an Enterprise MDI Implementation Team, or EMIT) has the insight to ask effective questions of prospective MDI solution providers to ensure a successful MDI implementation that meets the needs of the healthcare enterprise.

Some Tips on Selecting an MDI Solution

Selecting an MDI solution provider is, perhaps, as important as the particular technology employed within any one MDI solution offering. The following points have been published in summary form elsewhere[2] but form a good core around which to create an MDI solution provider checklist.

During the qualification process prior to procurement, each enterprise should determine whether:

1. The MDI solution provider can meet the medical device connectivity requirements for the healthcare enterprise spaces to be integrated. Questions regarding the mechanism(s) for data collection from bedside devices, as well as semantic data translation between the POC medical devices to the health IT system should be investigated. Availability of medical device drivers should be determined, and the MDI solution provider should be able to offer a list of existing medical device drivers contained within their vendor-specific library. Specific questions follow:

   a. Does the MDI solution provider have or can the vendor create the necessary medical device drivers?

   b. If the MDI solution provider does not currently have the desired medical device drivers in its present library, how much time will be required to develop new medical device drivers?

   c. Does the medical device driver development timeline unacceptably extend the overall project timeline, or is the timeline within schedule?

   d. What are the costs for the development of new medical device drivers?

   e. Who owns the medical device drivers once completed?

   f. Are medical device drivers able to be freely shared among all such devices (i.e., within all departments) in the enterprise, or is there a licensing fee for deployment beyond one unit/department or hospital?

   g. Is there a license fee for number of medical devices for which the medical device driver can be employed?

   h. How are medical device drivers maintained, and how does the MDI solution provider receive notification of updates to medical device firmware that may impact data communication?

2. Can the MDI solution provider seamlessly scale their system from the department(s) to the entire healthcare enterprise?

   a. Does the technology easily scale upward?

   b. What are the costs of scaling upward and at what rate (e.g. linear, exponential or geometric, logarithmic, etc.)?

   c. What capital hardware and software are required to scale the MDI system from department to enterprise?

3. Is the MDI solution provider revealing all of the costs required for the implementation up front?

   a. Is the healthcare enterprise expected to carry any of the cost burdens from a procurement, management, implementation, and support perspective?

   b. If so, what are these costs?

   c. What assumptions are built into the price structure from the implementation and from a support perspective?

4. Are facilities and other logistical costs anticipated?

   a. For example, network drops required, wireless infrastructure, etc.?

   b. Are these costs built into the overall project cost from the enterprise perspective?

   c. Are the timelines for facilities modifications built into the project schedule?

5. Sometimes the assumption is made that healthcare enterprises will maintain their own or a third party HL7 integration engine. These are often used for translating departmental HL7 messaging from laboratory, patient administration, orders and pharmacy systems to support health IT system integration. MDI systems will require similar translation to more standardized formats. How does the MDI solution provider translate proprietary formats into more standardized data formats?

   a. Does the MDI solution provider offer model or default translations and mappings of existing medical device parameters through an interface engine that they provide, or is a third-party interface or integration engine required as part of the offering?

   b. Can the MDI solution provider support direct interfaces to health IT systems?

   c. Is there a possibility to leverage an existing interface engine already in use within the environment?

   d. What are the costs to create new inbound communication ports to the health IT system?

   e. Who is required to manage the interface between the MDI solution provider's system and the health IT system?

6. What is the requirement for hardware at the POC?

    a. Does the MDI solution provider have a proprietary data collection appliance that is used for serial port data retrieval from medical devices, or does the vendor use off-the-shelf (OTS) computing hardware?

    b. What are the security requirements of the healthcare enterprise, and can the offering of the MDI solution provider meet these requirements?

    c. How are data protected as they are collected and transmitted from the POC (e.g., encrypted or otherwise secured) to the health IT system?

    d. What are the power, operating system software, and other requirements associated with the data collection appliances?

    e. Will the enterprise need to procure additional hardware to facilitate data collection, or is this all part of the MDI solution provider's offering?

    f. Will the data collection appliances meet with the requirements of existing clinical workflow?

    g. Are the data collection appliances approved for proximal use with patients at the POC (e.g., meet IEC 60601-1-X standards[17])? Do the appliances meet electrical safety and hazard requirements?

    h. Can the POC appliances be cleaned and disinfected using ordinary methods employed by the healthcare enterprise for medical equipment?

7. Is the MDI solution provider's offering minimally cleared by FDA as a Medical Device Data System (MDDS)?

    a. If not, is there a plan for this?

    b. If no plan, then what is the solution provider's philosophy in this regard? Is this philosophy acceptable to meet the policy requirements of the healthcare enterprise?

8. Is there a mechanism in place for providing notifications and alerts upon specific technical events? Examples:

    a. Failure of a device to communicate?

    b. Failure of the interface between the MDI and the health IT systems?

    c. Cable or attachment point failures between POC appliances and medical devices?

9. Is caching or storage of data supported?

    a. In the event of a network failure, can data be retained using a store and forward type mode from the POC appliance to the health IT system?

    b. Is there a way to adjust this caching behavior to meet the various technical and clinical needs within the environment?

10. If server software is employed, can it run on a standard virtualized partition in the enterprise data center, or does it require the purchase of standalone computing hardware?

    a. What are the operating system, memory, storage, database and networking requirements of the server?

b. How many POC appliances /medical devices can be managed through the server?

c. What are the server security requirements? Can enterprise antivirus and anti-malware be run on the server?

11. What are the performance requirements of the MDI solution?

a. How many beds/medical devices per bed can be communicated?

b. Are additional hardware and software required above certain bed/medical device quantities?

c. How many HL7 transactions can be supported on output per minute?

12. What mechanism, if any, is employed by the MDI solution provider for associating patient information, including patient identifiers (PIDs) with the data retrieved by the POC appliances?

a. Does the vendor support an inbound admission-discharge-transfer (ADT) feed?

b. Are POC methods such as barcode or radio frequency identification (RFID) tagging supported by the vendor?

c. In lieu of barcode or RFID tagging of medical devices, does the vendor provide a user interactive screen for associating or disassociating patients from medical devices?

d. What is the workflow for this association of a medical device to a patient and the accompanying disassociation workflows?

These are a sampling of key questions to ask based on what has been discussed thus far. In the following chapters, additional questions and insights will be raised to provide further detail in guiding the process of selecting and implementing an MDI solution.

SUMMARY

Medical device data collection has increasingly become a part of the fabric of health IT system deployment. Data gathered from medical devices is often used as a supplement for manual charting and provides a more complete, stabile, and accurate means of communicating information from medical devices associated with the patient to recipient health IT systems to augment bedside clinical decision making. Integrating data from medical devices at the POC is particularly important for technologically-dependent patients, such as in operating room or intensive care unit settings, or in cases in which a reliable means of regular data capture would assist the clinical decision-making process.

Today, many medical devices are standalone and still do not conform to specific messaging interface standards (such as HL7) but, rather, rely on proprietary, vendor-specific interface communication. Many medical devices communicate over serial ports and require medical device intermediaries to translate proprietary data from medical devices at the POC into a more standardized communication and messaging format acceptable for health IT systems. Proprietary, medical device manufacturer-specific interfaces also imply proprietary semantics that need to be translated into a common language and represent data collected that carries both consistent and enterprise clinical meaning.

Data collection from certain medical devices, such as physiologic monitors, can be accomplished using monitoring gateways or concentrators that relieve the requirement of POC serial or direct medical device communication.

Many standalone medical devices provide no means of direct patient association. Hence, associating data with specific patients must be carried out through separate applications, such as barcoding and radiofrequency identification (RFID). Associating medical devices with patients is important to minimize the possibility of incorrectly associating data from one patient with that of another patient. MDI solution providers may possess several means of associating patients with medical devices, including barcode, RFID, manual association, and via enterprise ADT messaging interfaces with the registration system.

CHAPTER 1

Medical Device Types and Classes Used and How They Communicate

HEALTHCARE ENTERPRISE DEPARTMENTS MOST OFTEN IN NEED OF MDI

Upon commencing an MDI implementation, frequently as part of the RFI or RFP, MDI solution providers need to understand the scope of the medical device integration rollout (quantities, locations) and the desired workflow objectives (e.g., health IT system integration, data warehousing, other). Aside from creating an accurate cost and implementation proposal, having a medical device inventory (e.g., maintained through clinical or biomedical engineering departments) that describes which types of medical devices are in use in each department also lends itself to better management of inventory in those environments.

In support of this objective, the following departments will be used as examples as part of MDI rollout objectives within the healthcare enterprise:

- Surgical services (OR, PACU)
- Critical/ICUs
- EDs
- Medical Surgical Units

These departments are good examples as they normally have medical device equipment from which medical device data can be extracted for use in patient charting and patient care management.

In deploying an MDI solution, it is often wise to consider taking small bites and implementing a unit or department at a time, particularly for the healthcare enterprise that is attempting this anew without any prior experience. The reason behind this is because there are usually significant workflow and technical changes involved in the MDI solution implementation process leading to go-live. These changes impact the clinical staff, as well as the supporting organizations of IT, clinical or biomedical engineering (BME) or clinical engineering (CE), facilities, and the workflow within these environments. Getting used to the implementation on a smaller scale minimizes the shock of change, as well as enables the organization to accommodate the new way of doing business and allows lessons learned to be brought forward to follow-on phases of implementation.

MEDICAL DEVICE TOPOLOGIES

Both serial port data and gateway medical device data will exist within the enterprise networking environment. An important step in the process of selecting an MDI solution provider is to determine how the vendor intends to integrate these separate data sources and whether it is necessary, cost-effective, or advisable to select only one vendor or vendor's method to communicate all data to the health IT system based on any one MDI solution provider's offerings or potential limitations.

The MDI solution provider, through their proprietary software and hardware appliances, fields medical device drivers that communicate with and poll the medical devices for the desired data. These medical device drivers or, simply, device drivers, are generally unique since no two medical devices from separate vendors (or possibly even different devices from the same vendor) communicate in precisely the same way. Nevertheless, there are exceptions, and sometimes medical device families (medical devices produced by a manufacturer that principally employs the same data communication specification) will have similar data communication architectures. By taking advantage of these similar architectures and query mechanisms, the MDI solution provider can take advantage of economies-of-scale and can reduce overall development timelines for new medical device drivers.[18]

To illustrate the range of medical device integration options, Figures 1-1 and 1-2 provide examples of data communication architectures using both serial and network data collection from different departmental systems and different medical devices. In Figure 1-1, the focus is on systems that communicate in operating suites (i.e., surgical environments). The medical devices usually employed in these environments for management and care of patients include anesthesia machines (basically, mechanical ventilators with anesthetic gas delivery capability), physiologic monitors, and specialty devices that can be used in conjunction with the anesthesia monitoring and management of the patient. The latter category includes devices such as bi-spectral index (BIS) monitors for assisting in the monitoring of depth of sedation; cardiopulmonary bypass machines for oxygenating blood externally from the body in instances of patients undergoing coronary artery bypass grafting (CABG); and end-tidal carbon dioxide monitoring, among many other specialty devices.

While most of these devices (e.g., anesthesia machine, BIS monitor, end-tidal CO2 monitor) typically communicate via serial port, the physiologic monitors generally have the capability to communicate both via serial port and over the LAN. The ability to communicate over the LAN is dependent on whether the enterprise already has or is planning to implement a medical device concentrator or gateway to span communication from the individual monitors over their own proprietary network to the healthcare enterprise LAN. Regardless of whether serial or concentrator-based communication is employed, however, the end result is the communication to the health IT system.

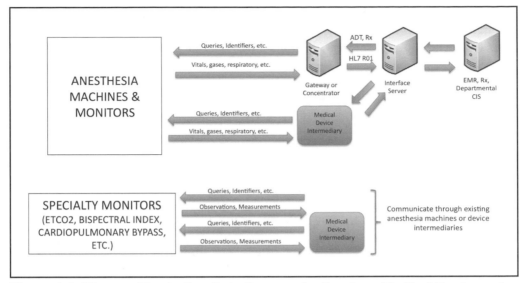

Figure 1-1: Diagram Illustrating Data Communication from Medical Devices at the POC in Operating Rooms (ORs), with Emphasis on the Specific Forms of Data Communication Modalities.

Note: The monitoring gateway or concentrator-based communication is shown versus serial port communication through medical device intermediaries. Also illustrated are the specialty medical devices that communicate according to their proprietary query-response interactions through the medical device integration solution providers.[19] Inbound HL7 data feeds such as ADT and pharmacy (Rx) are displayed along with outbound results (ORU) feeds.

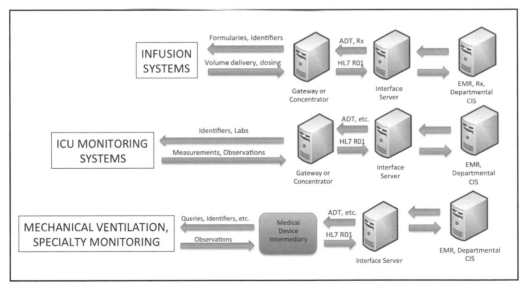

Figure 1-2: Diagram Extending the Concept of Medical Device Data Communication to Intensive Care Units (ICUs).[19]

In Figure 1-1, the medical devices represented are those specific to higher acuity settings, such as ORs. In these settings, medical devices that communicate via serial ports (e.g., anesthesia machines, cardiopulmonary bypass machines, etc.) can be co-mingled with medical devices that communicate through gateways (e.g., physiologic monitors). Alternatively, all medical devices may be routed via serial port connectivity through MDI POC appliances.

ICUs are high-acuity settings for monitoring and managing very ill patients, wherein these patients can receive focused treatment and, consequently, are monitored very closely. Figure 1-2 illustrates an example MDI architecture associated with the critical care environment. Monitoring of vital signs, management of respiratory and pulmonary performance, and the need to monitor the infusion of drugs all require capturing and monitoring the observations and findings derived from the patient care devices at the bedside.

Physiologic monitors, mechanical ventilators, infusion pumps, and specialty devices such as intra-aortic balloon pumps (IABPs) all produce data capable of being captured. Physiologic monitoring and infusion systems often communicate through their respective monitoring gateways while medical devices such as mechanical ventilators and IABPs often communicate through serial port connectivity. These latter devices require MDI hardware and software, whereas, the healthcare enterprise has typically invested in physiologic monitoring gateways to support both remote monitoring of vital signs (at the nursing station or other area), as well as providing the capability to communicate data through these gateways in a standardized (HL7) format.

As described in the preceding chapter, medical devices normally communicate in one of two ways: through serial ports or over LAN connections. In the case of medical device communication over LANs, physiologic monitors in ICUs represent a prime example of this type of medical device communication.

In this model, data are communicated to the physiologic monitoring gateway directly from the monitoring system, where they are translated into a more common format such as HL7. An MDI device driver applied to this model may need to do nothing more than transform the particular HL7 format of the monitoring gateway into a format amenable to the health IT system.

Examples of physiologic monitors that communicate with monitoring gateways include GE CARESCAPE, GE Solar™ 8000M/I or Dash monitors, Philips Intellivue monitors, Spacelabs, and Welch Allyn monitors (this list is not exhaustive). These monitors communicate on their respective proprietary, high-speed and dedicated network to their particular form of gateway server. The high-speed data network on which the physiologic monitors communicate is usually reserved only for those devices and is not to be shared with any other devices such as enterprise network computers or other types of general public access. The reason for this is the fact that interventional data, such as alarm notifications and alerts, together with waveforms and other high-frequency data, are communicated to CMS. These live and real-time data are used clinically for intervention (e.g., Code Blue or other emergency events).

Hence, extraneous traffic is forbidden to pass along these networks, which support the need for communicating events that result in possible intervention in real-time at the bedside.

The monitoring gateway server hardware will have two networks. One is dedicated to the proprietary, high-speed network upon which the physiologic monitors communicate their alarm and waveform traffic together with discrete vital signs. The second communicates only lower frequency discrete data to the enterprise network, specifically for delivery to the health IT system or MDI solution provider. The exact topology of configuration will depend on the physiologic monitoring manufacturer's specifications. These monitoring gateways are typically identified by their given proprietary names specific to the medical device manufacturer. For example, in the case of GE physiologic monitors, these are known as the GE CARESCAPE Gateway. In the case of Philips Intellivue monitoring environments, Intellivue Information Center (IIC) provides a bridge between the high-speed Intellivue Clinical network and the hospital network.[20]

The diagram in Figure 1-3 illustrates one example of a physiologic monitoring topology featuring a high-speed or proprietary network and the enterprise network. Oftentimes the device manufacturers provide an HL7 formatted interface from the gateway to the enterprise network, from which HL7 formatted data may be retrieved. In such cases where only discrete data are required for communication to the health IT system, there is no need for direct interaction with the physiologic monitors (no need for device-level or POC level communication with the physiologic monitors through, say, serial data ports). Receiving discrete physiologic data through the gateway is convenient and eliminates the need for MDI solution provider POC appliances at the bedside.

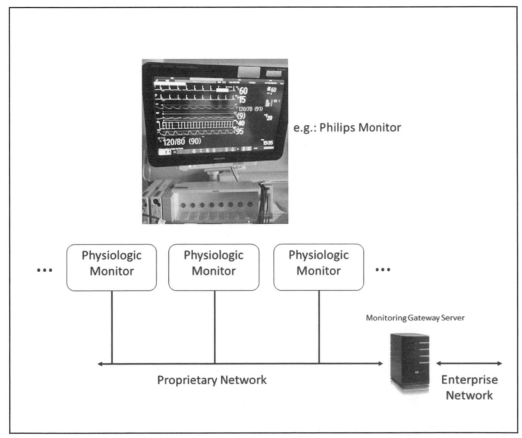

Figure 1-3: Physiologic Monitoring Gateway Featuring Two Separate Networks: Proprietary, High-speed Monitoring Network and Healthcare Enterprise Network.

Yet, with this convenience also comes restriction: enterprises wishing to engage in research and requiring specific information (e.g., waveform data from individual bedside monitors in ASCII format) may find that vendors do not support generalized data access at the frequencies desired when interacting with the physiologic monitoring systems through their gateways. Often, only high-frequency data are accessible through the proprietary networks reserved for central monitoring access. Data communication through physiologic monitoring gateways may have a minimum-reporting interval (e.g., 15 seconds) defined by the manufacturer and may also not communicate all possible data that are actually measured. If there is a need for high-fidelity data for research or clinical purposes that fall outside of the capability of the physiologic monitoring gateway, then it should be investigated whether other methods for data communication may be warranted, or whether the vendor can supply the requested data and at what cost.

SURGICAL SERVICES ENVIRONMENTS (OPERATING ROOM, OR; POST-ANESTHESIA CARE UNIT, PACU)

Surgical services normally consist of those areas/units that support the OR and environs. Units that are typically included in this category are as follows:

- ORs
- Post Anesthesia Care Unit(s) (PACU)
- Endoscopy
- Imaging (Magnetic Resonance, X-Ray, Interventional Radiology, Computed Tomography)
- Catheterization Lab
- Labor & Delivery

The medical device classes typically used for diagnostics, intervention, and from which data may be extracted and charted in these environments are listed in Table 1-1. Photographs of medical devices employed in the surgical services environment follow together with notes on the methodology for medical device data integration.

Table 1-1: Example Medical Devices Typically Used in Surgical Services Areas of the Hospital.

Hospital Area	Medical Device Types	Manufacturers & Example Medical Devices
OR	Physiological Monitors	Philips Intellivue, GE Solar™, Nihon Kohden, Draeger Infinity® Delta, ...
	Anesthesia Machines	Dräger Fabius®, Apollo®, Narkomed; GE Aespire, Aestiva; Mindray AS 3000 ...
	Cardiopulmonary Bypass	Sorin Socket S5; Maquet HL20; Terumo-CVS Advanced Perfusion System 1, ...
	End Tidal CO2	Covidien Capnostream® 20; Philips SureSigns; GE Dash ...
	BSI	Covidien Aspect BIS ...
PACU	Physiologic Monitors	Philips Intellivue, GE Dash, Datascope Passport®...
Endoscopy	Physiologic Monitors	Philips Intellivue, GE Dash, Datascope Passport®...
Catheterization Lab	Physiologic Monitors	Philips Intellivue, GE Solar™, Nihon Kohden, Draeger Infinity® Delta, ...
	Anesthesia Machines	Dräger Fabius®, Apollo®, Narkomed; GE Aespire, Aestiva; Mindray AS 3000 ...
Labor & Delivery	Physiologic Monitors	Philips Intellivue, GE Solar™, Nihon Kohden, Draeger Infinity® Delta, ...
	Anesthesia Machines	Dräger Fabius®, Apollo®, Narkomed; GE Aespire, Aestiva; Mindray AS 3000 ...
	Baby Warmers	Natus Infant Radiant Warmer SM 401; COBAMS LR 90; DISON BN-100A; GE Lullaby, Panda, Giraffe, ...
	Fetal Monitors	Hill Rom® Navicare® WatchChild®; Philips Avalon FM40, FM50; GF Corometrics 250cx, ...

A photograph illustrating devices used in ORs is shown in Figure 1-4. Various combinations of physiologic monitors and anesthesia machines are often employed. Figure 1-5 shows a Dräger Fabius® Tiro® anesthesia machine with a GE Solar™ 8000M/I physiologic monitor.

**Figure 1-4: Photograph of a Typical OR Anesthesia Machine (Dräger Fabius®
GS Premium) with Accompanying Physiologic Monitor (*left*—Philips Intellivue
MP70) and Bispectral Index Monitor (*center, top*—Covidien BIS Vista™).**

Note: Data communication from the anesthesia machine and the Bispectral index monitor is achieved
through serial port communication. The physiologic monitor can communicate either through the introduction of a serial port board or through network communication, as described in the previous section. (Photo
by Author)

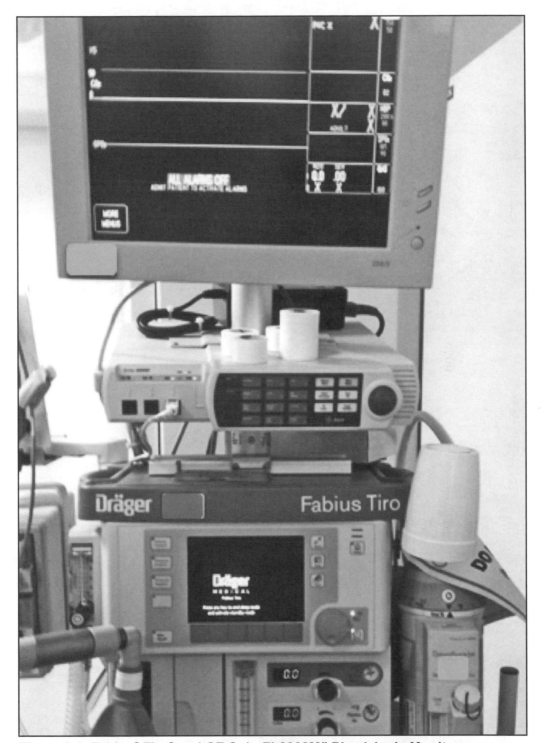

Figure 1-5: Fabius® Tiro® and GE Solar™ 8000M/I Physiologic Monitor.

Note: Data communication from both of these devices is achieved through serial port communication. The physiologic monitor can communicate over the Unity network, as well, if the hospital uses them in support of telemetry monitoring. Many OR environments do not have networked physiologic monitors. (Photo by Author)

An example of a cardiopulmonary bypass machine is shown in Figure 1-6.

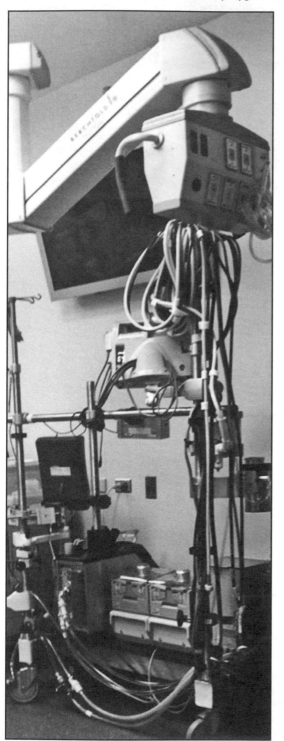

Figure 1-6: Cardiopulmonary Bypass Machine.

Note: These machines possess a serial data port for communication. (Photo by Author)

An example of a physiologic monitor used in a PACU is shown in Figure 1-7; a Philips Intellivue MX800 is shown in Figure 1-8.

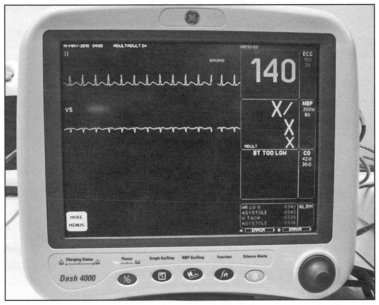

Figure 1-7: GE Dash 4000 Physiologic Monitor - An Example of a Monitor That Might Be Used in a PACU.

Note: These monitors can communicate either through a serial AUX port or with the Unity network via network port. Both ports are located on the back of the monitor. (Photo by Author)

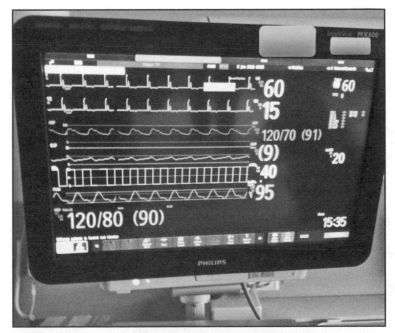

Figure 1-8: Philips MX 800 Physiologic Monitor.

Note: These monitors and other Intellivue class monitors can communicate over network port connection. Intellivue monitors can be outfitted with optional serial port cards that will also permit them to communicate discrete data over a standard serial interface using an RJ45 cable. (Photo by Author)

Figure 1-9 shows a GE Datex-Ohmeda anesthesia machine along with its accompanying Datex-Ohmeda Cardiocap™/5 physiologic monitor. Data communication on most of these devices is achieved through serial port access on the backside of the machines.

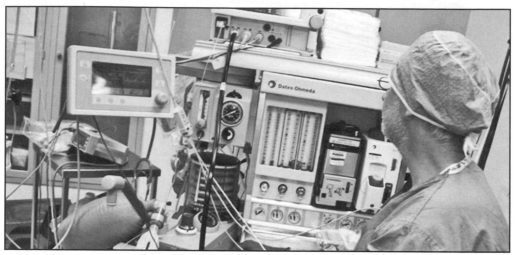

Figure 1-9: Photo of Author in Front of a Datex-Ohmeda Anesthesia Machine with Cardiocap™/5 Physiologic Monitor (partially cut off on top).

Note: Both the anesthesia machine and the Cardiocap™/5 monitor provide serial port communication. (Photo by Author)

Figure 1-10 shows a close-up view of the Cardiocap™/5 monitor accompanying the anesthesia machine.

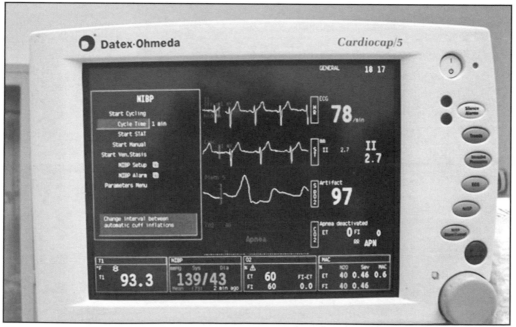

Figure 1-10: Close-up View of Cardiocap™/5 Physiologic Monitor.

(Photo by Author)

Figure 1-11 shows another type of physiologic monitor (Infinity® Delta) accompanying a POC anesthesia machine.

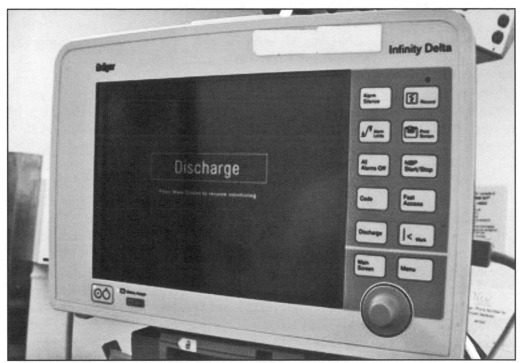

Figure 1-11: Dräger Infinity® Delta Physiologic Monitor.
(Photo by Author)

These latter physiologic monitors can either be networked to a central monitoring station and concentrator (i.e., gateway) or can be standalone. Their serial port communication employs a special adapter cable.

In the case of ORs, many of the physiologic monitors that accompany anesthesia machines may not be networked through their respective medical device gateways. The healthcare enterprise will need to perform the cost tradeoff between having these physiologic monitors communicate their data through the respective medical device vendor gateway or employing an MDI solution provider's POC data collection approach. If the solution provider's approach for POC medical device data collection involves the use of appliances that communicate serially with the medical devices, then both the physiologic monitors and the anesthesia machines may be integrated in this way. The question that will need to be addressed will be how these MDI solution provider appliances can be mounted. The preference here is highly dependent on the requirements of the healthcare enterprise. Some POC appliances can be wall-mounted, some can be mounted on the anesthesia machines themselves or mounted on or next to the anesthesia information management systems (AIMS) computer workstation on wheels (WOW).

Keep in mind that if it is decided to use a gateway for physiologic data collection, then it may be necessary (or preferred) to send data from the anesthesia machines through the physiologic monitors themselves, bypassing the need for a separate POC

MDI solution provider appliance. Most physiologic monitors will support some ancillary equipment communication through a medical information bus (MIB) that allows for external medical devices to transmit data through the physiologic monitor, with the monitor providing the concentration pathway for the data from these devices. It should be determined whether, in sending data this way, there is any loss of information (i.e., whether the physiologic monitor MIB limits the amount and frequency of data collected from ancillary devices). This can be determined through the physiologic monitoring manufacturer. Should there be a limitation on the type and quantity of data that can be transmitted, the healthcare enterprise will need to determine whether the available data elements are acceptable clinically for the management of patients.

ESSENTIAL OR DATA ELEMENTS

Key vital signs data elements obtained from the OR environment include electrocardiography, pulse oximetry, invasive and non-invasive blood pressure, invasive measurements such as cardiac output and wedge pressure, temperature, respiratory and pulmonary mechanics, ventilator settings, and level of sedation. The following tables[21] summarize data elements that, from experience, have been extracted and used for AIMS charting, as well as for data warehousing and patient care management.

These tables list primary or major parameters that are normally collected for charting purposes. Variations and additional parameters exist. During the MDI implementation process, the various parameters are normally validated by clinical staff for charting purposes and the health IT system or AIMS flow sheets are configured to receive them. The selection of parameters for charting is completely dependent on the clinical data requirements as specified by anesthesiology. The unified code names (i.e., the parameter naming conventions) are validated by clinical staff together with their units of measure (UOM).

We begin to illustrate the types of parameters normally charted with elements from electrocardiography. The parameter elements identified with electrocardiography, as shown in Table 1-2, are measured through physiologic monitoring. Not all parameter values are required measurements on each and every patient. In most instances, pulse (or heart rate) and ECG monitoring may be employed. The measurement of premature ventricular contractions (PVCs), ST segment elevations, and QT intervals is important, as well. The point is that the physiologic monitoring system and the MDI solution provider must provide the specific measurements as required by the anesthesiologist, and the MDI system must have the ability to communicate these findings to the AIMs or other health IT systems to support the clinical use cases (i.e., monitoring patients within OR or other surgical services setting).

Pulse oximetry measures the amount by which blood hemoglobin is oxygenated and is a non-invasive parameter that approximates the arterial blood oxygenation, SaO2, normally derived through laboratory measurement. Table 1-3 summarizes those parameters derived through pulse oximetry.

Table 1-2: Example of Parameters Measured Using Electrocardiography and Physiologic Monitoring.

Description	Unit of Measure
Heart Rate (HR)	/min
Premature Ventricular Contraction Count (PVC)	/min
QT Interval (QT)	Milliseconds
Six ECG Limb Leads: STI, STII, STIII, aVR, aVL, aVF	Millimeters
Six ECG Precordial or chest leads: V1, V2, V3, V4,V5, V6	Millimeters
Modified single-lead ECG (5 lead) ECGs can include the three bipolar leads, STI, STII, STIII plus two additional leads, MCL1 and MCL6, which are modified versions of V1 and V6 [22]	Millimeters

Table 1-3: Parameter Measurements Obtained Through Pulse Oximetry.

Description	Unit of Measure
Peripheral Oxygen Saturation measured through pulse oximetry (SpO2)	%
Peripheral Oxygen Saturation Heart Rate (SpO2-HR)	/min
Certain types of physiologic monitors will also provide details on measurement sources, measurement modes, strengths of signals. Because these are specific to the devices themselves, they are left intentionally vague save for the mention here as a reminder to the investigator to determine the specific reporting of the medical devices in question.	

Invasive and non-invasive measurements of blood pressure, venous pressure, and intracranial pressure are also made in this environment. A superset of the measured invasive and non-invasive blood pressure parameters are summarized in Table 1-4 and Table 1-5, respectively. These parameters are collected through the physiologic monitor present in the OR. Non-invasive parameters (e.g., blood pressure) are also normally measured using the physiologic monitors in PACU or in radiology. For example, Invivo or Medrad® physiologic monitors are often used in Magnetic Resonance departments, wherein pulse and blood pressure are determined in patients either during or prior to magnetic resonance imaging sessions.

Table 1-4: Invasive and Parameter Measurements of Blood Pressure.

Description	Unit of Measure
Arterial Blood Pressure (ABP-D,M,S)	mm(Hg)
Heart Rate Derived from Arterial Blood Pressure (ABP-HR)	/min
Aortic Blood Pressure – Diastolic Pressure (AoBP-D,M,S) mm(Hg)	
Cerebral Perfusion Pressure (CPP). Note: CPP = MABP – ICP	mm(Hg)
Central Venous Pressure (CVP)	mm(Hg)
Femoral Artery Pressure (FEM-D,M,S)	mm(Hg)
Intracranial Pressure (ICP)	mm(Hg)
Intraocular Pressure	mm(Hg)
Intra-Uterine Pressure	mm(Hg)
Left Atrial Pressure (LAP)	mm(Hg)
Pulmonary Artery Occlusion Pressure (PAOP)	mm(Hg)
Pulmonary Artery Wedge Pressure (PAWP) or Pulmonary Artery Pressure (PAP-D,M,S)	mm(Hg)
Right Atrial Pressure (RAP)	mm(Hg)
Umbilical Arterial Catheter Pressure (UACP)	mm(hg)
Umbilical Venous Catheter Pressure (UVCP)	mm(Hg)

Table 1-5: Parameters Associated with Non-invasive Blood Pressure and Its Measurement.

Description	Unit of Measure
Non-invasive Blood Pressure (NBP or NIBP-D,M,S)	mm(Hg)
Heart Rate derived from Non-invasive Blood Pressure Measurement (NBP-HR)	/min
Non-Invasive Blood Pressure - Time Stamp (NBP-TS)	Time Stamp (YYYY-MM-DD-hh:mm:ss:ms)

Arterial blood pressures, cardiac calculations including cardiac output (CO), and end-tidal carbon dioxide are tracked in the OR environment, as well. Table 1-6 and Table 1-7 summarize these findings and related observations.

Table 1-6: Parameters Associated with Hemodynamic Calculations.[23]

Description	Unit of Measure
Cardiac Output (CO)	l/min
Body Surface Area (BSA):[24] BSA (Dubois) = [Ht (cm)]$^{0.725}$ x [Wt (kg)]$^{0.425}$ x 0.007184 BSA (Jacobsen) = {[Ht (cm)] + [Wt (kg)] – 60} / 100	m2
Arterial Pressure – Mean (ABP-M) ABP-M = (2 x ABP-D + ABP-S)/3	mm(Hg)
Mean Pulmonary Artery (Wedge) Pressure (MPAP or MPAWP) MPAP = (2 x PAP-D + PAP-S) / 3	mm(Hg)
Cardiac Index (CI) CI = CO / BSA	L/(min/m2)
Stroke Volume (SV) SV = CO / HR x 1000	L/beat
Stroke Volume Index (SVI)SVI = CI / HR x 1000	L/m2/beat
Systemic Vascular Resistance (SVR) SVR = 80 x (ABP-M – RAP) / CO	Dynes-sec/cm5
Systemic Vascular Resistance Index (SVRI) SVRI = 80 x (ABP-M – RAP)/CI	Dynes-sec/cm5/m2
Stroke Volume Variation (SVV) SVV = (SVMAX – SVMIN) / SVMEAN x 100	%
Pulmonary Vascular Resistance (PVR) PVR = 80 x (MPAP – PAOP) / CO	Dynes-sec/cm5
Pulmonary Vascular Resistance Index (PVRI) PVRI = 80 x (MPAP – PAOP) / CI	Dynes-sec/cm5/m2
Left Ventricular Stroke Work (LVSW) LVSW = SV x ABP-M x 0.0144	g/m/m2
Left Ventricular Stroke Work Index (LVSWI) LVSWI = SVI x (ABP-M – PAOP) x 0.0136	g/m2/beat
Right Ventricular Stroke Work (RVSW) RVSW = SV x ABP-M x 0.0144	g/m/m2
Right Ventricular Stroke Work Index (RVSWI) RVSWI = SVI x (MPAP – CVP) x 0.0136	g/m2/beat
Continuous Cardiac Output (CCO)	L/min
Continuous Cardiac Index (CCI) CCI = CCO / BSA	L/min/m2

Note: L/min is liters per minute
L/beat is liters per beat
G is grams
mm(Hg) is millimeters of mercury

Table 1-7: Parameters Associated with End-tidal Carbon Dioxide Measurements.

Description	Unit of Measure
Expired CO2 /End-tidal CO2 (etCO2)	%
Inspired CO2 (FiCO2)	%
Respiration Rate – measured via CO2 cannula (CO2-RR)	breaths/min
Expired O2 (etO2)	%
Inspired O2 (FiO2)	%
Partial pressure of carbon dioxide in arterial blood (PaCO2)	mm(Hg) or kiloPascals (kPa)
Partial pressure of oxygen in arterial blood (PaO2)	mm(Hg) or kiloPascals (kPa)
CO2 Production (VCO2) or normalized by BSA	L/min or L/min/m2
Transcutaneous CO2 Pressure (tcpCO2)	mm(Hg)
Transcutaneous Oxygen Pressure (tcpO2)	mm(Hg)

Table 1-8 summarizes key anesthesia machine-derived parameters.

Table 1-8: Typical Anesthesia Machine Gas Parameter Measurements.

Description	Unit of Measure
Expired, Inspired Agent (iAGNT, oAGNT) (note: agent other than those specified below)	%
Agent # Name (Text)	-
Expired, Inspired Desflurane (eDES, iDES)	%
Desflurane flow rate	mL/hr
Expired, Inspired Enflurane (eENF, iENF)	%
Enflurane flow rate	mL/hr
Expired, Inspired Halothane (eHAL, iHAL)	%
Halothane flow rate	mL/hr
Expired, Inspired Helium (eHE, iHE)	%
Expired, Inspired Isoflurane (eISO, iISO)	%
Isoflurane flow rate	mL/hr
Mean Alveolar Concentration (MAC)*	%
Desflurane, Enflurane, Halothane, Isoflurane, Sevoflurane MAC Concentration	%
Expired, Inspired N2O (Nitrous Oxide)	%
N2O flow rate	mL/hr
Fresh Gas Flow Rate (FGF)	mL/hr
O2 flow rate	mL/hr

*Mean Alveolar Concentration is a measure of anesthetic potency and is defined as the amount of anesthetic in the lungs required to prevent movement in 50% of respondents associated with the toleration of surgical pain (e.g., scalpel incision).

BIS is also employed to assist in determining relative levels of sedation through four-channel EEG measurement during anesthesia. Parameters associated with BIS monitoring are provided in Table 1-9. BIS monitoring provides a relative measurement on depth of consciousness and level of sedation. The scale that is taken ranges from 0 to 100, with the following generally accepted convention:

- 0 – patient is comatose
- 40-60 – patient under general anesthesia
- 60-90 – patient is sedated
- 100 – patient is awake and conscious

Table 1-9: Parameters Associated with Bi-spectral Index Monitoring (BIS VISTA™).

Description	Unit of Measure
Bispectral (BIS) Monitoring Index	-
BIS Signal Quality Index (SQI) Note: percentage of good and suppressed epochs in the last 120 (61.5 seconds) that could be used in the BIS calculation[25]	%
BIS Suppression Ratio	%
BIS Total Power	-
BIS Burst Count	-

Table 1-9 summarizes principle parameters associated with the Covidien BIS Vista™ brand of BIS monitors—an example of a monitor used as an aid in monitoring the effect of anesthetic agents through the monitoring of four (4) channels of EEG.[26]

Other medical devices in these areas that will communicate data include cardiopulmonary bypass machines (i.e., heart-lung machines) and cerebral oximetry devices. Depending on the acuity of the surgical procedure, more medical devices may be required at the bedside to assist in monitoring and management of the patient.

PARAMETER TRANSMISSION INTERVALS—OR

Data collection in the OR is governed by the needs of the anesthesiologists in managing their patients. Normally, the rate at which data are collected is on the order of one set of observations per minute, which allows for minute-by-minute charting within the AIMS. Rates can be higher, depending on the needs for patient care management and specifics of the case. Changes in drugs or modifications in dosing are normally recorded when the dosing or infusion change is made and is governed by ad hoc moment-by-moment events.

Redundant Parameter Transmission—OR

Frequently, clinical staff will require that the same finding be obtained from different medical devices to provide corroborating evidence; for example, heart rates measured from non-invasive blood pressure cuffs versus heart rates measured from pulse oximetry cuffs. These values, while redundant, can provide confirming or otherwise corroborating evidence of values should an error occur—such as the failure of a blood pressure cuff, or accidentally detaching a pulse oximetry cuff. When seconds matter, measurements can be minutes away (e.g., blood pressure measurements). Hence, having backup or corroborating values can provide needed clinical information for the clinical end user to safely manage the patient.

In terms of charting redundant information in the health IT system or AIMS patient chart, the healthcare enterprise should determine whether this type of communication to the chart is required and whether the selected MDI solution provider can meet the need of sending redundant information from separate medical devices simultaneously. It should also be determined whether the health IT system can receive and chart the same parameters derived from two or more separate medical devices. This is a simple query to perform but can save problems down the road.

Examples of corroborating parameters:

- Pulse measured via ECG versus pulse oximetry cuff (ECG-HR vs SPO2-HR)
- Left arm versus right arm non-invasive blood pressure (NBP-L vs NBP-R)
- Spontaneous respiratory rate measured through end-tidal CO2 cannula (etCO2-RR) versus spontaneous respiratory rate measured via anesthesia machine inspiratory and expiratory lines (SPO-RR).

The need to chart redundant data may be a requirement specified by clinical staff to provide corroborating and independent findings as part of patient care management. Hence, clinical staff should be interviewed as to the need for redundant findings and in which clinical settings prior to introducing an MDI solution into the clinical environment.

Intensive Care Units (ICUs)/Critical Care Units (CCUs)

ICUs and CCUs, in general, are high-acuity settings with directed attention on patients who are very ill. Medical device types typically used in the critical care setting are listed in Table 1-10. Physiologic monitoring, and management and support of patient breathing are common functions in ICUs, particularly post-surgical critical care such as surgical intensive care units (SICUs), neuro-trauma intensive care units, cardiac care units (CCUs), pediatric care units (PICUs) and neonatal intensive care units (NICUs). Together with infusion of drugs and the use of specialty equipment for assisting in the pumping of blood (intra-aortic balloon pumps, or IABPs) and monitoring of blood gas exchange, the need to closely manage patients in these units is critical to maintaining life. Because of the dependency on medical devices to sustain life in these environments, patients in ICUs are sometimes referred to as technologically-dependent patients: many of them require mechanical ventilation to sustain breathing; drug infusions to maintain blood pressure and cardiac function; and monitoring of cardiac performance.

As in the previous section, the parameters cited in the tables that follow are those principally monitored and charted within the health IT system. Differing brands of medical devices will provide for some variation in parameters, and semantic mappings will not always be precisely the same between differing brands of equipment. Modes of operation can vary, as well. This is particularly true among some brands of mechanical ventilators: some offer many differing and complex modes of mechanical ventilation, while others do not. This should not be taken to imply that one brand of mechanical ventilator is better than another; simply, it is to point out that the health-care enterprise needs to be aware of these differences which will become evident when defining the key parameters to be charted within the health IT system. The findings recorded within the health IT system will usually be based on clinical requirements.

Table 1-10: Medical Device Types Typically Associated with Use in ICU Settings.

Hospital Area	Medical Device Types	Manufacturers / Example Medical Devices
Critical Care Unit	Physiological Monitors	Philips Intellivue, GE Solar™/Dash, Nihon Kohden, Draeger Infinity®, …
	Mechanical Ventilators	Draeger Evita®, Nellcor N-395, Puritan Bennett™ 840, Respironics V60, Maquet Servoi, Viasys Avea®, Draeger Evita® V500, …
	IntraAortic Balloon Pumps	Maquet CS 300, Datascope, …
	Standalone Infusion Systems	Hospira, Carefusion, B|Braun, …
	Beds	Stryker, Hill-Rom, Sizewise, …
	End-tidal CO2 Monitoring	End-tidal CO2 monitors (Covidien, Philips, …)

Physiologic Monitors

The physiologic monitoring variables described in the previous section on surgical services apply for the most part in the ICU. A key difference between physiologic monitors employed in the ICU versus the OR is the central monitoring station: most ICUs employ central monitoring achieved through networking the monitors to the central station for live monitoring of patients. The specific parameter measures charted within a health IT system for a given patient in the ICU are based on those required or ordered by the attending physician. Normally, most physiologic monitors, depicted in Figure 1-12, provide the capability to maximally monitor electrocardiography (i.e., measurement of electrical activity in the heart) and hemodynamic (i.e., monitoring of blood pressure and blood movement through the arteries and veins) performance of the patient. The ability to provide certain observations or measurements is usually dependent on the use of specialty modules that can be attached to the physiologic monitor (e.g., invasive blood pressure measurement through arterial catheters and measurement of cardiac output). Baseline measurements of ECG, HR, pulse oximetry, and NBP are usually available on all monitors without requiring any special attachments, and most monitors employ standard disposable leads and cuffs to ensure a sanitary environment.

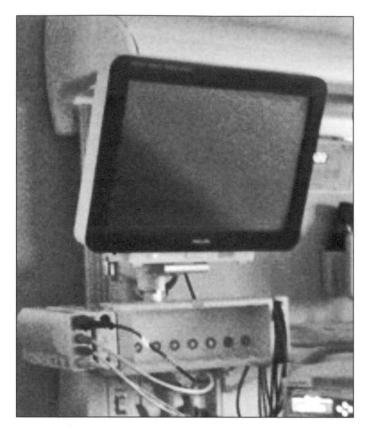

Figure 1-12: Philips MX 800 Physiologic Monitor—A Type of Monitor Frequently Used in Intensive/Critical Care Units.

Note: These monitors and those of other manufacturers employed within the intensive care unit environment are normally networked to a central monitoring station (CMS) where vitals and waveforms from each patient within the unit can be displayed simultaneously and where alerts and alarms can be communicated to staff dedicated to the monitoring of critical events. (Photo by Author)

Mechanical Ventilators

Mechanical ventilators are frequently used in critical care settings to support patients with questionable pulmonary performance or to assist patients who have degraded performance owing to surgical procedures.

Figure 1-13 and Figure 1-14 show the Puritan Bennett™ ventilator and its serial communication port, respectively. Other examples of mechanical ventilators employed in these environments: the Philips Respironics V60 and the Viasys Avea® mechanical ventilators, shown in Figure 1-15 and Figure 1-16, respectively.

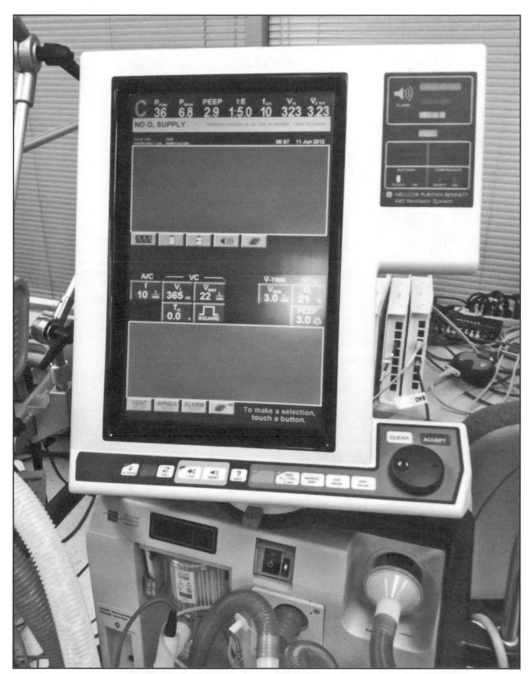

Figure 1-13: Puritan Bennett™ 840 (PB840) Brand Mechanical Ventilator.

(Photo by Author)

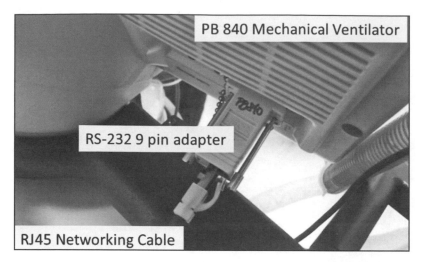

Figure 1-14: Serial Data Collection Port on Back of Puritan Bennett™ (PB840) Mechanical Ventilator, with Serial 9-pin Adapter Attached to Unit.

(Photo by Author)

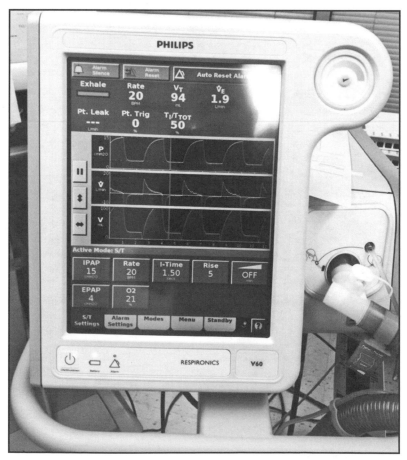

Figure 1-15: Philips Respironics V60 Mechanical Ventilator.

(Photo by Author)

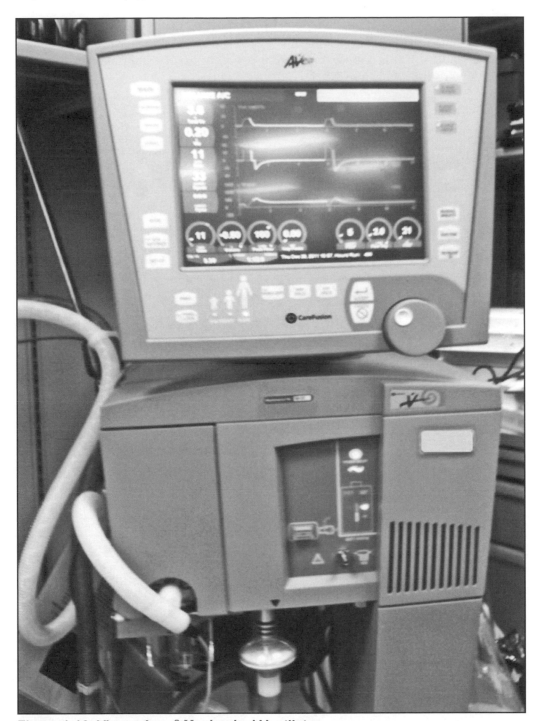

Figure 1-16: Viasys Avea® Mechanical Ventilator.

(Photo by Author)

Parameters associated with mechanical ventilators usually relate to settings, or mandatory values, and measurements, or spontaneous values. Mechanical ventilators operate in one of several different modes, and newer mechanical ventilators allow for combinations of modes or hybrid modes. Mechanical ventilators breathe for patients when the patients cannot breathe for themselves, or assist in the gas exchange process by enabling the infusion of pure oxygen or mixtures of oxygen and room air from 100 percent O_2 down to room air (21% O_2).

Most mechanical ventilators communicate using serial ports, via RS232 adapters, as shown on the Siemens Servo-i® brand of mechanical ventilator in Figure 1-17. The serial port is depicted in Figure 1-18.

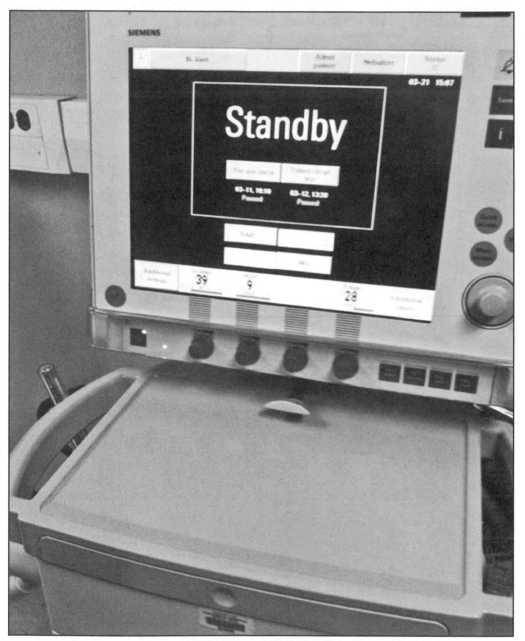

Figure 1-17: Siemens Servo-i® Mechanical Ventilator.

Note: Servo-i® later acquired by Maquet. (Photo by Author)

Figure 1-18: RS-232 9-pin Serial Port with Cable Attached on the Servo-i® Mechanical Ventilator.

(Photo by Author)

Table 1-11 and Table 1-12 list the types of ventilator settings and measurements that can be retrieved from many of the mechanical ventilators that are used within the ICU setting. A note on terminology: the use of the term setting in the context of mechanical ventilation connotes the offered or mechanical ventilator-initiated values. The term spontaneous refers to those patient-initiated parameters. For example, a spontaneous breath is a patient-initiated breath. A respiratory rate setting of 10 breaths per minute in a mandatory ventilation mode implies that the mechanical ventilator will provide 10 breaths in a given minute, despite how the patient is breathing. On the other hand, a respiratory rate setting of 10 breaths per minute in a ventilation mode of Synchronous Intermittent Mandatory Ventilation (SIMV) will offer 10 breaths per minute to the patient unless the patient can initiate breaths on his or her own. In pressure support or spontaneous modes, the mechanical ventilator offers no breaths to a spontaneously breathing patient. Hence, the spontaneous parameters are what they imply: patient-offered or patient-initiated breathing not governed by mechanical ventilator settings.

Hence, patients who are recovering from the effects of anesthesia (such as those undergoing heart surgery or are injured) would most likely be placed in either mandatory or SIMV ventilation mode, while those being weaned from mechanical ventilation or are otherwise conscious may be managed in a more spontaneous mode of mechanical ventilation. Clinical use cases vary widely, and mechanical ventilators may offer many different modes and sub modes of mechanical ventilation to support various patients from neonates to adults.

Table 1-11: Mechanical Ventilator Parameter Settings.

Description	Unit of Measure
Respiratory Rate Setting (RRm or RR-SET)	Breaths/min
Apnea Delay Setting (SET-APN-DELAY)	Seconds
Set Apnea IE Ratio (SET-APN-IE)	-
Set Apnea IE-Expiratory Component (SET-IEE)	Seconds
Set Apnea IE-Inspiratory Component (SET-IEI)	Seconds
Setting Apnea Inspiratory Pressure (SET-APN-IP)	cmH2O
Set Apnea Respiration Rate (SET-APN-RR)	/min
Set Apnea Time (SET-APN-T)	Seconds
Set Apnea Tidal Volume	Liters or milliliters
Set Assisted Spontaneous Breath (SET-ASB)	cmH2O
Set Assisted Spontaneous Breath End-Flow (SET-ASB-EFLW)	L/min
Inspired Oxygen Concentration Setting (SET-FIO2)	%
Set Flow Rise (SET-FLW-RISE)	L/min
Set Flow Trigger (SET-FLW-TRG)	L/min
Set Fresh Gas Flow (SET-FGF)	L/min or mL/min
High-Frequency Ventilation Flow Setting (SET-HF-FLW)	L/min
Set End-Tidal CO2—High Limit (SET-HI-CO2-EX)	%
Set Inspiratory CO2—High Limit (SET-HI-CO2-IN)	%
Set Exhaled Minute Volume–High Limit (SET-HI-MVe)	L/min
Set Inspiratory Oxygen—High Limit (SET-HI-O2-IN)	%
Set PEEP High Setting—Refers only to BILEVEL Ventilation (SET-HI-PEEP)	cmH2O
Set High Peak Inspiratory Pressure (SET-HI-PIP)	cmH2O
Set High Respiratory Rate Limit (SET-HI-RR)	/min
Set Expiratory Tidal Volume—High Limit (SET-HI-TV)	L/breath or mL/breath
Set Inspiration Pause (SET-INSP-HLD)	%
Set I:E Ratio (SET-IE)	-
Set I:E Expiratory Component (SET-IEE)	Seconds
Set I:E Inspiratory Component (SET-IEI)	Seconds
Set Inspiratory Time (SET-INSPT)	Seconds
Set PEEP (SET-PEEP)	cmH2O
Set End-tidal CO2—Low Limit (Set-LO-CO2-EX)	%
Set Low Exhaled Minute Volume Limit (SET-LO-MVe)	L/min
Set Inspiratory O2—Low Limit (SET-LO-O2-IN)	%
Set PEEP Low— Refers only to BILEVEL Ventilation (SET-LO-PEEP)	cmH2O
Set Low Peak Inspiratory Pressure (SET-LO-PIP)	cmH2O

Table 1-11: Mechanical Ventilator Parameter Settings. (cont.)

Description	Unit of Measure
Set Low Respiratory Rate Limit (SET-LO-RR)	Breaths/min
Set Low Exhaled Tidal Volume Limit (SET-LO-TV)	L/breath or mL/breath
Set Max Inspiratory Flow (SET-MFLW)	L/min
Set Max Inspiration Pressure (SET-MIP)	cmH2O
Set Mandatory Minute Volume (SET-MVm)	L/min
Set Inspired Oxygen (SET-O2)	%
Set Pressure Trigger (SET-P-TRG)	cmH2O
Set Positive End Expiratory Pressure (SET-PEEP)	cmH2O
Set Peak Inspiratory Flow (SET-PIF)	L/min
Set Peak Inspiratory Pressure (SET-PIP)	cmH2O
Set Plateau Pressure (SET-PLAT)	cmH2O
Set Pressure Support Ventilation (PSV) Rise Time (SET-PSV-RT)	Seconds
Set Assisted Spontaneous Breath (ASB) Ramp (SET-RAMP)	Seconds
Set Respiration Rate (also Mandatory Respiration Rate) (SET-RR or RRm)	Breaths/min
Set Support Pressure (SET-PSUP)	cmH2O
Set Endotracheal Tube Size (SET-ETT-SIZE)	Millimeters
Set Endotracheal Tube Type (SET-ETT-TYPE)	String
Set Tidal Volume or Mandatory Tidal Volume (SET-TV or TVm)	L/breath or mL/breath
Set Inspiratory Tidal Volume (SET-TVIN or TVm)	L/breath or mL/breath
Set Ventilation Mode (SET-VNT-MODE)	String
Set High Airway Pressure (SET-AWP)	cmH2O
Set Inspiratory Pressure (SET-INSP-P)	%
Set Apnea Peak Flow (SET-APN-PF)	L/min
Set Pressure Sensitivity (SET-PSENS)	cmH2O
Set Pressure Support (SET-PPS)	cmH2O
Set Maximum Circuit Pressure (SET-MCP)	cmH2O
Set Apnea Flow Rate (SET-APN-FLW)	L/min
Set High Inspiratory O2 (SET-HI-FIO2)	%
Set High PEEP Limit (SET-HI-PEEP)	Mbar
Set Low Spontaneous RR (SET-LO-SPO-RR or SET-LO-RRsp)	Breaths/min
Set High Spontaneous RR (SET-HI-SPO-RR or SET-HI-RRsp)	Breaths/min
Set Low Tidal Volume (SET-LO-TV or SET-LO-TVm)	L/breath or mL/breath
Set High End Tidal CO2 (SET-HI-ETCO2)	mm(Hg)

Table 1-12: Mechanical Ventilator Spontaneous Parameters.

Description	Unit of Measure
Spontaneous Respiration Rate (SPO-RR or RRsp)	Breaths/min
Respiration Rate Source	String
Airway Respiration Rate	Breaths/min
Alveolar Ventilation (AL-VNT)	Milliliters
Apnea Time/Duration (APN-T)	Seconds
Mean Airway Pressure (MAWP)	cmH2O
Base Flow (BS-FLW)	L/min
Static Compliance (C-STAT)	mL/cmH2O
Dynamic Compliance (C-DYN)	mL/cmH2O
Dynamic Resistance (D-RAW)	cmH2O/(L/sec)
Expiratory Time (EXP-T)	Seconds
Fraction of Inspired CO2 (FICO2)	%
Fractional Inspired Oxygen (FIO2)	%
Flow Trigger (FL-TRG)	L/min
Flow Rate (FLW-RT)	L/min
High Frequency Ventilation Peak-to-Peak Pressure (HF-PP)	cmH2O
High Frequency Ventilation Flow Rate (HFV or HF-FR)	Hz
I/E Ratio (I:E)	String
I:E Ratio Expiratory Component (IE-E)	Seconds
I:E Ratio Inspiratory Component (IE-I)	Seconds
Inspiration Hold Time (IN-HLD)	Seconds
Inspiratory Time (INSP-T)	Seconds
Intrinsic PEEP (I-PEEP)	cmH2O
Intrinsic PEEP Time (I-PEEPT)	Seconds
Minimum Airway Pressure (MIN-AWP)	cmH2O
Mandatory Minute Volume (MVm)	L/min
Measured PEEP (M-PEEP)	cmH2O
Mandatory Respiration Rate (RRm)	Breaths/min
Mandatory Tidal Volume (TVm or Vt-m	L/breath or mL/breath
Total Minute Volume (MV-TOT or MVt)	L/min
Expired Minute Volume (MV-EXP)	L/min
Inspired Minute Volume (MV-IN)	L/min
Negative Inspiratory Pressure (NIP)	cmH2O
Airway Occlusion Pressure OCL-AWP	cmH2O
Positive End Expiratory Pressure (PEEP)	cmH2O
Peak Expiratory Flow (PEF)	L/min

Table 1-12: Mechanical Ventilator Spontaneous Parameters. (cont.)

Description	Unit of Measure
Peak Inspiratory Flow	L/min
Peak Inspiratory Pressure (PIP)	cmH2O
Plateau Airway Pressure (PPLAT)	cmH2O
Positive Pressure Support (PPS)	cmH2O
Ramp (Rise time)	Seconds
Rapid Shallow Breathing Index	Breaths/min/L
Spontaneous Minute Volume (SPO-MV or MVsp)	L/min
Spontaneous Respiration Rate (SPO-RR or RRsp)	Breaths/min
Spontaneous Tidal Volume (SPO-TV or TVsp)	L/breath or mL/breath
Total PEEP (T-PEEP)	cmH2O
Tachypnea Frequency (TACFR)	Breaths/min
Tidal Volume (TV)	L/breath or mL/breath
Expired Tidal Volume (TV-EXP)	L/breath or mL/breath
Inspired Tidal Volume (TV-IN)	L/breath or mL/breath
Vital Lung Capacity (VC)	Milliliters
Ratio of Dead Space to Tidal Volume (VD/VT)	-
Dead Space Volume (VDS)	Milliliters
Ventilator Leakage (VNT-LEAK)	mL/min
Total Respiratory Rate (TOT-RR or RRt)	Breaths/min
Ventilator Mode (VNT-MODE)	String
Functional Residual Capacity (FRC)	Ml
Duration Session Hours	Hours
Duration Session Minutes	Minutes
Transcutaneous Bilirubinometry (RTSB)	L/min
Work Of Breathing (WOB)	Joules

Mechanical ventilators from different manufacturers may not offer equivalent mappings of certain parameters, even when designed for use in support of the same function. Furthermore, mechanical ventilators can operate in different modes, and not all mechanical ventilators operate or offer the same modes of operation.

For example, the Puritan Bennett™ 840 brand of mechanical ventilator is one that is in operation widely and is in use in critical care units in many hospitals. This mechanical ventilator can operate in one of several modes. These modes are listed next, together with tables that list sample output taken directly from this brand of mechanical ventilator:

SIMV =   Synchronous Intermittent Mandatory Ventilator, or a mode of breathing whereby the mechanical ventilator provides mandatory minimum number of breaths per minute when patient does not initiate a breath but will not over breathe or force termination of a patient-initiated breath.

Bi-Level =   BIPAP ventilation, or noninvasive airflow through a facemask in which airflow through the expiratory phase is reduced over inspiratory to facilitate exhalation.

CPAP =   Continuous Positive Airway Pressure, also synonymous with PEEP (positive end-expiratory pressure) in which continuous airflow at a preset end expiratory pressure is maintained to ensure alveolar recruitment to maximize areas of alveolar exposure for oxygenation.

CMV =   Continuous Mandatory Ventilation, or a preset inspiratory breath and flow pattern delivering breaths at fixed tidal volumes. Patient-initiated breaths are not possible in this mode of ventilation.

A listing of parameters obtained from this mechanical ventilator for the SIMV mode is provided in Table 1-13. Parameter values are representative of those taken during ordinary use of the device. The parameter labels are those associated with the device specification. Medical devices such as mechanical ventilators contain many parameters associated with settings and measured or spontaneous values from the patient. Yet, mechanical ventilators from different manufacturers do not ordinarily possess the same software method for data extraction (not to mention physical interface), nor do they necessarily possess exactly overlapping semantic naming conventions. Hence, an important part of the data validation process as part of the MDI implementation is the mapping of parameters from medical devices of different manufacturers to common definitions within the health IT system. It is not an overstatement to suggest that the process of performing this mapping and validating the data from each individual device type can take significant effort in terms of clinical and IT personnel—perhaps several months. Furthermore, mechanical ventilators from different manufacturers sometimes do not support the same specific modes of operation (Dräger Evita® XL and Puritan Bennett™ 840, are examples of such machines). This means that some of the modes of operation of the PB840 do not map explicitly to certain modes of the Evita® XL mechanical ventilator. While the clinical function of these machines is sound, obviously, for the uses intended, the issue at hand is the mapping of functions and parameters registered from the devices. The modes of operation may approximately overlap one another, and this may be sufficient in terms of equivalency for mapping terms in the health IT system.

Table 1-13: Example of the Typical Parameters Reported by the PB840 Mechanical Ventilator while in SIMV Mode.

PB840 Parameter	Description	Example Value	Unit of Measure (UOM)
VNT-MODE	Ventilator mode	SIMV	N/A
SET-RR	Respiratory rate setting	12	/min
SET-TV	Tidal volume setting	0.44	Liter
SET-MFLW	Mean flow setting	65	L/min
SET-O2	O2 fraction setting	21	%
SET-PSENS	Pressure sensitivity	0.0	cmH2O

Table 1-13: Example of the Typical Parameters Reported by the PB840 Mechanical Ventilator while in SIMV Mode. (cont.)

PB840 Parameter	Description	Example Value	Unit of Measure (UOM)
SET-PEEP	Positive end expiratory pressure setting	5.0	cmH2O
IN-HLD	Inspiratory hold	0.0	cmH2O
SET-APN-T	Apnea time setting	22	Seconds
SET-APN-TV	Apnea tidal volume setting	0.60	cmH2O
SET-APN-RR	Apnea respiratory rate setting	12	/min
SET-APN-FLW	Apnea flow rate setting	60	L/min
SET-APN-O2	Apnea O2 fraction setting	21	%
SET-PPS	Pressure support setting	0	cmH2O
SET-FLW-PTRN	Flow pattern	RAMP	N/A
O2-IN	O2 supply	OFF	N/A
VNT-RR	Respiratory rate—total	12	/min
TV	Exhaled tidal volume	0.39	Liter
MV	Exhaled minute volume	4.58	L/min
SPO-MV	Spontaneous minute volume	0.0	Liter
SET-MCP	Maximum circuit pressure	6.4	cmH2O
AWP	Mean airway pressure	6.4	cmH2O
PIP	Inspiratory pressure	20	cmH2O
IE-E	Expiratory component of I:E ratio	9.80	Seconds
SET-HI-PIP	High circuit pressure limit	50	cmH2O
SET-LO-TV	Low exhaled tidal volume limit	0.20	Liter
SET-LO-MV	Low exhaled minute volume limit	1.0	L/min
SET-HI-RR	High respiratory rate limit	40	/min
ALR-HI-PIP	High circuit pressure alarm status	NORMAL	N/A
ALR-LO-TV	Low exhaled tidal volume alarm status	NORMAL	N/A
ALR-LO-MV	Low exhaled minute volume alarm status	NORMAL	N/A
ALR-HI-RR	High respiratory rate alarm	NORMAL	N/A
ALE-NO-O2	No O2 supply alarm status	ALARM	N/A
ALR-NO-AIR	No air supply alarm	NORMAL	N/A
ALR-APN	Apnea alarm status	NORMAL	N/A
SET-FLW-BASE	Ventilator set base flow	4	L/min
SET-FLW-TRG	Flow sensitivity setting	3	L/min
SET-PIP	Inspiratory pressure or PEEP high setting	0	cmH2O

Table 1-13: Example of the Typical Parameters Reported by the PB840 Mechanical Ventilator while in SIMV Mode. (cont.)

PB840 Parameter	Description	Example Value	Unit of Measure (UOM)
SET-INSPT	Inspiratory time or PEEP high time setting	0.00	Seconds
SET-APN-T	Apnea interval setting	22	Seconds
SET-APN-IT	Apnea inspiratory pressure setting	0	cmH2O
SET-APN-RR	Apnea respiratory rate setting	12	/min
SET-APN-O2	Apnea O2% setting	21	%
SET-PMAX	High circuit pressure limit	50	cmH2O
ALR-MUTE	Alarm silence state	OFF	N/A
ALR-APN	Apnea alarm status	NORMAL	N/A
ALR-VNT	Severe occlusion/disconnect alarm status	NORMAL	N/A
SET-IEI	Inspiratory component of I:E ratio	0.00	Seconds
SET-IEE	Expiratory component of I:E ratio	0.00	Seconds
SET-APN-IEI	Inspiratory component of apnea I:E ratio	0.00	Seconds
SET-APN-IEE	Expiratory component of apnea I:E ratio	0.00	Seconds
SET-CONST	Const. during rate set. chn. for PCV mandatory breaths		
IE	Monitored value of I:E ratio	1:9.80	N/A

Table 1-14 lists a major subset of the raw data collected from an PB 840 mechanical ventilator[27] associated with the proprietary "SNDA" command (i.e., a command identified in the manufacturer's specification used to query the medical device for data), shown to illustrate the proprietary manner in which the data are communicated. These data were collected through serial RS232 port on the mechanical ventilator.

Table 1-14: Puritan Bennett™ (PB 840) Mechanical Ventilator Example Raw Data Response to "SNDA"Command–Mechanical Ventilator in SIMV Mode.

Note: The left-hand data represent the HEXADECIMAL equivalent of the ASCII response from the mechanical ventilator.

```
MEDICAL DEVICE: PB 840
QUERY: SNDA
HEXADECIMAL EQUIVALENT                                    ASCII RESPONSE
-----------------------------------------------------    ----------------
4D 49 53 43 41 2C 37 30 36 2C 39 37 2C 02 31 33          MISCA,706,97,.13
3A 32 33 20 2C 38 34 30 20 33 35 31 30 30 38 33          :23 ,840 3510083
36 37 35 20 20 20 20 2C 20 20 20 20 20 20 2C 53          675     ,        ,S
45 50 20 30 33 20 32 30 31 30 20 2C 53 49 4D 56          EP 03 2010 ,SIMV
20 20 2C 31 32 2E 30 20 20 2C 30 2E 34 34 20 20          ,12.0  ,0.44
2C 36 35 20 20 20 2C 32 31 20 20 20 20 2C 30             ,65    ,21     ,0
2E 30 20 20 2C 33 2E 30 20 20 20 2C 30 2E 30             .0  ,3.0   ,0.0
20 20 20 2C 20 20 20 20 20 20 2C 20 20 20 20 20              ,          ,
20 2C 20 20 20 20 20 20 2C 20 20 20 20 20 20 2C          ,        ,       ,
32 32 20 20 20 20 2C 30 2E 36 30 20 20 2C 31 32          22    ,0.60  ,12
2E 30 20 20 2C 36 30 20 20 20 20 2C 32 31 20 20          .0  ,60     ,21
20 20 2C 30 20 20 20 20 20 2C 52 41 4D 50 20 20          ,0       , RAMP
2C 20 20 20 20 20 2C 20 20 20 20 20 20 2C 4F             ,        ,        ,O
20 20 2C 20 20 20 20 20 20 2C 31 32 20 20 20             ,         ,12
20 2C 30 2E 33 39 20 20 2C 34 2E 36 35 20 20 2C          ,0.39  ,4.65  ,
30 2E 30 20 20 20 2C 32 34 2E 30 20 20 2C 36 2E          0.0  ,24.0  ,6.
32 20 20 20 2C 32 30 2E 30 20 20 2C 35 2E 38 30          2   ,20.0  ,5.80
20 20 2C 35 30 20 20 20 20 2C 20 20 20 20 20 20          ,50     ,
2C 20 20 20 20 20 20 2C 30 2E 32 30 20 20 2C 31          ,        ,0.20  ,1
2E 30 20 20 20 2C 34 30 20 20 20 20 2C 4E 4F 52          .0   ,40    ,NOR
4D 41 4C 2C 20 20 20 20 20 2C 20 20 20 20 20 20          MAL,     ,
20 2C 4E 4F 52 4D 41 4C 2C 4E 4F 52 4D 41 4C 2C          ,NORMAL,NORMAL,
4E 4F 52 4D 41 4C 2C 41 4C 41 52 4D 20 2C 4E 4F          NORMAL,ALARM ,NO
52 4D 41 4C 2C 4E 4F 52 4D 41 4C 2C 4E 4F 52 4D          RMAL,NORMAL,NORM
41 4C 2C 20 20 20 20 20 2C 20 20 20 20 20 20             AL,     ,
2C 31 33 3A 32 33 20 2C 20 20 20 20 20 20 2C 53          ,13:23 ,        ,S
45 50 20 30 33 20 32 30 31 30 20 2C 30 2E 30 20          EP 03 2010 ,0.0
20 20 2C 30 2E 30 20 20 20 20 2C 33 31 2E 30 20          ,0.0   ,31.0
2C 31 36 2E 30 30 20 2C 30 20 20 20 20 2C 30             ,16.00 ,0     ,0
2E 30 30 30 20 2C 30 20 20 20 20 2C 34 20 20             .000 ,0      ,4
20 20 20 2C 33 20 20 20 20 20 2C 20 20 20 20 20          ,3       ,
20 2C 20 20 20 20 20 20 2C 20 20 20 20 20 20 2C          ,        ,       ,
20 20 20 20 20 20 2C 20 20 20 20 20 20 2C 20 20              ,          ,
20 20 20 20 2C 20 20 20 20 20 20 2C 20 20 20 20          ,         ,
20 20 2C 20 20 20 20 20 20 2C 20 20 20 20 20             ,         ,
2C 20 20 20 20 20 20 2C 4E 4F 4F 50 20 43 2C 32          ,         ,NOOP C,2
30 2E 30 30 20 2C 30 20 20 20 20 20 2C 30 2E 30          0.00 ,0        ,0.0
30 20 20 2C 32 32 20 20 20 20 20 2C 30 20 20 20          0  ,22     ,0
20 2C 31 32 2E 30 20 20 2C 30 2E 30 30 20 20 2C          ,12.0  ,0.00  ,
32 31 20 20 20 20 2C 35 30 20 20 20 20 2C 4F 46          21    ,50     ,OF
46 20 20 20 2C 4E 4F 52 4D 41 4C 2C 4E 4F 52 4D          F   ,NORMAL,NORM
41 4C 2C 30 2E 30 30 20 20 2C 30 2E 30 30 20 20          AL,0.00  ,0.00
2C 30 2E 30 30 20 20 2C 30 2E 30 30 20 20 2C 20          ,0.00  ,0.00  ,
20 20 20 20 20 20 20 20 2C 31 3A 35 2E 38 30 2C                  ,1:5.80,
03 0D
```

By way of comparison, Table 1-15 lists the general modes of mechanical ventilation for Dräger mechanical ventilators,[28,29] and Table 1-16 lists the ventilator mode settings for the PB 840 mechanical ventilator.[30]

Table 1-15: Mechanical Ventilation Modes for Dräger Evita® XL Mechanical Ventilators.

Ventilation Type	Mode
Volume-Controlled (VC) Ventilation: set tidal volume is supplied at a constant flow. Breaths divided among inspiratory and expiratory phases (with AutoFlow)	VC-CMV (Continuous Mandatory Ventilation): volume-controlled, machine-triggered
	VC-AC (Assist Control): volume-controlled, machine- or patient-triggered; patient always receives the set tidal volume
	VC-SIMV (Synchronized/Synchronous Intermittent Mandatory Ventilation): volume-controlled, machine- or patient-triggered; spontaneous breathing permitted during end expiration phase
	VC-MMV (Mandatory Minute Volume): volume-controlled, machine- or patient-triggered; patient always receives the set minute volume
Pressure-Controlled (PC) Ventilation: PEEP and upper level Pinspiratory are maintained as constant	PC-CMV (Continuous Mandatory Ventilation): pressure-controlled, machine-triggered, spontaneous breathing permitted during entire breathing cycle
	PC-AC (Assist Control): pressure-controlled, machine- or patient-triggered, breathing attempts at PEEP triggers a mandatory breath, spontaneous breathing permitted during entire breathing cycle
	PC-SIMV (Synchronized/Synchronous Intermittent Mandatory Ventilation): pressure-controlled, machine- or patient-triggered, spontaneous breathing permitted during entire breathing cycle, patient can breathe spontaneously but mandatory breaths minimum
	PC-BIPAP (Biphasic Positive Airway Pressure): pressure-controlled, machine- or patient-triggered, inspiration & expiration synchronized, spontaneous breathing permitted during entire breathing cycle
	PC-APRV (Airway Pressure Release Ventilation): pressure-controlled, machine-triggered, spontaneous breathing permitted under continuous positive breathing pressure
	PC-PSV (Pressure Support Ventilation): pressure-controlled, machine- or patient-triggered, guaranteed minimum frequency, patient can breathe spontaneously at PEEP level
Spontaneous/Assisted (SPN) Ventilation: patient performs majority of work of breathing. Pressure level (PEEP) can be adjusted.	SPN-CPAP/PS (Continuous Positive Airway Pressure/Pressure Support): spontaneous breathing, continuous positive pressure with or without pressure support
	SPN-CPAP/VS (Continuous Positive Airway Pressure/Volume Support): spontaneous breathing, continuous pressure level, with or without volume support
	SPN-PPS (Proportional Pressure Support): spontaneous breathing, flow- and volume-proportional pressure support
Spontaneous (SPN) Neonatal Mode	SPN-CPAP (Continuous Positive Airway Pressure): spontaneous breathing, manually triggered, time-cycled pressure-controlled breathing at PEEP level
Pressure Control (PC) Neonatal Mode	PC-HFO (High Frequency Oscillation): pressure-controlled, high frequency oscillatory at level of average pressure
	PC-MMV (Mandatory Minute Volume): volume-ensured, machine- or patient-triggered, patient can breathe spontaneously and always receives the set minute volume

Table 1-16: Mechanical Ventilation Modes for the Puritan Bennett™ (PB 840) Mechanical Ventilators.

Modes	Mandatory Breath Types	Spontaneous Breath Types	Breathing Policy
Assist/Control (A/C)	INVASIVE: Pressure Control (PC), Volume Control (VC), Volume Control+ (VC+)	N/A	Ventilator-, patient-, operator-initiated breaths
	NON-INVASIVE: Pressure Control (PC), Volume Control (VC)	N/A	
Synchronous Intermittent Mandatory Ventilation (SIMV)	INVASIVE: Pressure Control (PV), Volume Control (VC), Volume Control+ (VC+)	Pressure Support (PS), Tube-compensated (TC), or Continuous Positive Airway Pressure (CPAP)	New breaths require mandatory interval during which patient initiation results in a mandatory synchronized breath. If not patient-initiated breath, ventilator delivers mandatory breath
	NON-INVASIVE: Pressure Control (PC), Volume Control (VC)	Pressure Support (PS) or Continuous Positive Airway Pressure (CPAP)	
Spontaneous (SPONT)	N/A except Pressure Control (PC) and Volume Control (VC) permitted by operator for manual inspirations	INVASIVE: Pressure Support (PS), Tube-Compensated (TC), Volume Support (VS), Proportional Assist (PA), Continuous Positive Airway Pressure (CPAP)	All spontaneous
		NON-INVASIVE: Pressure Support (PS) or Continuous Positive Airway Pressure (CPAP)	
BILEVEL	Pressure Control (PC)	Pressure Support, Tube-Compensated (TC), Continuous Positive Airway Pressure (CPAP)	Mandatory and spontaneous modes combined

On the Evita® XL mechanical ventilator, the selectable modes of mechanical ventilation are as follows and are drawn from the published intended use document:[31]

- Intermittent Positive Pressure Ventilation (Referred to as IPPV or CMV): volume-controlled ventilation with fixed mandatory minute volume. Options:
  - Continuous Positive Pressure Ventilation (CPPV)—controlled ventilation with continuous positive airway pressure (CPAP)
  - Pressure-Limited Ventilation (PLV)—Pressure limited constant-volume ventilation
  - AutoFlow®—automatic regulation of inspiratory flow and inspiratory pressure

  ▫ Inverse Ratio Ventilation (IRV)—ventilation with inverse inspiration/expiration ratio
- Synchronized Intermittent Mandatory Ventilation (Referred to as SIMV): combines mechanical volume-controlled ventilation with spontaneous breathing. Options:
    ▫ PLV
    ▫ AutoFlow®
- Mandatory Minute Volume Ventilation (MMV): spontaneous breathing with automatic adjustment of mandatory ventilation to patient minute volume requirement. Options:
- PLV
- AutoFlow®
- Spontaneous Breathing (SB): spontaneous breathing at ambient pressure
- Continuous Positive Airway Pressure (CPAP): spontaneous breathing with positive airway pressure
- Assisted Spontaneous Breathing (ASB): pressure-assisted spontaneous breathing
- Biphasic Positive Airway Pressure (BIPAP): pressure-controlled ventilation combined with spontaneous breathing during complete breath cycle with pressure adjustable to CPAP level
- Biphasic Positive Airway Pressure Assisted (BIPAPAssist): pressure-controlled assisted ventilation
- Airway Pressure Release Ventilation (APRV): Spontaneous breaths on two pressure levels with long, independently adjustable time ranges
- Proportional Pressure Support (PPS): Optional. For differentiated proportional support of spontaneous breathing with pathological compliance and/or resistance
- Independent Lung Ventilation (ILV): separate, differentiated, synchronized ventilation with two separate Evita XL units independently ventilating each lung

The following text messages are available on output from the Evita® XL mechanical ventilator. These are the explicit annotations that indicate the selected mode of mechanical ventilation settings on this brand of Dräger ventilator:[28]

Mode IPPV
Mode IPPV/ASSIST
Mode SIMV
Mode SIMV/ASB
Mode BIPAP
Mode BIPAP/ASB
Mode SIMV/AutoFlow
Mode SIMV/ASB/AutoFlow
Mode IPPV/AutoFlow
Mode IPPV/ASSIST/AutoFlow
Mode APRV
Mode MMV
Mode MMV/ASB
Mode MMV/AutoFlow

Mode MMV/ASB/AutoFlow
Mode CPAP
Mode CPAP/ASB
Mode APNEA VENTILATION
Mode CPAP/PPS
Mode SYNCHRON MASTER
Mode SYNCHRON SLAVE
Mode BIPAP/ASSIST
Mode Adults
Mode Pediatrics
Mode Neonates
IV-Invasive Ventilation
NIV-Non-Invasive Ventilation
Ventilator STANDBY

Several of these messages can be seen in OBX segment 37 in Table 1-17.

By comparison, the Puritan Bennett™ 840 mechanical ventilator identifies four specific modes, as outlined in Table 1-16. These are the following:[30]

- **Assist/Control (A/C):** the ventilator delivers only mandatory breaths. Breaths may be patient-, ventilator-, or operator-initiated.
- **Spontaneous (SPONT):** the ventilator delivers only spontaneous, patient-triggered breaths. There is no set mandatory respiratory rate on the part of the ventilator.
- **Synchronous Intermittent Mandatory Ventilation (SIMV):** the ventilator provides one mandatory breath per breath cycle and as many spontaneous breaths as can be triggered by the patient during the remainder of the breath cycle.
- **BILEVEL:**[32] establishes two levels of PEEP setting.

Despite differences in terminology, some modes can be mapped to each other from different brands or manufacturers. Discussion over specific modes and the mapping of same across mechanical ventilators is beyond the scope of this text. Much has been written on modes of mechanical ventilation and mechanical ventilation, in general.[33] A simple treatment of the modes is included here to illustrate the points made in regard to differences across medical device manufacturers.

The most basic modes of mechanical ventilation shared by most mechanical ventilators include the following:

- Mandatory ventilation: volume-controlled or pressure-controlled
- Spontaneous ventilation: spontaneous or assisted modes

Table 1-17 and Table 1-18 list example HL7 transactions from these two mechanical ventilators. More discussion on HL7 will be taken up in Chapter 4. As can be seen from these two tables, some data elements are specified differently between the two medical devices. While many medical devices are employed in different use cases in the hospital (example: adult versus neonatal intensive care), an exercise in caution and careful planning must take into account the fact that the mapping of parameters to health IT system patient flow sheets may require tailoring for these specific use cases. For example, certain mechanical ventilators (such as the 840) may by default be set to report tidal volumes (TV) in liters whereas the Evita® XL normally reports in milliliters. These seemingly simple yet subtle variations translate into work effort to ensure that the patient charts employ common units of measure and that data are reported unambiguously and clearly so that clinical staff are clear as to the values. Thus, there can be an impact on patient safety if not addressed during the installation and rollout of an MDI implementation.

Table 1-17: Sample HL7 Result Listing for the Dräger Evita® XL Mechanical Ventilator (note: 1 mbar = 1.0197 cmH2O).

```
MSH|^~\&|<Sending_App>|<Sending_Fac>|<Receiving_
  App>|Receiving_Fac>|20140119102934||ORU^R01|IDC0020064
  6|P|2.3
PID|123456|||||^^
PV1||I|
OBR|1||||||20140119102934|||||||||
OBX|1|NM|COMP||41.3|L-1
OBX|2|NM|RAW||12.4|mbar*L-1/s
OBX|3|NM|LNGTC||643|cL
OBX|4|NM|MINAWP||6|mbar
OBX|5|NM|AWP||11|mbar
OBX|6|NM|PEEP||6|mbar
OBX|7|NM|SPO-MV||0|L/min
OBX|8|NM|PIP||24|mbar
OBX|9|NM|TV||468|mL
OBX|10|NM|SPO-RR||0|/min
OBX|11|NM|MV||7|L/min
OBX|12|NM|TRG-FR||0|/min
OBX|13|NM|RR||15|/min
OBX|14|NM|SET-O2||21|%
OBX|15|NM|SET-TV||540|mL
OBX|16|NM|SET-TI||12|s
OBX|17|NM|SET-IEI||1|
OBX|18|NM|SET-IEE||2.3|
OBX|19|NM|SET-RR||15|/min
OBX|20|NM|SET-PEEP||6|mbar
OBX|21|NM|SET-APN-T||20|s
OBX|22|NM|SET-TACFR||100|/min
OBX|23|NM|SET-FLW-TRG||2|L/min
OBX|24|NM|SET-RAMP||2|s
OBX|25|NM|SET-TUBE-COMP||100|%
OBX|26|NM|SET-TUBE-DIAM||8|mm
OBX|27|NM|SET-CPAP-ASB-T||40|s
OBX|28|NM|SET-EOF-TRS||2.5|%
OBX|29|ST|SET-IE||1:2.3|
OBX|30|ST|DEV-MODEL||EvitaXL|
OBX|31|ST|DEV-CODE||8260|
OBX|32|ST|DEV-PROT||MEDIBUS|
OBX|33|ST|DEV-PROT-VER||04.00|
OBX|34|ST|DEV-VER||07.00|
OBX|35|ST|DEV-TXT-TS||10:2014-Jan-19|
OBX|36|TS|DEV-TS||20140119102934|
OBX|37|ST|DEV-MODE||mode Adults\IV - Invasive Ventilation\Mode
  IPPV/ASSIST/AutoFlow
```

Table 1-18: Sample HL7 Result Listing for the PB 840 Mechanical Ventilator.

```
MSH|^~\&|<Sending_App>|<Sending_Fac>|<Receiving_App>|Receiving_Fac>|20100
   519102934||ORU^R01|IDC00200646|P|2.3
PID|123456|||||^^
PV1||I|
OBR|1||||||20100519102934||||||||
OBX|1|ST|DEV-TIME^Ventilator time||10:29|
OBX|2|ST|DEV-ID^Ventilator ID||840 3510010508|
OBX|3|ST|DEV-DATE^Ventilator Date||JAN 19 2014|
OBX|4|TS|DEV-TS^Device Timestamp||20100519102934|
OBX|5|ST|VNT-MODE^Ventilator Mode||CMV|
OBX|6|NM|SET-RR^Respiratory rate||10.0|/min
OBX|7|NM|SET-TV^Tidal volume||0.50|L
OBX|8|NM|SET-MFLW^Peak flow setting||0|L/min
OBX|9|NM|SET-O2^O2% setting||21|%
OBX|10|NM|SET-PSENS^Pressure sensitivity||0.0|cmH2O
OBX|11|NM|SET-PEEP^PEEP||5.0|cmH2O
OBX|12|NM|IN-HLD^Plateau||0.0|cmH2O
OBX|13|NM|SET-APN-T^Apnea interval||20|s
OBX|14|NM|SET-APN-TV^Apnea tidal volume||0.50|cmH2O
OBX|15|NM|SET-APN-RR^Apnea respiratory rate||16.0|/min
OBX|16|NM|SET-APN-FLW^Apnea peak flow||60|L/min
OBX|17|NM|SET-APN-O2^Apnea O2%||100|%
OBX|18|NM|SET-PPS^Pressure support||0|cmH2O
OBX|19|ST|SET-FLW-PTRN^Flow pattern|||
OBX|20|ST|O2-IN^O2 Supply||OFF|
OBX|21|NM|VNT-RR^Total respiratory rate||21|/min
OBX|22|NM|TV^Exhaled tidal volume||0.39|L
OBX|23|NM|MV^Exhaled minute volume||9.51|L/min
OBX|24|NM|SPO-MV^Spontaneous minute volume||0.0|L
OBX|25|NM|SET-MCP^Maximum circuit pressure||22.0|cmH2O
OBX|26|NM|AWP^Mean airway pressure||14.0|cmH2O
OBX|27|NM|PIP^End inspiratory pressure||21.0|cmH2O
OBX|28|NM|IE-E^1/E component of I:E||1.00|
OBX|29|NM|SET-HI-PIP^High circuit pressure limit||60|cmH2O
OBX|30|NM|SET-LO-TV^Low exhaled tidal volume limit||0.20|L
OBX|31|NM|SET-LO-MV^Low exhaled minute volume limit||2.0|L
OBX|32|NM|SET-HI-RR^High respiratory rate limit||40|/min
OBX|33|ST|ALR-HI-PIP^High circuit pressure alarm status||NORMAL|
OBX|34|ST|ALR-LO-TV^Low exhaled tidal volume alarm status||NORMAL|
OBX|35|ST|ALR-LO-MV^Low exhaled minute volume alarm status||NORMAL|
OBX|36|ST|ALR-HI-RR^High respiratory rate alarm status||NORMAL|
OBX|37|ST|ALR-NO-O2^No O2 supply alarm status||NORMAL|
OBX|38|ST|ALR-NO-AIR^No air supply alarm status||NORMAL|
OBX|39|ST|ALR-APN^Apnea alarm status||NORMAL|
OBX|40|NM|SET-FLW-BASE^Ventilator-set base flow||3|L/min
OBX|41|NM|SET-FLW-TRG^Flow sensitivity setting||2|L/min
OBX|42|NM|PIP^End inspiratory pressure||21.00|cmH2O
OBX|43|NM|SET-PIP^Inspiratory pressure or PEEP High setting||0|cmH2O
OBX|44|NM|SET-INSPT^Inspiratory time or PEEP High time setting||1.44|s
OBX|45|NM|SET-APN-T^Apnea interval setting||20|s
OBX|46|NM|SET-APN-IP^Apnea inspiratory pressure setting||0|cmH2O
OBX|47|NM|SET-APN-RR^Apnea respiratory rate setting||16.0|/min
OBX|48|NM|SET-APN-IT^Apnea inspiratory time setting||0.00|s
OBX|49|NM|SET-APN-O2^Apnea O2% setting||100|%
OBX|50|NM|SET-PMAX^High circuit pressure limit||60|cmH2O
OBX|51|ST|ALR-MUTE^Alarm silence state||OFF|
OBX|52|ST|ALR-APN^Apnea alarm status||NORMAL|
OBX|53|ST|ALR-VNT^Severe Occlusion/Disconnect alarm status||NORMAL|
OBX|54|NM|SET-IEI^Inspiratory component of I:E ratio||1.00|
OBX|55|NM|SET-IEE^Expiratory component of I:E ratio||3.17|
OBX|56|ST|SET-APN-IEI^Inspiratory component of apnea I:E ratio||0.00|
OBX|57|ST|SET-APN-IEE^Expiratory component of apnea I:E ratio||0.00|
OBX|58|ST|SET-CONST^Const. during rate set. chn.for PCV mandatory
   brths||I-TIME|
OBX|59|ST|IE^Monitored value of I:E ratio||1.00:1|
```

Note in Table 1-17 that OBX segment 30 through 34 list specifics associated with the device type, its firmware version and data communication protocol. This type of information may be available from medical devices, depending on what the interface specification details, and can be useful for managing the medical device inventory and maintaining firmware versions, as well. Sometimes alarm-specific information is communicated by the devices through the RS232 port, as in the case of OBX segment 33-39 in Table 1-18. This information can be provided to nurse call or other related notification systems for communication in the event of device-specific notable events that can impact the patient.

Infusion Systems and Tourniquet Pumps

Infusion systems (medication pumps) are also widely used in most environments within the hospital setting. Infusion pumps in critical care are a major medical device component, and some patients in critical care can receive multiple drugs. Because patients in intensive care may be on multiple drugs, oftentimes many pumps are employed to infuse drugs into a single patient. It is not unusual for a patient in intensive care to receive multiple infusions, all delivered through separate pumps. Hence, drug delivery through infusion systems can be rather complicated and requires careful management in terms of the type and dosage of the drug, often normalized or titrated by patient size and weight. Thus, control and measurement of drug delivery is essential to maintenance of patient systems and is critical to preservation of life.

Infusion systems are often tightly integrated with pharmacy systems and medication administration systems. Hence, the individual pumps themselves, such as the Carefusion pump depicted in Figure 1-19, are often integrated through a medical device manufacturer's infusion gateway. These gateways provide for inbound patient information, including admission, discharge and transfer (ADT) type HL7 transactions to support patient identification and workflow management, in addition to integration from computerized provider order entry (CPOE) systems to provide feedback relative to completion and fulfillment of drug orders. Integration with pharmacy (Rx) systems also provides for updates of drug database formularies. Hence, the complexity of the integration of these infusion systems would suggest that direct integration from individual infusion pumps from the perspective of taking raw data (e.g., flow rate, volume delivery, time to go, etc.) is rather impractical: given that the data from the infusion systems must be tightly integrated with the health IT system and clinical workflow, some infusion pump vendors recommend or will only permit integration via their published interfaces available through their infusion gateways.

Before attempting to integrate pumps through MDI solution vendors, first inquire of the pump manufacturer and your health IT system vendor whether they support direct integration of infusion systems. Integration mechanisms would typically employ the newly-minted interoperability profiles or standards proffered by IHE Patient Care Device Technical Framework pertaining to the POC Infusion Verification (PIV) implementation profile.[34,35,36] The IHE-PCD Transaction Map, shown in Table 1-19, defines those PCD transactions related to infusion: The PCD-03 and PCD-10 transactions define the infusion order communication and the outbound events from the infusion system, respectively. The PIV Profile seeks to verify the order and the patient. The PIV Profile accomplishes this by ensuring that the "5 Rights of Medication Administration" are adhered to.[36] These include verifying:

- The Right Patient
- The Right Drug
- The Right Dose
- The Right Route
- The Right Time

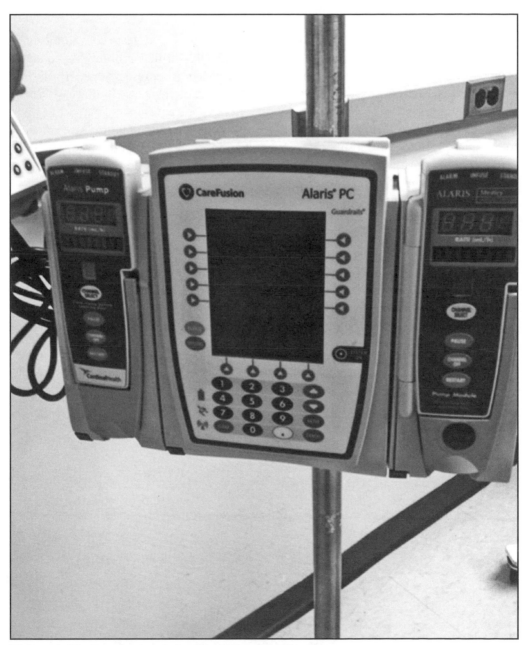

Figure 1-19: Carefusion Infusion Pump on Stand.

(Photo by Author)

Table 1-19: Partial IHE-PCD Transaction Map Related to Infusion-based Transactions.

Transac-tion ID	Transaction Name or Title	Profile	Source Actor	Receiving Actor
PCD-03	Communicate Infusion Order	PIV	Infusion Order Pro-grammer (IOP)	Infusion Order Con-sumer (IOC)
PCD-10	Communicate Infusion Pump Event	IPEC	Device Observation Reporter (DOR)	Device Observation Consumer (DOC)

The Infusion Pump Event Communication (IPEC) Profile seeks to communicate clinical and technical data from the Patient Care Device—infusion pump(s)—to an information system. In this case, the information system is represented generically as a Device Observation Consumer (DOC). The Patient Care Device—in this case, the infusion pump system—is the Device Observation Reporter (DOR).

Specialty devices, such as the Tourniquet by Stryker shown in Figure 1-20, control tourniquet pressure during surgery. While not an infusion pump in the traditional sense, it does control cuff pressure and provides for data integration through a serial port. A view of the RS232 serial adapter attached to this pump is shown in Figure 1-21.

Specialty Medical Devices

Other specialty devices are used in the critical care environment, including dialysis machines and intra-aortic balloon pumps. These devices both support medical device integration through serial ports and network ports. Figure 1-22 depicts a Gambro Prismaflex dialysis machine used at the bedside of critically ill patients. Figure 1-23 illustrates an Intra-Aortic Balloon Pump (IABP) formerly manufactured by Datascope but acquired by Maquet. Some types of dialysis equipment can communicate over network ports while others communicate over serial ports. Figure 1-24 shows the reverse side of a Fresenius 2008T model of dialysis machine with the RS232 adapter disassembled to illustrate pin connections for data communication. Figure 1-25 shows a frontal view of the same machine.

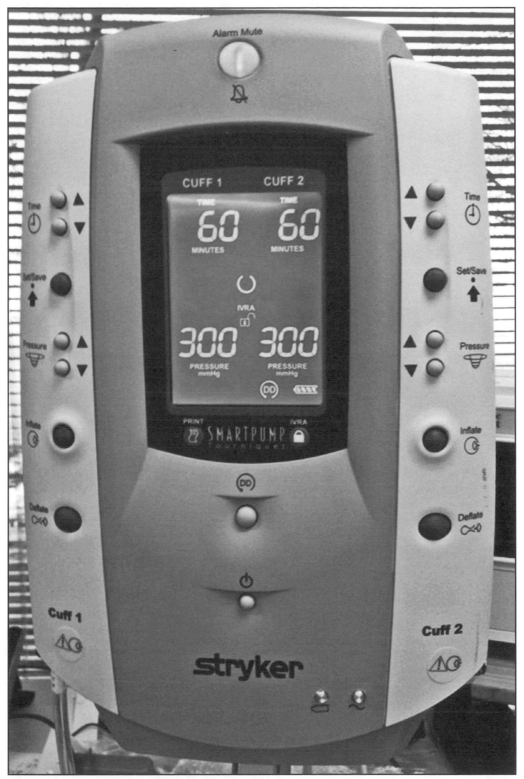

Figure 1-20: Stryker Tourniquet Pump.

(Photo by Author)

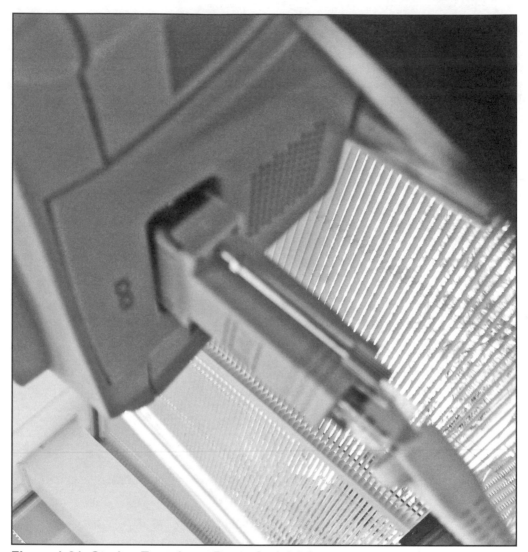

Figure 1-21: Stryker Tourniquet Pump Serial Adapter.

(Photo by Author)

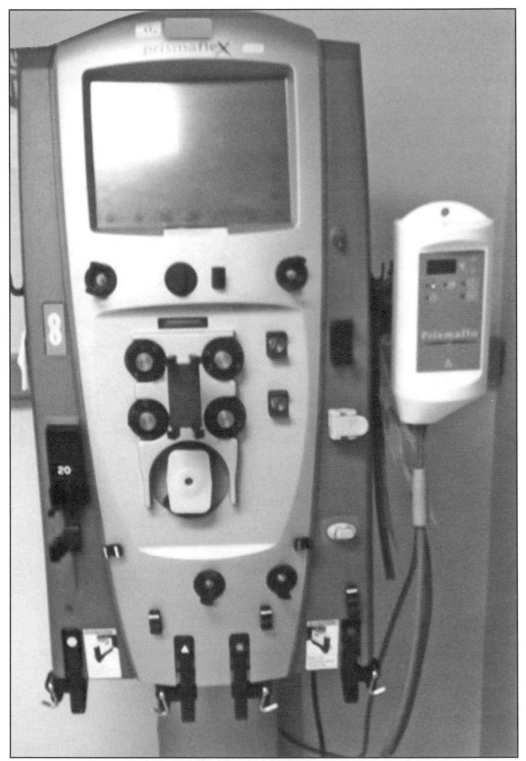

Figure 1-22: Gambro Prismaflex Dialysis Machine.

(Photo by Author)

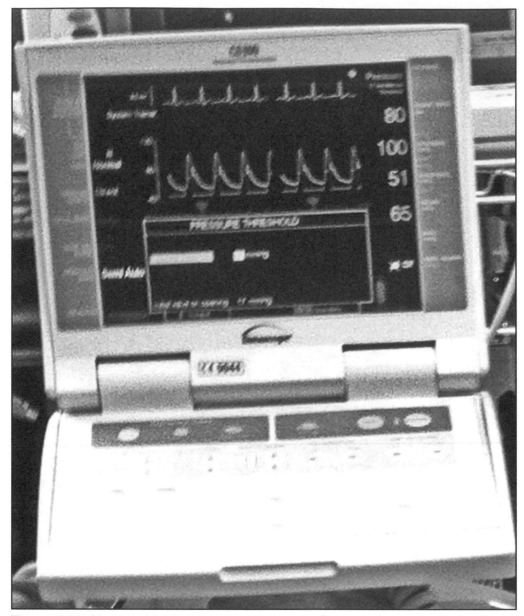

Figure 1-23: Maquet CS 300 Intra-Aortic Balloon Pump (IABP).

(Photo by Author)

Figure 1-24: Fresenius Dialysis Machine Showing Serial RS232 Port and Adapter Taken Apart to Illustrate Pin Connections.

(Photo by Author)

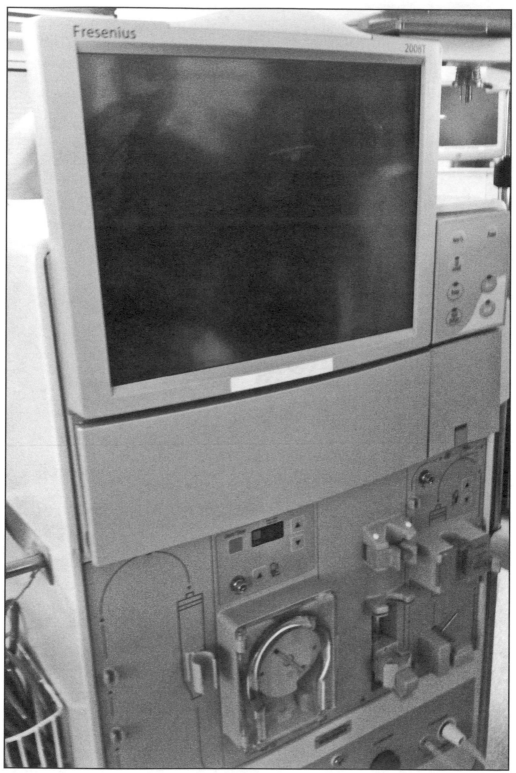

Figure 1-25: Fresenius 2008T Front View.

(Photo by Author)

Emergency Departments (EDs)

Emergency departments (EDs) often use physiologic monitors and other equipment at the bedside for electrocardiography (ECG). Many of the devices that have been illustrated in the previous sections can be used in EDs, as well. Nonetheless, physiologic monitors are most often the medical devices that are readily available and deployed within these units. Figure 1-26 illustrates one brand of monitor used in these environments. These are usually attached to wall mounts in convenient locations at the bedside. Data may be retrieved from physiologic monitors, depending on brand, through network or serial port connectivity, as has previously been described.

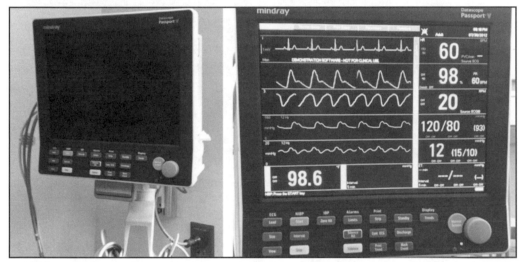

Figure 1-26: Example Physiologic Monitor As Might Be Used in an Emergency Department (ED) or Endoscopy Department (Passport® V).

(Photo by Author)

In the case of the Datascope monitor shown, data may be retrieved via direct access through serial ports on the back of the units, illustrated in Figure 1-27. Hence, data may be extracted through a medical device intermediary at the POC and then communicated over a network connection to the health IT system.

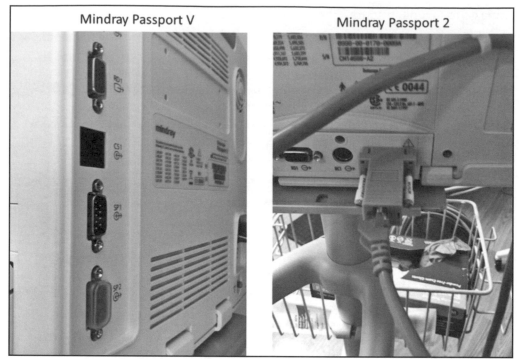

Figure 1-27: Datascope Passport® V & Passport® 2 RS-232 Serial Port.

(Photo by Author)

Other devices can be brought to bear in the ED environment, and many physiologic monitors may be configured to communicate through their monitoring gateways. In these cases, there is no need for individual monitor communication, as the data are normally communicated to central stations and telemetry monitoring rooms, as illustrated in Figure 1-28. Data obtained from these gateways is translated into a more standardized form via a dedicated gateway or concentrator and then these data are transmitted in an HL7 or related format to the enterprise network for consumption by the health IT system.

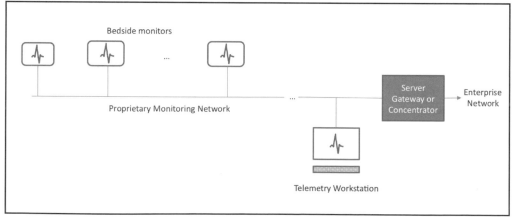

Figure 1-28: Physiologic Monitors Communicating Over a Proprietary Local Area Network to a Telemetry Workstation and Concentrator or Gateway.

An example of the physical network connection to the enterprise LAN is shown in the photograph in Figure 1-29.

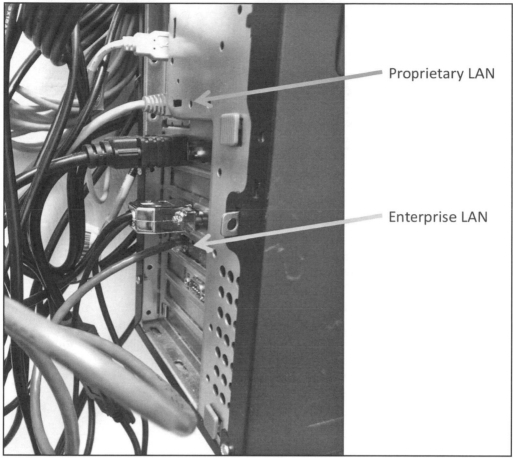

Figure 1-29: Enterprise and Proprietary Networks Attached to Physiologic Monitoring Gateway (Philips Intellivue database server shown).

Note: The upper orange network cable is attached to the proprietary or monitoring side and the blue network cable is attached to the enterprise network.(Photo by Author)

Medical Surgical/Step-Down Units

Medical devices in general medical/surgical units can vary, as well. Infusion pumps for pain management, physiologic monitors for aperiodic monitoring of vital signs, and other devices (e.g.,capnography monitors used in the end tidal CO_2 measurement for patients on opioids for pain) are often used in these environments. Standalone spot vital signs monitors are also frequently used to assist in ad-hoc vitals collection throughout the day and evening hours. Figure 1-30 is a close-up of one type of spot vital signs monitor: the GE Dinamap ProCare. These monitors provide measurements of non-invasive blood pressure, oxygen saturation from pulse oximetry cuffs, temperature measurement and heart rate pulse measurement either through the pulse oximetry cuff or the non-invasive blood pressure monitoring cuff.

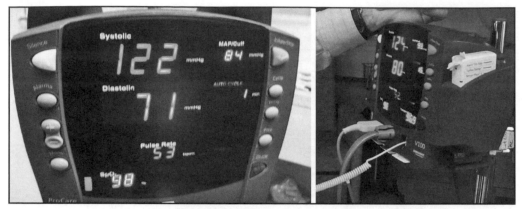

Figure 1-30: GE Dinamap Spot Vital Signs Monitor. (Photo by Author)

Table 1-20 summarizes an HL7 transaction typically derived from the data reported by the GE Dinamap ProCare monitor. Despite the fact that the clinical parameters of non-invasive blood pressure, temperature, oxygen saturation, and pulse represent only a handful of data, the machine itself produces much more information related to settings that can be used from a workflow or an alarm notification perspective. For example, high and low values associated with oxygen saturation, blood pressure, temperature, device state indicators, signal quality indicators, and device model and modes can be retrieved from the Dinamap. This information can be used by subsequent systems (e.g., health IT systems or EHRs) to compare patient measured values relative to known thresholds for alarm management, as well as to establish measurement context.

Table 1-20: HL7 Listing of Parameters Available from the GE Dinamap Spot Vital Signs Monitor.

```
MSH|^~\&|<Sending_App>|<Sending_Fac>|<Receiving_App>|Receiving_Fac>|20130
    518205032||ORU^R01|IDC00200646|P|2.3
PID|123456|||||^^
PV1||I|
OBR|1|||||20130518205032
OBX|1|NM|HR^^||54|/min
OBX|2|ST|HR-SRC^^|||Pulse Oximeter|
OBX|3|NM|SPO2^^||97|%
OBX|4|ST|SPO2-CHSTAT^^||Operate mode OK|
OBX|5|NM|SPO2-SIGNAL^^||9|
OBX|6|NM|SPO2-PLSINT^^||1|
OBX|7|ST|SPO2-MTSTAT^^||No Motion Detected|
OBX|8|ST|NBP-DTSTAT^^||Busy|
OBX|9|ST|NBP-TYPE^^||Unknown|
OBX|10|ST|NBP-DTTYPE^^||Normal mode|
OBX|11|TS|NBP-TS^^||20100518204952|
OBX|12|NM|NBP-S^^||126|mmHg||||||20130518204952||20130518204952
OBX|13|NM|NBP-D^^||69|mmHg||||||20130518204952||20130518204952
OBX|14|NM|NBP-M^^||85|mmHg||||||20130518204952||20130518204952
OBX|15|NM|NBP-CUFFSTAT^^||0|
OBX|16|NM|NBP-CUFFP^^||31|mmHg
OBX|17|NM|NBP-HR^^||52|/min
OBX|18|NM|SET-NBP-S-LO^^||80|mmHg
OBX|19|NM|SET-NBP-S-HI^^||200|mmHg
OBX|20|NM|SET-NBP-D-LO^^||30|mmHg
OBX|21|NM|SET-NBP-D-HI^^||120|mmHg
OBX|22|NM|SET-NBP-M-LO^^||0|mmHg
OBX|23|NM|SET-NBP-M-HI^^||255|mmHg
OBX|24|NM|SET-SPO2-LO^^||90|%
OBX|25|NM|SET-SPO2-HI^^||100|%
OBX|26|NM|SET-HR-LO^^||50|/min
OBX|27|NM|SET-HR-HI^^||150|/min
OBX|28|NM|SET-TP1-LO^^||0|F.
OBX|29|NM|SET-TP2-HI^^||0|F.
OBX|30|NM|DEV-MODEL^^||7280|
OBX|31|NM|DEV-MODE^^||1|>
```

Data are extracted from the GE Dinamap through the serial port on the rear of the unit, shown in Figure 1-31. The RS-232 connection from the GE Dinamap involves a 15-pin connector.

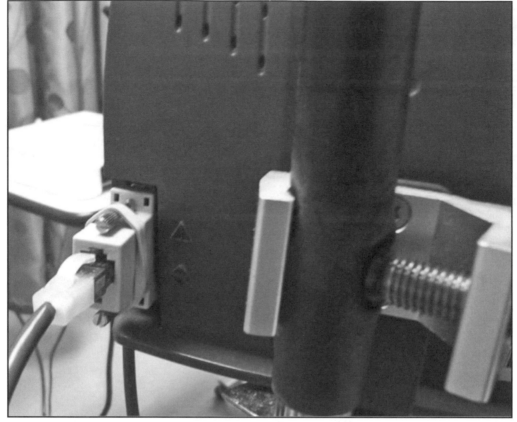

Figure 1-31: An Example of a 15-pin Serial Port for Data Access on the GE Dinamap Spot Vital Signs Monitor.

(Photo by Author)

SUMMARY

This chapter's objective was to provide examples of the various device types that can be expected to be seen in the major in-patient environments. While not exhaustive, as there are many thousands of other types of medical devices that can be accessed in these environments, the major device types were presented together with their typical data export capabilities and use cases.

In summary:

- Operating room environments normally employ each of the following:
  - Physiologic monitoring
  - Anesthesia machines
  - Bi-spectral index monitoring for level of sedation management (may be optional and may be present either as a standalone machine or as an extension to physiologic monitoring)
  - Infusion devices
  - Additionally, specialty operating rooms, or those dedicated to specific types of surgeries (e.g., open heart surgeries) may include the following:

- Cardiopulmonary bypass machines
- Cerebral oximetry monitoring
- End-tidal carbon dioxide monitoring (may be present as a standalone machine or as an extension to either physiologic monitoring system or anesthesia machine)
- Critical care units normally employ one each of the following for individual rooms:
  - Physiologic monitoring
  - Mechanical ventilation (for dependent patients or patients who are recovering from surgery)
  - Infusion
- Additionally, specialty devices that may be employed include one or more of the following:
  - Intra-aortic balloon pumps
  - End-tidal carbon dioxide monitoring (present either as a standalone machine or as an extension to either physiologic monitoring system or anesthesia machine)
- Step-down, medical surgical units, and post-anesthesia care units (PACUs) employ physiologic monitoring and may employ (in addition) standalone ad-hoc spot vital signs monitors, mechanical ventilators, and infusion systems.
- Emergency departments physiologic monitoring and other devices, such as infusion systems, can be brought to the bedside as required.
- Catheterization laboratories, radiology departments, and other areas within the surgical services domain will also maintain physiological monitoring and anesthesia machines. Infusion systems will also be present at these locations.
- Labor and delivery units will frequently have dedicated operating rooms, which feature standalone physiological monitoring, as well as anesthesia machines, infusion systems and mechanical ventilation. In addition, fetal monitoring systems, baby warmers, and incubators are employed in these units.
- Pediatric and neonatal intensive care units will feature principally the same machinery as adult operating rooms: physiologic monitoring, as well as anesthesia machines and mechanical ventilation and specialty devices, such as nitrous oxide administration.

Each of these departments will have their specific peculiarities in terms of use cases and medical devices that will provide data for charting and integration. The common denominator across most of these units is physiologic monitoring, followed by respiratory management fulfilled in part by mechanical ventilation and anesthetic gas administration as part of the therapeutic and treatment protocols required for each of these domains.

Part of the task of the MDI hospital integration team is to implement an MDI solution that best communicates the data across these environments and integrates them into the health IT system in the most cost-effective way that meets the requirements of the "client" (i.e., clinical end-user). If the enterprise is seeking to begin the integration in one department (say, operating rooms and other units related to perioperative management), then the best MDI approach should be used that can scale from this department to multiple departments. These requirements include asking (and answering) the following questions:

1. Is the healthcare enterprise seeking to integrate physiologic monitors into the health IT system using vendor-supplied medical device gateways or via serial POC connectivity?

    a. If so, does a gateway-based approach enable integrating ancillary devices?

    b. Will all data from the ancillary devices be available if reported through the existing physiologic monitors or will data be truncated?

    c. If the integration of ancillary medical devices through existing MIB connection to physiologic monitors is limiting in terms of data reporting, is it possible to support a hybrid approach whereby gateway-based physiologic monitoring can coexist with POC data collection via medical device serial ports?

2. How does the MDI solution provider specifically solve the problem of data association to patients when collected separately through physiologic monitoring gateways and separate POC serial port data collection?

3. Is it possible to retrieve data from the physiologic monitors at the bedside via their serial ports while not disturbing any central monitoring capability required of these same monitors? Can existing central monitoring capabilities be supported simultaneously while separately pulling data integration with health IT systems?

4. Can the data from the various medical devices be communicated to the health IT system at the desired rates, regardless of whether communicated through gateways or from POC medical device serial ports?

These questions are designed to trigger the MDI team within the healthcare enterprise to investigate the various complexities and interrelationships of the aforementioned items, particularly as relates to deciding upon an MDI solution provider.

MDI Solution Acquisition and Implementation

There is no substitute for experience when it comes to MDI implementation. In this chapter, the objective is to provide guidance on building the implementation team, preparing for the implementation, and estimating implementation timelines.

STARTING THE MDI ACQUISITION PROCESS: BUILD OR BUY

The healthcare enterprise may develop or acquire an MDI solution. The home-grown development of MDI carries with it certain responsibilities, as does acquiring a vendor-based solution. Therefore, the enterprise should be cognizant of the pros and cons of either approach.

Building an MDI Solution

Home-grown MDI solutions have been employed quite successfully. The tradeoff on time, personnel, regulatory requirements, and project management of an in-house-developed solution must be considered in light of the native talent and capabilities of the IT and clinical engineering teams in place within the healthcare enterprise. The availability of native talent may restrict internal development to institutions that either are staffed appropriately or can afford to hire these resources. This implies that large research institutions are typically those that engage in such a practice as developing or tailoring an enterprise-specific solution, although this is not a strict rule.

The implications of building an MDI from the ground up:
- The clinical or biomedical engineering and IT teams can develop and field POC data collection hardware and software; have access to medical device specifications and interface protocols; and have the software development capability to write and maintain medical device drivers.

- Software development personnel must be available on hand to maintain medical device drivers and/or develop new medical device drivers (e.g., hiring of external consultants).
- Support teams must be in place to provide 24/7 coverage and maintenance of the MDI solution. This team would include those in the clinical or biomedical engineering organization, as well as the health IT organization to manage bedside hardware and the data interfaces to the health IT system.
- POC serial data communication will require hardware to communicate from the medical devices. This hardware will need to be acquired or developed and maintained.
- Quality and regulatory management of the system, inclusive of the necessary artifacts such as testing documentation, will also be required.

Building an MDI solution internally is, in essence, equivalent to creating a custom product for medical device integration within the healthcare enterprise. A key benefit of this undertaking is that the enterprise has the opportunity to create precisely what it needs to meet its MDI requirements. And this can be done unfettered by MDI solution provider offerings, which, of necessity, must be made market-generic to meet the needs of multiple prospects and clients. The healthcare enterprise can also specifically focus on integrating the most needed medical devices on a timeline that is beneficial to the needs of the enterprise and availability of resources including clinical, IT, and biomedical staff.

One challenge associated with this approach is that the enterprise takes on the role of an MDI solution provider development shop and may expose itself to the need for quality and regulatory oversight (e.g., FDA clearance). Nonetheless, maintenance of a quality system and compliance with practices consistent with good manufacturing and development processes will need to be undertaken. A discussion of this topic is reserved for Chapter 7.

If the enterprise has neither the experience nor resources for developing and maintaining an MDI solution, then that becomes a challenge to be overcome as part of development and implementation. Again, for larger enterprises, this may be acceptable and even welcome, as it ensures that the developed solution is tailored most precisely to the enterprise needs.

Clinical stakeholder requirements will most likely require developers to consider usability of the system and human interaction. Such usability requirements translate into taking into account workflow interaction requirements, as well as visual end-user requirements. The MDI solution will also need to interoperate with an existing health IT system. Therefore, these interface requirements will need to be taken into account throughout the development process.

To illustrate what is meant here, consider the use of patient demographic information for the purpose of patient association and disassociation with POC medical devices. If patient identifiers are to be associated with the medical devices and communicated to the health IT system, then patient-to-medical device association mechanisms will need to be acquired or fabricated, and fielded. To accomplish this requires workflow analysis; software development to conform to the end-user workflow requirements, which can vary by department; user validation testing; training; implementation; and support.

Because the scope of this effort can be vast, involving much in the way of resources, this can discourage smaller healthcare enterprises from developing their own home-grown MDI solutions and suggests that only larger healthcare enterprises may be able to muster the resources needed to meet the challenges associated with home-grown MDI development.

Acquiring an MDI Solution

One of the benefits of purchasing a vendor-based solution is the MDI solution provider takes on the development responsibility and delivers an end product that, in theory, will be as close to turnkey as possible. A key challenge is that the healthcare enterprise is dependent on the MDI solution provider for upgrades and development of new medical device drivers. Furthermore, because customization is not often possible, this implies that the healthcare enterprise may be required to change or modify workflow to accommodate the operational behavior of an MDI system. Hence, healthcare enterprises may find themselves having to make necessary changes to clinical, IT and support workflow. For smaller healthcare enterprises that do not possess extensive IT infrastructure in terms of staff and fiscal resources, this approach is the one that may be favored.

Unlike their larger healthcare enterprise counterparts, smaller enterprises may not need a highly tailored and customized solution that provides needed data for health IT systems, data warehousing, and other recipients.

The acquisition of an MDI solution should be conducted in a manner similar to that of acquiring other software and hardware systems within the healthcare enterprise. MDI solutions, however, span both hardware and software and, as such, may require a collaboration between clinical engineering and IT system expertise. Alternatively, healthcare enterprises may opt to develop a new type of position within the enterprise: that of device integration analyst. Such individuals must possess skills that span software, interfacing, and clinical engineering. Because of this skill mix, the acquisition of an MDI solution will most assuredly require the services of a broad team of individuals.

The RFI/RFP Process

Acquiring an MDI solution usually begins with a request-for-information (RFI) or request-for-proposal (RFP) process. The process of acquiring an MDI solution provider starts with an elaboration of the requirements of the healthcare enterprise. An evaluation of the stakeholder needs must be undertaken to determine what is actually required, and for what reasons. For example, prior to beginning the RFI process, the healthcare enterprise should have a clear understanding of the following:

- What strategic need or goal must be supported by MDI? For example, which departments are to be integrated? What medical device types?
- Which health IT system is to receive the data? What are the clinical expectations for MDI from the perspective of the clinical stakeholders?
- What are the near-term and long-term objectives of the MDI solution? For example, is the near-term objective (i.e., current fiscal year) deployment and

integration of a single department? Is the long-term objective an enterprise rollout to the entire healthcare system?

- What is the timeframe for the rollout? Will the rollout be conducted in stages?
- What is the budget for the MDI solution? Is the MDI solution budget contained within the overall budget of a health IT system rollout or independent of it? Are there budget timeline restrictions in terms of when the budget must be allocated and spent? What types of cost or fiscal restrictions are in place within the healthcare enterprise, and what has or is being budgeted to implement the project?
- Is an existing MDI solution in place within the healthcare enterprise that will be replaced or does this represent a net-new implementation?
- What are the expectations and requirements within the healthcare enterprise surrounding security, maintenance, support, and training?

An example of a medical device integration planning matrix is shown in Table 2-1 (and Appendix 1). This tool or a close variant should be maintained by the healthcare enterprise and shared with a prospective MDI solution provider. It is intended to assist the enterprise in planning, enumerating, and quantifying the types, methods, and quantities of medical devices to be integrated on a per-department basis; the kind of physical connectivity required; and in determining, per the various MDI solution vendors considered, whether existing medical device drivers are available from the vendor or whether they need to be created. This information will be helpful for the MDI solution provider to refine overall costs and the implementation timeline and, thus, serves the healthcare enterprise in increased efficiency and in improved confidence in the success of the MDI solution rollout.

Table 2-1: Example MDI Solution Provider Costing and Quantity Planning Tool.

Department	Medical Device Types	Deployment Timeline	Quantities of particular medical devices	Serial or network connectivity? If Serial, Adapter Type?	Device Model (if known)	Current Data Communication Protocol (if known)	MDI Solution Vendor Has Driver?	If Driver Development Required, Estimated Time to Completion
SICU	Mechanical Ventilators	Phase II	20	Serial / 9-pin RS232; Female null-modem	PB 840	TBD	Yes	N/A
OR	Physiologic Monitors	Phase I	18	Serial / 9-pin RS232 Male	GE SolarM/I	TBD	No	8 Weeks
Med / Surg	Spot Vital Signs Monitors	Phase III	25	Serial / 15-pin Male	Dinamap ProCare 300	TBD	Yes	N/A
OR	Anesthesia Ventilators	Phase IV	18	Serial / 9-pin RS232 Female	Dräger Fabius® GS Premium	Medibus	Yes	N/A
…	…	…	…	…	…	…	…	…

As the long-term objective may be to start small at the departmental level and expand, based on the budget, it is important to understand the overall costs of the MDI investment—not just acquisition of the initial system, but the overall cost of expansion as capital equipment, software, licensing and computing power. The ability to grow economically can be a very important guideline in terms of selecting an overall MDI solution provider: how will the costs to implement and maintain, in terms of capital investment, maintenance, support and management, accrue over time? Figure 2-1 illustrates the qualitative possibilities in terms of the overall cost to deploy a system in stages.

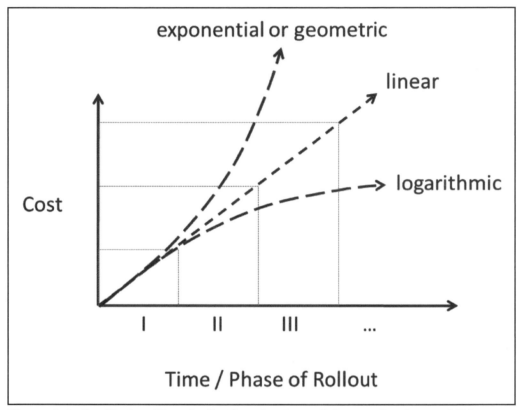

Figure 2-1: Qualitative Chart Indicating the Overall Cost to Deploy an MDI Throughout Phases of the Effort.

Note: The chart indicates whether the costs will increase (e.g., exponential or geometric), will increase and scale linearly with size of rollout (e.g., linear), or will decrease overall costs over time (e.g., logarithmic).

When deploying the MDI solution in stages (i.e., one department at a time), whether based on budgetary restrictions or other factors, there is most likely going to be a long-term relationship established with the MDI solution provider, similar to investments in health IT systems. The rollout will impact not only the IT staff but will also affect clinical workflow. Staff training to use and become comfortable with the new technology, how it is used, and how to interact with it at the POC, is important to overall acceptance. Hence, the investments are great in terms of not only money but also time and effort, as the technology will become embedded in the clinical operations of the healthcare enterprise.

There is also a potential impact on workflow from the perspective of clinical provider-patient interaction, so the enterprise brand in terms of the patient experience is an important component of the MDI solution rollout.

All of this is rather a long way of saying that the decision on which technologies to employ and which vendors to select is an extremely important one.

To illustrate the investment aspect of the MDI rollout, let's suppose that the enterprise envisions a phased approach for the overall implementation, perhaps coinciding with different departments or areas of the hospital system. Examples might be

- Phase 1 → Surgical Services (e.g., operating rooms, radiology, endoscopy, L&D, etc.)
- Phase 2 → Critical Care (e.g., SICU, MICU, PICU, NICU, etc.)
- Phase 3 → Medical Surgical or Step-Down Units

The curves in Figure 2-1 represent the qualitative cost, measured in terms of money, staff time, effort, etc., required for the phased implementation. The shape of the curves is an attempt to indicate the degree by which previous phases can be leveraged to reduce the costs and implementation/training time of follow-on phases.

The linear curve indicates that the cost to expand into the next phase is equal across all phases. That is, if an enterprise is currently live in one department and endeavors to expand to another, the cost of the expansion will be the same as in the previous phase, and is additive 1:1 with respect to the current investment. This implies that efficiencies in the previous phase, or hardware and software licensing required for the follow-on phases, do not translate into efficiencies gained from a previous phase that can be brought to bear in the next phase. Examples of this approach could be the requirement for additional server hardware per phase, expanded training and deployment costs, additional required software licensing for device drivers, or additional bed licensing.

The logarithmic curve makes the case that additional departments draw on efficiencies from previous phases, thereby resulting in lower overall costs as the MDI solution is extended to other departments. Examples of this case include being able to leverage existing server hardware, software, and device drivers for use with expanded beds without requiring additional bed licensing.

The exponential curve indicates that the cost actually increases over time. This is an extension of the linear profile, with the possibility that new device drivers need to be developed or additional software and hardware procured to support the additional rollouts. This case, admittedly, is an extreme one. Yet, the case should prompt questions regarding long-term, continuing, and incidental costs associated with the MDI solution. For example, does the MDI solution provider:

- Charge per bed licensing or do they provide an enterprise-license up front?
- Can device drivers be used anywhere in the hospital system, or must they be licensed per bed, per department, or per hospital?
- How does the MDI solution scale? Is it possible to make an enterprise investment in certain items while starting with a departmental rollout?
- Are performance degradations experienced as more departments are rolled out, which would necessitate additional server deployments and, if so, what is the general limit on number of beds from a performance perspective relative to enterprise-wide rollouts?

COMMUNICATING ENTERPRISE REQUIREMENTS TO MDI SOLUTION PROVIDERS

To gain an understanding of how an MDI solution provider can meet the MDI requirements of the healthcare enterprise, and to gain this understanding as quickly as possible, it is recommended that a full picture of the intended rollout be provided to the solution provider. This would usually include the following:

- Department(s) to be rolled out
- Health IT system with which to integrate
- Rollout timeline, including live date and testing/validation requirements and dates associated with the integration to the health IT system
- The size of the enterprise in terms of the number of beds per department to be rolled out
- The quantity of medical devices, the medical device types (including brands and specific medical device models)
- The existence (in detail) of current and planned physiologic monitoring gateways and the preference for medical device data communication from these medical devices (that is, through the gateway or through serial port connection)

Regarding deployment of the MDI solution at the bedside:

- Does the MDI solution support mobile medical devices, and medical devices fixed at the bedside, and what are the approaches for both types of implementations?
- What type of mechanism and/or method is desired to associate data from the medical devices with individual patients?
- Is wireless medical device communication permitted/desired/required in the environment or is hardwiring of medical devices the preferred method for data communication?

The information discussed next is an example of the type of information that might be provided to a vendor.

- Location of the deployment (department)
- Timeline for deployment, either in absolute time or by phase (deployment timeline)
- Medical device types usually associated with the environment that the healthcare enterprise wishes to have integrated
- Specific models of medical devices
- Quantity of medical devices of specific types
- Type of connectivity—serial or network based

Implicit within the need to identify what medical devices are to be integrated with the health IT system is the availability of medical device drivers. The MDI solution provider will have a library of existing medical device drivers. It will be important for the healthcare enterprise to understand the timeline for new medical device driver development should they be needed. The following sub-section provides a brief background on medical device drivers and requirements on their development.

MEDICAL DEVICE DRIVER DEVELOPMENT AND TIMELINES

Medical device driver software is a collection of methods normally written in standard computing languages (e.g., C, C++, C#, Java, etc.) that cause the polling of medical devices to trigger the receipt of data from those same devices. Figure 2-2 is a sequence diagram that illustrates at a high level the process of medical device data query and response. The software method that queries the medical device is normally identified as a medical device driver: it is responsible for either (i) querying the medical device in the device's own proprietary query language, causing the medical device to issue data associated with the query via the medical device communication port; or, (ii) listens for data automatically issued by the medical device in situations in which the medical device requires no query but simply communicates data one-way outbound through its communication port.

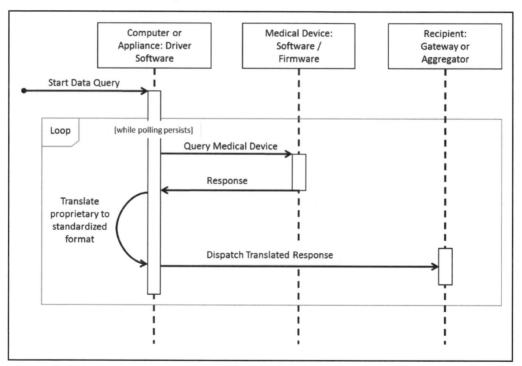

Figure 2-2: Sequence Diagram Illustrating the Process of Querying a Medical Device for Data and Translating Those Data into a Format Acceptable to a Recipient Health IT System.

The medical device driver software method will continue querying in a loop until caused or requested to stop. The interval of request (that is, the frequency of the query) can be dependent on several conditions:
- The core query frequency of the medical device software method, which may be controlled through an external update interval or polling frequency
- The base or minimal polling capability of the medical device—the minimum interval or maximum frequency of data collection with which the medical device can respond

- The maximum rate or frequency of collection that can be supported by the recipient health IT system
- The desired data collection rate with which the clinicians wish to see data reported within the EHR system

Because each medical device is unique, their mechanisms for communication via this query-response mechanism may also be unique. The term may is used because, while many medical devices employ proprietary methods for data communication, there are instances in which classes of medical devices from a single medical device vendor may use the same or similar protocols (e.g., Dräger MEDIBUS or MEDIBUS.X protocol; Mindray DIAP protocol; Philips Intellivue, etc.). Thus, for certain types of medical devices, economies of scale are possible, which can translate into reduced time to develop new or related drivers.

Because of the wide variation in medical devices and their protocols, the need for MDI providers to establish libraries of such drivers is necessary. These libraries can be extensive and, as might be inferred, their maintenance becomes an important and continuing task. Medical device driver software is simply not developed once and never changed again; MDI solution providers are upgrading their medical device drivers regularly. Prudence and good manufacturing practices dictate that when firmware are updated on an existing medical device, the associated medical device driver software must be re-evaluated through regression testing to validate that the medical device upgrades did not materially impact or change the functional operation or performance of the driver. Changes in medical device specifications, which can accompany firmware changes by medical device manufacturers, could also invalidate medical device driver software. Hence, the medical device driver software development process is rarely static.

A continuing dialog is required between the MDI solution providers and medical device manufacturers to ensure that MDI solution provider's medical device driver software is always current. Some MDI solution providers impose a formal process as part of acceptance testing for new medical device firmware and will make part of their contracts with healthcare enterprises the requirement that no medical device firmware be updated without first notifying the MDI solution provider. While this may seemingly add a level of unnecessary administration and red tape into the process, the reasons for the restriction is to mitigate the likelihood that patient safety risks and hazards are not introduced. Should a new medical device firmware upgrade result in a change in the specification or operation of the medical device, the information retrieved using a medical device driver could be materially impacted up to and including retrieving data incorrectly or mapping data to the wrong data fields either within the driver itself or within the health IT system. The result of this could be quite detrimental to the patient or even dangerous if these data are to be used for clinical decision making.

The key takeaway is that the medical device drivers are non-trivial pieces of software that require development, maintenance, validation, verification, and review. Quality processes and oversight of the medical device drivers are essential functions of the MDI solution provider.

Part of the reason for publishing the medical device list to the MDI solution provider is to assist the latter in assessing whether medical device drivers need to be developed to meet the overall enterprise needs, ultimately affecting rollout timeline. Ergo, the development timelines and costs associated with the development of these medical devices must be incorporated into the overall implementation timeline for MDI solution rollout.

It is important to determine those medical devices for which driver development is required up front with the MDI solution provider, as this will translate into both time and cost. Depending on the types of medical devices that need to be developed, the availability (or lack of availability) of medical device drivers can impact the scheduled timeline. Hence, it is important to determine the timeframe within which an MDI solution provider can develop a tested and certified medical device driver (including the timeframe required for acceptance testing and any other requirements pertinent to quality and regulatory considerations).

From a purely development-based perspective, this can vary by MDI solution provider. From experience, a timeframe of 8 to 12 weeks for medical device driver development is not out of the norm. And the estimate of the amount of time required for development must also take into account both the complexity of the driver, as well as the availability of medical device manufacturer specifications required for development.

It may be necessary for the healthcare enterprise to facilitate the transfer of specification information from the medical device manufacturer to the selected MDI solution provider, as this proprietary information may require prearranged non-disclosure agreements between the MDI solution provider and the medical device manufacturer. The process of establishing these relationships can take time, and if the healthcare enterprise is on a tight schedule, delays in access to information can result in delays in implementation.

The cost of medical device driver development is another key measure. Hence, this leads to a list of questions that should be asked of the MDI solution provider:

- What is the timeframe required to build a medical device driver and certify said driver for use in the production environment at the healthcare enterprise?
- What is the overall cost of development for medical device drivers? Is the healthcare enterprise expected to subsidize this cost?
- Once available, are there restrictions on use of the medical device drivers within the enterprise environment?
- Who owns the intellectual property associated with the medical device driver, and what is the MDI solution provider's freedom to market said driver to other clients?
- How will testing of the medical device driver be conducted and in what environment(s)?
- What constitutes acceptance testing for the medical device driver by the healthcare enterprise, and what are the parameters surrounding support for the driver should errors be discovered or further modifications be desired?

This list of questions is not all-inclusive, yet provides a fairly robust basic list with which the healthcare enterprise can evaluate the MDI solution provider. If a particular MDI solution provider does not have a medical device driver (and no one has everything), the solution provider should provide answers to these questions.

In terms of implementation, the specific physical hardware and software required for the solution provider-specific solutions will dictate what type of physical appliance or computing hardware on which the medical device drivers are to be deployed. Nonetheless, and particularly for serial-port communication, whether a computer or dedicated appliance is employed at the POC, the method for data collection will involve running the device driver on that piece of computing hardware. Hence, the previous discussion applies to many different MDI solution provider physical implementations.

COMMUNICATING WITH THE HEALTH IT SYSTEM

Communication of data from the POC would not be complete without transmitting it in a standardized format to the health IT system. The communication outbound to the EHR is normally accomplished using an HL7 unsolicited observation reporting (ORU) format consistent with the 2.x (i.e., 2.3, 2.5, 2.6, etc.) version of that standard. Most MDI solution providers have standardized interfaces and experience in communicating with many different health IT system vendors. The medical device driver provides for the basic collection of data from the medical device. Queries for data result in (usually) non-standard results (i.e., text-based, no specific standardized formats). In some MDI solution provider architectures, data retrieved from the medical device are then communicated to a data aggregation point. This data aggregation point can be a gateway-like appliance or software that can reside on a server, sometimes located within the enterprise-based data center. A single aggregation point for MDI data from POC medical devices serves an analogous role to that of physiologic monitoring gateways: the aggregation point provides a single point of communication for receiving all data from the POC medical devices and providing a single network communication point for transmission to the health IT system. An example of this topology is expressed in Figure 2-3. On the left-hand side of this diagram, data are collected from the POC medical devices to the MDI solution provider appliance or computing hardware. The medical device driver queries the medical device and the data are retrieved. The data are then translated to the Data Aggregator (i.e., MDI gateway) where they are further conditioned and then communicated to the EHR or health IT system. The Data Aggregator serves to receive information from the individual data collection appliances and to transform the raw data received into a more standardized format—most likely into an HL7 set of observation transactions. A more complete treatment of HL7 will be provided in Chapter 4.

As part of the integration process, the healthcare enterprise should inquire of the MDI solution provider as to their experience integrating with the healthcare enterprise's particular health IT system. Some key questions that can be asked:

- How many implementations with this particular health IT system has the MDI solution provider performed?
- What types of specific interfaces are supported (e.g., for outbound results; for inbound ADT; other types of systems)?
- Can the MDI solution provider support multiple independent interfaces that can be tailored (e.g., in terms of HL7 results formatting; in terms of outbound data communication rate)?

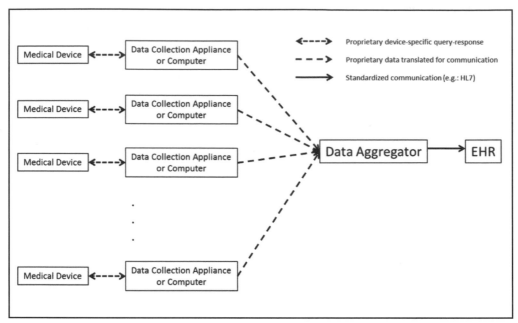

Figure 2-3: Diagram Illustrating Communication of Medical Device Data from Initial Retrieval to Health IT System.

In addition to being able to transmit data in a standardized format, the question as to the customization of the datafeed also needs to be addressed; frequently, the data need to be formatted or translated into different units of measure for a specific health IT system. Furthermore, separate feeds are sometimes required and need to be created for different health IT systems, particularly where different health IT systems coexist (e.g., departmental versus enterprise health IT systems) that require simultaneous communication across separate interfaces. For instance, separate datafeeds may be required for independent health IT systems within the environment.

Given this possibility, it would be necessary to be able to copy or split the feeds from the MDI solution provider's Data Aggregator and send them to these separate recipients. If an enterprise has a third-party integration engine, this may be used to accomplish this end goal. However, should the MDI solution providers offer this feature separately, that can add to the flexibility of deployment.

Some questions that may be worthwhile to ask in regard to integration:

- Can the MDI provider quantify the number of simultaneous transactions they can process through their system (i.e., system throughput)?
- Can the MDI provider support the data throughput of multiple departments simultaneously to the health IT system?
- Can the MDI provider tailor the feeds from multiple departments to different charting systems and control the rates of data transmission, as well as customizations (e.g., unified code variations) for each feed?

HOSPITAL FACILITIES AND ENTERPRISE NETWORKING REQUIREMENTS

POC data collection using bedside computers or dedicated MDI appliances requires that these be connected to the medical devices and to the enterprise network. Enterprise network connections are either made through hardwired LANs or through the wireless LANs. Hardwired networking requires that the POC MDI appliances have network access at each and every location where they are to be used. This implies that network access must be enabled for these appliances and may require that the healthcare facilities department install these additional network drops. Retrofitting rooms with LAN ports can be a time consuming and expensive process. On the other hand, wireless data collection, to be used reliably, requires sufficient quality of service to ensure no data dropouts while in use wherever data are intended to be collected. Thus, part of the consideration for the healthcare enterprise is evaluating the time and expense required for additional network access required for POC MDI implementation.

Building the MDI Implementation Team

MDI implementation requires the skills and talents of multiple individuals, roles, responsibilities, and departments. Integration of medical device data into the health IT system and its introduction into the healthcare environment is not purely an IT function, nor is it purely a clinical/biomedical engineering function. For hospitals that are unfamiliar with or have never conducted an MDI implementation, this can mean stepping into unfamiliar territory. Hence, the approach taken will be to focus on those roles that, from the author's experience, have been employed in highly efficient implementations.

Project Management

Implementation of MDI normally comes under the aegis of the chief information officer or director of IT. This individual may assign a project manager or a team led by one or more individuals as part of the acquisition of an MDI solution provider. This individual is charged with the overall planning and execution of the project.

As a first step, it is necessary to consider:
- Determining how the rollout is to be executed—single department or entire enterprise
- Identifying who needs to participate and the roles of team members
- Establishing team member responsibilities for the overall integration
- Selecting the MDI solution provider
- Estimating timelines for completion
- Installation
- Testing
- Go-live

From experience, determining how the rollout is to be executed is dependent on both the strategic objectives of the enterprise, as well as the available budget. Even if the objective is to budget the project all at once to deploy to the overall enterprise, whether single or multi-entity, in practice preferred approaches are those that involve departmental rollouts that expand to the entire enterprise over time, particularly when the healthcare enterprise is new to MDI solution implementations. There are several reasons why this approach makes sense. First of all, given an enterprise is undertaking the MDI implementation for the first time, a large learning curve exists for all involved, including IT, clinical staff, networking and facilities. Taking a smaller bite provides early lessons learned and experience necessary to ensure smooth expansion to the remaining departments within the enterprise. Secondly, for the enterprise inexperienced with rollout of MDI, the change in workflow and education required to ensure smooth operation in a clinical environment merits a smaller initial footprint where issues can be quickly resolved with a minimum impact to clinical staff. Finally, validating data from the MDI solution to the health IT system can be a significant effort involving clinical, IT and biomedical engineering/clinical engineering individuals. Finally, there may need to be time to acclimate to the additional support and maintenance burden associated with implementation of an MDI solution. By starting at the departmental level or in a single location, the various team members are able to refine support and maintenance issues to smooth these out before a large-scale deployment across the entire healthcare enterprise occurs.

Staging the MDI Solution Implementation

The decision of where to begin is, perhaps, the hardest. Some suggest starting with the easiest, least complex departments while others suggest the most complex. One approach that has been found to work well in terms of enterprise MDI solution rollout is to begin with the surgical services departments, as these high acuity areas involve a controlled set of medical devices that usually span the operating rooms, post anesthesia care units, endoscopy, radiology, labor and delivery rooms, and catheter labs. Their fixed locations together with the relatively high frequency of data collection merits the most attention to detail.

As described in Chapter 1, the surgical services department involves data collection in the operating rooms from anesthesia machines, physiologic monitors, and possibly from bi-spectral index monitors and cardiopulmonary bypass machines. Other devices typically monitored in these environments include cerebral oximetry or end-tidal carbon dioxide monitoring. The most robust of data collection requirements are usually in operating rooms: data collection at intervals of one minute or less is often required for AIMS, and close monitoring of patients mandates that data from all devices be available for review by anesthesiology and other clinical staff as quickly as possible. Patient association of the medical devices to the patients is usually accomplished through the health IT systems.

Following surgical services department deployment, intensive care units/critical care units can be a logical next step. Of course, the order of the rollout is dependent on the strategic and tactical requirements of the healthcare enterprise. However, the medical devices in the intensive care unit/critical care unit have analogs in the surgical services settings: physiologic monitors, mechanical ventilators (anesthesia machines), infusion systems, end-tidal carbon dioxide monitoring, and other specialty devices. Furthermore, both the surgical services and the intensive care units/critical care units involve mostly fixed location settings, whereby medical device data collection is affixed to the location of the patient (i.e., patient room). That is, patients are usually admitted for a period of time in a single unit and then moved to other units. Hence, there is a one-to-one mapping or association of medical devices to patients for a period of time. From a patient-to-medical device association perspective, this makes the workflow much more straightforward than lower acuity settings wherein the medical devices are free to roam throughout the department. The focus in the higher acuity settings in which the medical devices are fixed to a given room makes for a cleaner and more direct clinical workflow.

Once the decision is made as to the department in which to begin the actual roll-out, the next step is to assemble the team.

Assembling the MDI Implementation Team

Successful MDI rollouts require participation from members of IT staff, clinical staff, biomedical/clinical engineering staff, network engineering staff, and facilities departments. This is the minimally recommended team makeup for implementation and rollout:

- **Information Technology:** The IT team is usually the department responsible for the health IT system integration, data interfaces, computing and server hardware, and the mapping of parameters to meet health IT system charting requirements and clinical documentation (i.e.,charting) configuration. The enterprise health IT organization's role is essential in terms of verifying the mapping of parameters from the medical devices to the health IT system and ensuring that data are properly flowing through the system.
- **Clinical Staff:** The objective of MDI is to provide the necessary information required to facilitate the management of the clinician-patient relationship and to ensure that information is not compromised and is provided in a timely manner to the end users. The clinical staff is responsible for ensuring that the data needs and workflow essentials are communicated to the remaining team so that the care delivery needs can be met in a timely manner. The role of the clinical staff is also essential in terms of validating medical device parameters, validating charting content, and units of measure. The clinical staff are an essential part of the MDI team since the data produced by medical device must ultimately be used by them to care for, diagnose, and treat patients. Their participation during validation testing is also mandatory.
- **Biomedical/Clinical Engineering**: These individuals serve as the bridge between IT and the medical devices at the POC. When issues arise in the medical devices or in the appliances that interact with them to collect data from the POC, clinical engineering staff are normally notified. Clinical engineering must also work with facilities and clinical staff to physically place POC MDI solution appliances where they will not interfere with clinical workflow (e.g., on head boards, on medical devices, behind medical devices, etc.)
- **Networking:** The POC MDI solution appliances and computers communicate on the LAN. It is necessary to ensure that wherever POC data collection occurs, whether through hardwired for wireless means, data can be communicated in an uninterrupted manner. Some healthcare enterprises restrict access to the LAN. Hence, network engineering must ensure that appliances or computers placed at the POC receive IP addresses either through dynamic host configura-

tion protocol (DHCP) or through static IP mapping, and to properly route data from the POC to the health IT system.

- **Facilities:** The facilities team is essential to locating appliances at the POC. The actual physical mounting of MDI solution appliances and computers must be planned around clinical usage of the facilities (e.g., access to patient rooms when not in use). Frequently, the mounting of appliances must occur after hours. If MDI solution appliances are used, ensuring that the appliances meet POC usage standards, particularly IEC and UL requirements associated with proximal use with patients, is an important consideration.

Project management must organize the team so that specific tasks are assigned and progress is measured. Each member of the team holds equal weight in terms of importance to the overall implementation effort. A weekly meeting associated with the planning and deployment should be carried out following an initial kickoff meeting. Once the POC appliances are deployed, the IT and clinical teams must work together with the MDI solution provider to validate implementation and data mapping. This will culminate in a dry run of the implementation, sometimes referred to as a shadow run of the system in which clinical staff use the health IT system in parallel with the older approach (e.g., manual charting) to assist in identifying flaws and to correct data mapping and workflow errors. A shadow run may operate with both the new system and the old system concurrently for anywhere from several days to several weeks. The duration of shadow runs will depend on the clinical user needs, the comfort level of the clinical, IT and clinical engineering staff, and the smoothness with which the system operation proceeds without the identification of support issues that need to be resolved.

An important adjunct to this team is the MDI solution provider. If an external MDI solution provider is contracted, they need to be part of the overall project team. The MDI provider becomes a member of the healthcare enterprise MDI project team. From experience, the most successful teams are those in which the walls and barriers of an organization are erased and the roles of individuals are instead made the focus. The relationship between the healthcare enterprise and an MDI solution provider is a long-term one and the team, like a family, works best when it works together to solve problems. The MDI solution provider must be able to understand the scope of the implementation schedule and workflow requirements.

It is important as part of the MDI solution provider selection process, following the RFI/RFP, to ensure that complete and total information exchange occurs between the healthcare enterprise and the MDI solution provider. Incomplete information at this stage can lead to delays or other misunderstandings down the road. Hence, it is very important that ALL members of the healthcare enterprise MDI team meet with those members of the MDI solution provider team who will be involved in the implementation and management of the overall installation and implementation effort.

Installing and implementing an MDI solution is a practice; it is an art. There are certain aspects of the implementation process that are absolutely repeatable and predictable. Yet, there are challenges that will be revealed during the rollout that are unpredictable. For example, networking reliability and availability can be stressed by the MDI solution, depending on the amount and type of data to be communicated to the health IT system, and unless detailed and thorough testing are conducted, there may be no way of evaluating ahead of time whether the existing infrastructure will support every situation or use case for MDI implementation.

Another example of uncertainty is the comfort level of the clinical staff, particularly if the MDI implementation is being experienced for the first time. A clinical staff that is comfortable with paper charting may experience culture shock when exposed to the automated charting made possible by the availability of medical device data for health IT system charting.

The MDI solution provider, as part of the RFP process, should estimate costs associated with deployment in a testing and a production environment, and, ideally, a disaster recovery or education environment. Minimally, two environments should be budgeted for in the MDI solution proposal and should be requested by the healthcare enterprise project management team. A test environment is essential to stage new medical device drivers and for testing of the end-to-end MDI system prior to rolling into production. A production environment is, of course, a necessary one, as this is the live environment in which the operational system will operate and communicate to the health IT system. However, the testing environment is necessary to facilitate the creation of new medical device drivers and for staging software upgrades, facilitate regression testing, and to provide a platform for troubleshooting prior to rolling upgrades or new software into the production environment. A disaster recovery or education environment may augment the testing and production environments to support demonstrations, as well as to support failover, if the vendor provides that capability.

Estimating Timelines for MDI Implementation Completion

In order for the project manager to establish the timeline for completion overall, it is necessary for the MDI solution provider to:

- Develop a statement of work for the healthcare enterprise detailing the installation and implementation process to a high degree of confidence in terms of overall work effort and estimated timeline for medical device driver development, testing, and rollout.
- Create a list of medical devices in the environment, complete with quantities, firmware versions, and preferred medical device connectivity approaches. An example of a table describing these areas is included in Appendix 1, and a populated table was illustrated in this chapter in Table 2-1 (previously presented).
- Estimate the amount of time required to deploy POC computers or appliances for serial data collection, together with an estimate of the number of individuals required to complete this deployment.
- Quantify the number of individuals on the MDI solution provider team, as well as the healthcare enterprise team required to install and configure at the POC as expeditiously as possible. The healthcare enterprise must also assist the MDI solution provider with access to those POC environments (e.g., access to operating rooms and high-acuity areas as required to facilitate deployment). This may mean assisting the MDI solution provider in obtaining access badges; communicating to clinical staff the presence of MDI solution provider personnel; and facilitating access to departments, rooms and medical device equipment as required.

- Identify which medical device drivers are required that currently exist within the MDI solution provider's library and those that do not currently exist, and the timeline associated with creating net-new drivers. This is very important to determine sequencing in the deployment rollout. If departments that are part of the rollout require net-new drivers, it may be more worthwhile to focus on those departments for which device drivers exist, allowing the MDI solution provider time to develop new medical device drivers for follow-on deployment.
- Estimate the testing and integration of the back-end communication to the health IT system. This process can involve adjusting or modifying unified codes to enable receipt of the data by the recipient health IT system.

INSTALLATION

The MDI solution provider must communicate to the healthcare enterprise a reliable timeline on delivery of POC appliances or computers as required and a plan for assisting with the installation of the same in the various environments. Delivery timelines for medical device adapters, cables, and related hardware need to be ordered, and the timeline associated with these deliveries must be projected accurately to the healthcare enterprise so as to enable management to assemble a reliable project plan. For example, hardware appliance installation in a single operating room suite is highly dependent on the specifics of the MDI solution provider technology, as well as access to the environment. Access to the OR suites or to any room is dependent on whether the room is in use. Hence, installation may have to occur after hours. Critical care units may be in use for days at a time so attempting to predict the timeline associated with the implementation of hardware in these environments is more difficult. However, planning several weeks for the implementation of hardware for a single department may be sufficient to improve the uncertainties in gaining access to specific areas within the environment.

Specific items to estimate for the installation process:

- Reliable access to the environments in which deployment of POC appliances or computers are to be carried out (e.g., Friday or Saturday evenings from 10 p.m. to 4 a.m.).
- Availability of representatives from clinical engineering, networking, facilities, and IT personnel during these installation times to ensure that snags can be worked through as they arise.
- If POC appliances are to be installed by facilities or clinical engineering personnel and not by the MDI solution provider, then a reliable estimate of the completion timeline for this installation needs to be made.
- Access to enterprise computing environments for installation of software and hardware, which may be necessary to ensure deployment within the production enterprise software environment, will need to be ascertained before hardware deployment actually begins.
- Availability of medical device adapter hardware, communication cabling, and power for all of the POC appliance or computing hardware within a given department environment must be ensured prior to actually configuring within the ORs or other environments.

Testing

Medical device drivers that have already been developed and are certified should only require testing to validate data communication to the health IT systems. New medical device drivers will require testing and validation through the test environment before they can be placed into production. The healthcare enterprise should assist the vendor by providing the IT resources to validate the data entries in the EHR and to inform the vendor of non-compliance or errors in mapping of data should that occur.

Medical device driver data should be reviewed by the vendor to validate that what is being collected from the medical devices is indeed reported by the medical device drivers. On the back end, the data need to be mapped to appropriate fields within the health IT system. The data validation process must, therefore, be end to end: what is received at the POC must be mapped to specific fields within the health IT system charts and flow sheets. This testing can consume a significant amount of time—perhaps several weeks—to be thorough.

In total, the time required to install, test and deploy an MDI solution within a department can take anywhere from one to several months, depending on complexity. The healthcare enterprise should proceed with eyes open and understand that this timeframe is driven from the ground up by the complexity of and details involved in verifying the system of systems integration activities involved.

A summary of example tools used in the evaluation, testing and triage of data, networks and generating HL7 transactions is included in the Appendix 2 and 3. Testing tools in Appendix 2 should assist in HL7 communication, validation, and debugging. The simulator provided in Appendix 3 was developed by the author as a tool to generate HL7-based data for medical device drivers and integration engine testing at the medical device gateway level (e.g., emulates physiologic monitor gateway data communication), and to validate parameters being sent to the health IT system. The simulator provides for random generation of parameter values, ensuring variability and facilitating testing. These tools and methods are provided by the author as suggestions to aid the prospective enterprise in the rollout of the MDI solution.

Transition to Go-Live

Once medical device drivers have been validated in terms of production of reliable and accurate data verified through the health IT system, and have received clinical signoff in terms of accuracy and workflow, then the healthcare enterprise can plan the transition from the testing environment to production.

The MDI solution provider should be on hand for the actual go-live schedule. Some healthcare enterprises prefer a transition period whereby the old and new way of charting (i.e., pre- and post-MDI deployment) are conducted in parallel so that clinical staff can wean themselves off of the older system and become comfortable with the newer system. Plus, this process also allows for verification that data are accurate in the health IT system in comparison with the legacy charting experience.

Transitions to live operations can take as little time as one day or as much time as several weeks. In practice, the transition to go-live, if planned well, is nothing more than a cutover process, which should involve a minimum of technical changes to the

MDI solution provider's system other than a repointing from test to production health IT systems.

Once the MDI solution has rolled to live and the clinical, IT, and clinical engineering staff are comfortable with the operation, it is necessary to monitor and maintain a support system to report tickets and issues occurring in the live production environment. It is important for the healthcare enterprise to mandate that the MDI solution provider executes a clear and process-driven approach for reporting issues together with an estimate for resolution of various types of issues that might occur.

SUMMARY

The objective of this chapter was to delineate the key activities associated with an MDI solution implementation. The start of this process is the RFI/RFP phase in which a decision as to the best MDI solution provider is made, followed by a step-by-step implementation that features project planning through rollout to a go-live of the production system. To aid the prospective healthcare enterprise with the selection and rollout, a list of questions is provided next to aid the enterprise in covering the topics that need to be addressed as part of the MDI solution provider selection and implementation process. This is not an exhaustive list, but serves to specify the basic questions that need to be answered:

- Does the MDI solution provider charge per bed licensing or do they provide an enterprise-license?
- Can medical device drivers be used anywhere in the hospital system or must they be licensed per bed, per department, or per hospital?
- Is additional computing hardware required to support additional departments?
- Are performance degradations experienced as more departments are rolled out and, if so, what is the general limit on number of beds from a performance perspective relative to enterprise-wide rollouts? How does the MDI solution scale as more beds are added?
- Can the MDI provider quantify the number of simultaneous transactions they can process through their system (i.e., system throughput)?
- Does the MDI solution provider connect to all of the medical devices intended for integration within the environment?
- Is the MDI solution communicating with the enterprise network? If so, how?
- Which health IT system is on the receiving side of MDI transactions, and does the MDI solution provider have experience in working with this health IT system?
- What type of data security and patient protection safeguards are in place within the MDI solution?
- What is the MDI solution provider's approach and philosophy on support and maintenance?
- What is the architecture associated with the MDI solution?
- Does the MDI solution provider have all of the necessary medical device drivers for the rollout?
- How are new medical device drivers developed, tested, and deployed in the environment?

- What is the average length of time required to develop a new device driver? What are the costs to the healthcare enterprise, if any, to develop a new medical device driver?
- How are software upgrades to MDI solution software and firmware conducted? How often can they be anticipated? Are planned system downtimes required for upgrades?
- What are the provisions for high availability and system redundancy?
- Can the MDI solution be managed over the Internet or must thick client applications be installed in order to change settings, manage online POC data collection appliances, and interfaces to the health IT system?
- Can the MDI solution provider support the data throughput of multiple departments simultaneously to the health IT system?
- Can the MDI solution provider customize the feeds from multiple departments to different health IT systems simultaneously and control the rates of data transmission, as well as the unified code values to each feed?
- Does the MDI solution support mobile medical devices, medical devices fixed at the bedside, and what are the approaches for both types of implementations?
- What type of mechanism and/or method is desired to associate data from the medical devices with individual patients?
- Is wireless medical device communication permitted/desired/required in the environment or is hardwiring of medical devices the preferred method for data communication?

CHAPTER 3

Semantic Data Alignment and Time Synchronization of Medical Devices

Once data are extracted from medical devices, they are translated into a common format (e.g., HL7) and transmitted to the target health IT system. More often these health IT systems are EHRs. In this chapter, we investigate two key aspects of the integration of data into EHRs and health IT systems: the semantic and temporal alignment of data, or synchronization, to ensure proper posting into the record at the appropriate time.

Semantic alignment or synchronization refers to the consistent definition and naming of the data—to ensure that data that are transmitted is correctly interpreted from the perspective of its meaning and then used correctly based upon this meaning. More specifically, semantic alignment seeks to ensure the unambiguous definition of the data and associated UOM of data so that any clinician reviewing the same data will have no question as to its meaning or its possibility of being reinterpreted as something other than its intended purpose. Temporal alignment or synchronization refers to the correct and homogeneous time association of the collected measurements so that they are associated with a commontime of collection (frequently, network time) and communicated to the health IT system with this time.

INTEROPERABILITY CONTINUUM

AAMI published in their proceedings from the 2012 conference on "MDI: A Safer Path Forward," these four dimensions of interoperability:[38]

- **Data Interoperability:** Agreement/consistency in formatting, storage, querying, and synchronization of data.
- **Communication Interoperability:** Consistency in transmission and reception of messages between modes.
- **Semantic Interoperability:** Agreement/consistency between systems on the meaning of communicated information.

- **Workflow Interoperability:** Agreement/consistency on how technology supports/shapes the workflow. Processing or sequencing tasks between participants according to a set of procedural rules; formatting or displaying information; user interfaces; penetration of decision support.

Others[38] have published definitions and challenges related to semantic interoperability. From the perspective of practical implementation of MDI systems in the healthcare enterprise, all of these dimensions of interoperability are important and can and do impact the clinical environment from the perspectives of safety, clinician time and effort, support personnel time and effort, and, ultimately, the net effect in terms of cost. These statements may seem to be grand generalizations. However, consider the following:

- **Incorrectly associating medical device data measured on one patient with another patient.** Associating parameters from a medical device with the wrong patient or incorrectly identifying them in the clinical record can result in misinforming the clinical end user. Best case, this can be an irritation to the clinical user and result in delays in terms of requiring recollection of measurements. Worst case, the parameter values could be misinterpreted or could present a false appearance for clinical decision making, resulting in a delayed decision or a decision being made in error. For instance, heart rate measured on one patient is reported in the chart of another patient.
- **Failure to display a measurement in the patient chart.** This scenario involves retrieving the correct parameter from the medical device, but failing to populate the value in the patient chart. This can occur if (i) the parameter is not correctly mapped into the health IT system (that is, not mapped as a discrete parameter); or, (ii) syntax errors exist that cause the measured value to be rejected by the health IT system.
- **Failure to report the correct units of measure on a medical device parameter.** A parameter may be mapped correctly into the health IT system, but the UOM reported from the medical device do not match with the UOM reported within the health IT system. This issue can be minimized if the health IT system takes the UOM from the medical device and reports that. However, some health IT systems may require that the UOM be premapped into the clinical chart and will not use that UOM as reported from the medical device.
- **Medical device data that contain incorrect time stamps.** Incorrect timing or errors in the time associated with measurements from a medical device (e.g., blood pressure taken at 10:00 is stamped as 10:02) can have a clinical impact. When the measurement of parameters is associated with clinical decision making, the impact can be acute, for instance, when administration of a drug is dependent upon the value of a measurement (e.g., blood pressure measurement and the administration of a vasodilator). Alternately, measurement of medical device parameters, such as blood pressure or pulse, and administration of anesthetics during surgery, where anesthesiologists are using the measured values to determine the administration of anesthetic dosing, can have profound effects on patient care management.

  There are also technical and record-keeping implications associated with errors in measurement time recording: the time stamps of the medical device

parameters are recorded in the patient chart based upon the time stamp associated with the data received from the medical device. The source of this issue is
the use of a time stamp taken from the medical device itself wherein the medical device time is not synchronized with a common or accepted universal time
clock. Many medical devices in service today cannot have their internal clocks
synchronized with a common or external time source. As a result, their internal
clocks tend to drift over time. If not maintained regularly, the internal medical device clocks can deviate from the network or universal time appreciably.
Clinical or biomedical engineering typically will need to resynchronize medical device clocks on a regular interval. This can serve to reduce the impact of
medical device time deviation, but will not eliminate it. The best approach, save
medical devices that can synchronize automatically with a common time clock,
is to employ time stamps from an external clock through the use of the MDI
solution. The MDI solution should be able to assign time stamps to medical
device data so that these are synchronized with the network time or universal
time (for example, from a source such as the National Institute of Standards and
Technology, NIST).

- **Errors caused by differences in the interpretation of measurements obtained
  from different medical devices.** Errors in associating measurement values
  from one medical device with those of another that perform similar functions
  can also have clinical impacts. For example, a health IT system may have a
  patient chart tailored for a specific type of mechanical ventilator, in which all of
  the parameters are recorded and the clinical staff is familiar with the expected
  data and the location in which they are to appear in the patient chart. Should a
  different medical device be employed, however, that performs the same clinical function (e.g., a second brand of equivalent mechanical ventilator), and the
  parameters do not post into the chart properly, are missing, or have different
  UOM, then this can impact workflow. The misinterpretation of the parameter
  values can result in patient safety hazards and in lost staff time associated with
  correcting parameter values, as well as requiring a remapping of the parameter
  values within the health IT system patient chart.

SEMANTIC HARMONIZATION OF MEDICAL
DEVICE DATA

Medical device data have manufacturer-supplied definitions which, for the most part,
will map with standard clinical terminology. In medicine, the National Library of
Medicine (NLM) freely distributed the Systematized Nomenclature of Medicine—
Clinical Terms (SNOMED CT).[39] The SNOMED CT is

> *"...a comprehensive clinical terminology, originally created by the College
> of American Pathologists (CAP) and, as of April 2007, owned, maintained,
> and distributed by the International Health Terminology Standards Develop-
> ment Organisation (IHTSDO), a not-for-profit association in Denmark. The
> CAP continues to support SNOMED CT operations under contract to the*

IHTSDO and provides SNOMED-related products and services as a licensee of the terminology."[39]

Although SNOMED CT is intended to provide such a common nomenclature reference for medical use, medical device parameters communicated from one medical device do not necessarily map one-to-one to other medical devices of similar or precisely the same function: parameter names, their UOMs and even usage may vary slightly in coding (sometimes referred to as unified codes), thereby necessitating the process of mapping such parameters, their UOMs, and validating such mappings prior to clinical use within the health IT system patient chart.

During the process of validation, and prior to going live with medical device data integration to the health IT system, designated clinical, IT and engineering staff must review the data that are being received from the medical devices and verify their parameter names, unified codes, UOMs, and mappings within the patient chart. The unified codes refer to the acronyms or accepted naming representation within the health IT system patient chart. Furthermore, "[Data] must be mapped to specific parameters that clinicians normally validate. Different medical devices can and do produce [data] with different names and units of measure (UOMs). Some medical devices from different vendors ... can ... produce [data] for which direct one-to-one mappings are not possible."[2]

For example, suppose two different physiologic monitors produce parameters as shown in Table 3-1.

Table 3-1: Example Parameters Produced by Physiologic Monitors from Two Different Physiologic Monitoring Manufacturers.

Parameter Name	Definition	Example Unified Code Mapping	Unit of Measure
Heart Rate	Pulse measurement	HR	Beats/min (or /min)
Oxygen Saturation	Measurement of blood hemoglobin content as measured via pulse oximetry	SPO2	%
Non-Invasive Blood Pressure	Blood pressure as measured via automated sphygmomanometer; three components – Systolic, Diastolic and Mean	NBP-S NBP-M NBP-D	mmHg (millimeters of Mercury)
Cardiac Output	Volume of blood pumped through each heart ventricle per minute	CO	L/min
Premature Ventricular Contractions (PVC)	Contraction of lower heart chambers earlier than expected because of abnormal electrical activity in the heart	PVC	per minute (or / minute)
End-tidal carbon dioxide	Measured level of carbon dioxide exhaled from the lungs	CO2-EX or ETCO2	mmHg (millimeters of Mercury)

The different medical devices may be physiologic monitors produced by two different manufacturers. The unified codes would be mapped to a common set of attributes within the clinical record so that regardless of which specific physiologic monitor employed, the output will always be pointed to the correct unified code mappings representing the aforementioned attributes. Thus, regardless of whether each monitor produces a value for a parameter with the same unified code mapping as each other, they can be mapped to a common unified code or data dictionary that holds a common definition for the specific parameter(s).

This mapping is illustrated qualitatively in Figure 3-1, in which a mapping of these parameters to a common set for a generic pair of physiologic monitors is shown. The key assumption is that the parameter values from both devices are interpreted as precisely the same so that regardless of which device, there will be no ambiguity in the mapping of the unified codes from one device to the clinical record.

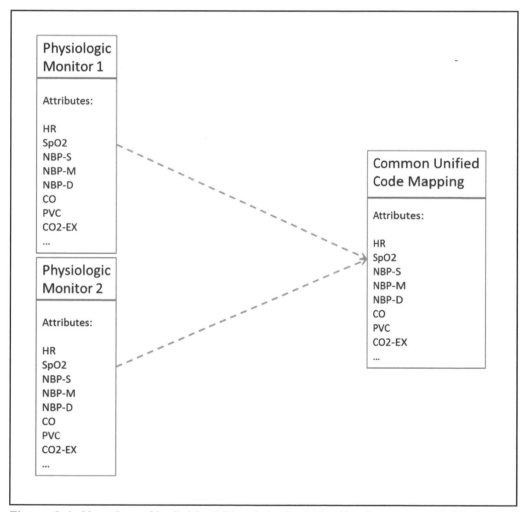

Figure 3-1: Mapping of Individual Physiological Monitor Parameter Unified Codes to Unified Codebook or Data Dictionary Definition.[40]

Similarly, the illustration of Figure 3-2 shows two mechanical ventilators that have parameters unique to one brand but not the other. The common mapping of unified codes must take these unique situations into account and the clinical and IT staff must decide whether the parameters associated with the one medical device should be displayed in the health IT system patient chart. Furthermore, clinical staff and IT must determine from a workflow perspective whether this action would introduce confusion for the end users when that particular medical device is used or when it is not in use.

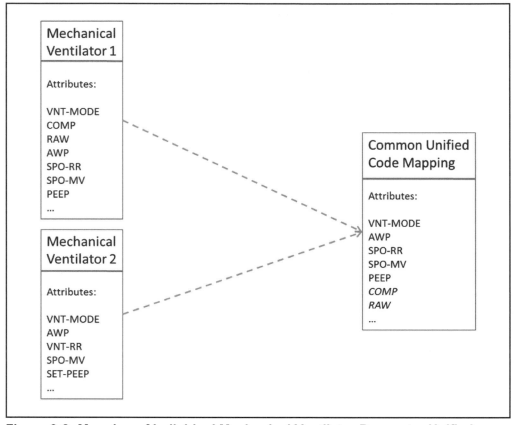

Figure 3-2: Mapping of Individual Mechanical Ventilator Parameter Unified Codes to Unified Codebook or Data Dictionary.

Note: Certain parameters may not map between devices (e.g., Compliance & Airway Resistance). In the case of mechanical ventilator 1, it produced parameters of compliance (COMP) and airway resistance (RAW), while mechanical ventilator 2 does not. Ergo, there is no mapping of these parameters between the two separate medical devices.

In the case of the mechanical ventilators, the following parameters are shown:
- Ventilator mode: Unified code = VNT-MODE
- Compliance: Unified code = COMP
- Airway resistance: Unified code = RAW
- Airway pressure: Unified code = AWP
- Spontaneous respiratory rate: Unified code = SPO-RR
- Spontaneous minute volume: Unified code = SPO-MV
- Positive end-expiratory pressure: Unified code = PEEP

In the case of Mechanical Ventilator 2, two of the parameters are not available (i.e., COMP & RAW). Hence, in terms of the data dictionary or common Unified Code mapping, the decision must be made whether the missing parameters shall be included in health IT system patient charting. If the lowest common denominator is selected as the option to move forward, then these parameters may be excluded or, from a workflow perspective, clinical staff may be instructed that these parameters may be entered manually by staff whenever Mechanical Ventilator 2 is used.

The key point from this simple example is that the end user workflow may be impacted depending on the option selected. The validation process of medical device parameters must, therefore, be conducted thoroughly for each department to verify that the necessary parameters can be charted and will remain consistent across the available medical devices.

Temporal Alignment of Medical Device Data

When communicating from medical devices through MDI solution POC appliances (in particular), each medical device communicates at its own rate. Unless the clocks of each medical device are synchronized, they will communicate time stamps for each data record asynchronously with respect to a common reporting time—defined with respect to the health IT system. In most cases, the MDI solution POC medical device integration appliance will assign a time stamp to data collected from each medical device, usually in accord with a network time server established within the healthcare enterprise. This is the first step in aligning data from medical devices to a common timeframe; each medical device, particularly those associated with a specific patient, must be reporting data with respect to a common reference point in time.

To illustrate the concept of temporal data alignment, an architecture for a hypothetical MDI solution will be presented, wherein the data collection at the POC (i.e., patient bedside) will be through a Data Collection Appliance (DCA), representative of a generic hardware component that can run medical device drivers and communicate physically with the medical device. The DCA will then transmit data from the medical device to a Data Aggregator or gateway, which serves to receive, translate, and communicate those data obtained from the POC to the health IT system patient chart.

Figure 3-3 illustrates this concept of each medical device communicating at its own rate. In the figure, data are shown as being collected through an MDI solution DCA, which may be a dedicated computing platform or hardware platform specifically designed to communicate with the medical device at the POC. The data that are communicated will vary in message size and frequency from the DCA at the POC to the Data Aggregator (or gateway) that is responsible for receiving, aggregating, and translating it into a standardized format for transmission to the health IT system. Once data are received at the Data Aggregator or gateway, they are aligned in terms of time and transmitted either separately or as a collection of messages associated with a common time interval, as illustrated in Figure 3-4.

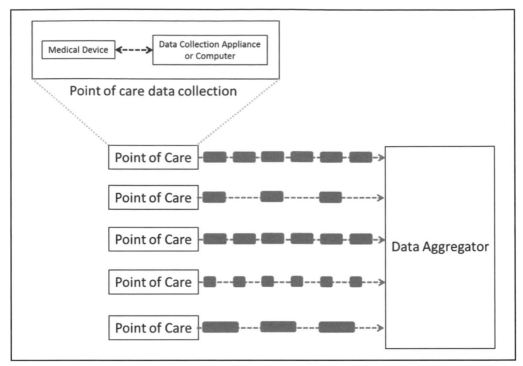

Figure 3-3: Medical Devices Communicating from the POC MDI Solution Data Collection Appliances at the Data Communication Rates Dictated by the Medical Device.

Note: Each Medical Device reports to the Data Aggregator at its own rate and using particular syntax specific to each Medical Device.[40]

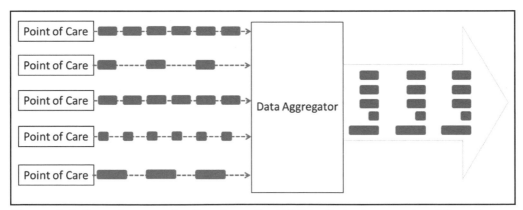

Figure 3-4: Data Communication from the POC to Data Aggregator Aligned According to a Common Time Interval and Transmitted from the Data Aggregator to the Health IT System.

Data communication from the Data Aggregator is normally at set intervals defined by the needs of the clinical end users, and the health IT system will post data into the patient chart as received from the MDI solution at the set intervals. These intervals can vary depending on use case and hospital department. For example, ORs may require data at intervals of one minute or less, whereas critical care units may only require data at 5-15 minute intervals and other departments may require data only when requested. Qualitatively, Figure 3-5 shows these intervals applied to the outbound data from the Data Aggregator.

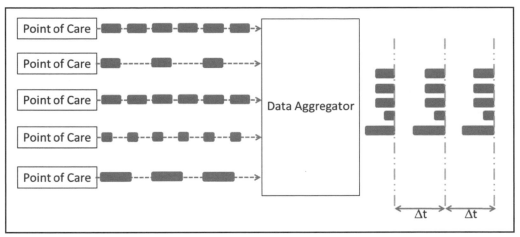

Figure 3-5: Data Intervals (Δt) for Communication from the Data Aggregator Usually Defined According to the Needs of the Health IT System.

Note: The interval is identified as Δt Here, the intervals Δt, are normally independent of the arriving data from the points of care and usually sample the POC data at the interval closest to the time of communication from the Data Aggregator to the health IT system.

Requirements on the values of these intervals will be dependent on the clinical requirements of the end users. Some healthcare enterprises may request data as frequently as it can be collected from the medical devices and then govern the rate down based upon validation requirements at the POC. In other words, the requirement to display data as frequently as it is collected may exist in the environment, with the assumption that the clinical end user will validate and select data for communication to the health IT system patient chart at a rate based on the clinical need. Related to this is the idea of time synchronization: ensuring that the data, when collected from the medical device and communicated through the Data Aggregator, are aligned with a common time source so as to ensure homogeneous and accurate communication and recording for the EHR and other recipients.

IHE has established an implementation profile related to time synchronization and consistency. The implementation profile is referred to as Consistent Time Integration (CT). The IHE Wiki provides the following detail:[41]

> *"[CT] provides a means to ensure that the system clocks and time stamps of the many computers in a network are well synchronized. This profile specifies synchronization with a median error less than 1 second… [CT] requires the use of the Network Time Protocol (NTP) defined in RFC 1305. When the Time Server is grouped with a Time Client to obtain time from a higher tier Time Server, the Time Client shall utilize NTP."*

The objective of this profile is to define implementation mechanisms to synchronize the time base between multiple actors, computers, and, ultimately, the data arriving from the medical devices.

Figure 3-6 provides some detail behind the process of time synchronization. As illustrated in the diagram, each medical device has its own time clock. This time clock may or may not be able to be synchronized with an existing common external source and is reported with respect to Universal Coordinated Time (UTC), such as a Network Time Service, which may be managed through the healthcare enterprise or externally (e.g., clock managed by NIST). At the POC, each medical device communicates at its own proprietary rate. This is indicated by the tick marks below the clocks associated with each medical device. The clocks themselves correspond to and indicate that each medical device may have its own clock—and these clocks need not be (and most probably are not) synchronized.

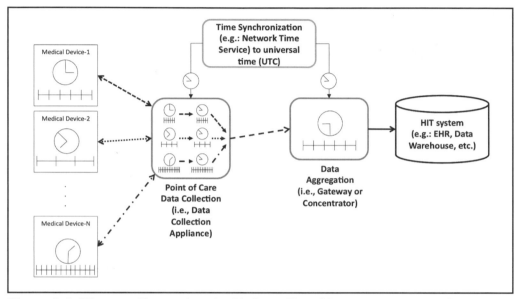

Figure 3-6: Diagram Illustrating the Various Time Measurements and Clocks that Define the Data Collection from the POC and Communicated to the Data Aggregator.[40]

The POC data collection is accomplished using a Data Collection Appliance. This appliance communicates with individual medical devices (a total of N), which report data at their own individualized rates (indicated by the line segments with tick marks that vary in terms of spacing). The individual medical devices may also report time stamps using their own localized clocks (illustrated by clock icons showing different times from individual medical devices). The DCAs receive these data, align to a common UTC while maintaining the individualized rates of data collection from each medical device, and then communicate to a Data Aggregator (i.e., a gateway or concentrator responsible for receiving and translating all received data into a common format). Data are then communicated according to a final, aggregated time aligned with UTC at a rate specified by the receiving system and communicated to that receiving system (e.g., an EHR or other health IT system).

The medical device data are collected through the POC DCA or computer. Potentially, multiple medical devices may be collected through this appliance or computer and the data polling from each of the medical devices via medical device drivers running on the appliance or computer. Each tick mark represents individual time stamps associated with measurements from the medical devices. At the DCA, data from the individual medical devices are accumulated and communicated to the Data Aggregator or gateway. Here, the data are aligned according to a common time, reflected by the common timeline with tick marks contained within the Data Aggregator.

Figure 3-7 illustrates the details of data reporting through a Data Aggregator, in which the data arriving from each medical device (through the DCA) is received and the reporting time, t^R, endeavors to take the data associated with each medical device that is closest proximally in time to the specific reporting time. The individual device reporting times from, say, the Nth medical device, are given by $(...t_N^{R-1}, t_N^R, t_N^{R+1},...)$ where the time of the measurement just prior to the common reporting time, t^R, is given by t_N^R.

The time between the common reporting time and the last reporting time of the individual medical device is at most equal to the individual medical device reporting interval, given by the time between medical device measurements, which, for the first medical device, is represented in the diagram of this figure as $\Delta t_1^{R,R-1}$. This is the interval between the measurement time at the current reporting interval and the measurement time of the reporting interval immediately preceding this one for this particular medical device.

Given the objective to synchronize data from multiple medical devices associated with a particular POC, the propagation of individual medical device measurements to a common reporting time can ensure that data transmitted to the health IT system does not contain gaps. It is important to note that, from the perspective of HL7 data communication, this common reporting time could be assigned to either the messaging time or the common observation reporting time (OBR) (i.e., the time of the Observation Request segment time). If it is important to maintain the actual observation time of the individual measurements (i.e., each observation has its own distinct time measurement) then the reporting time of the individual measurements can be communicated as OBX (i.e., the Observation/Result segment) time stamps within the individual HL7 messages. In this way, all time granularities would be maintained (i.e., common reporting time associated with message, individual time reporting of individual observations).

Some medical devices can communicate their internal clock information. That is, they maintain their internal clocks and can report this as a parameter. However, unless these medical devices can be synchronized to a system time defined by a time server, these times will not necessarily be synchronized with the current base time of the healthcare enterprise, which may be maintained via network time server.

To illustrate the native medical device time versus network or system time, Table 3-2 shows an HL7 transaction associated with an anesthesia machine. The native time stamp associated with the internal clock of the anesthesia machine is shown in bold in OBX segment 68.

The time stamp of the transaction is listed in the OBR segment:
`20131001113233:`   October 1st, 2013; 11:32:33

The time stamp in OBX segment 68 reads as follows:
`11:33:0001-OKT-13`   October 1st, 2013; 11:33:00

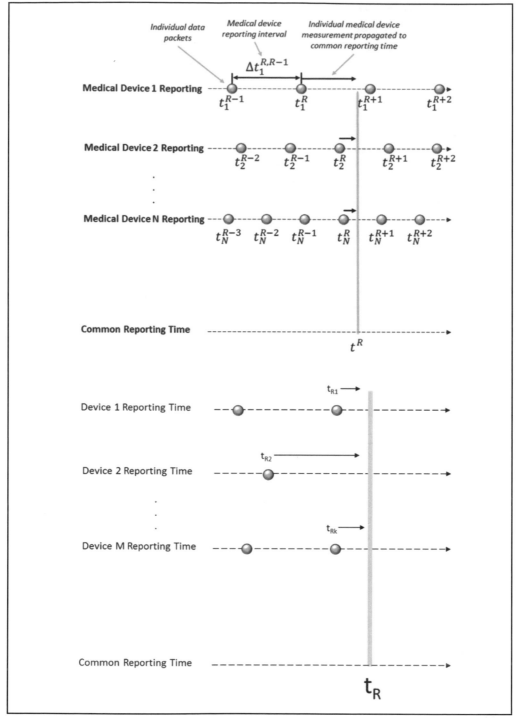

Figure 3-7: Depiction of Data Arriving from Medical Devices to Data Aggregator Where Measurements are Propagated to Common Reporting Time, t^R.

Note: Individual medical device reporting times are described with respect to the common reporting time. The last measurement received from each medical device prior to the common reporting time is then propagated to the common reporting time, thereby achieving a consistent set of data for health IT system at each reporting interval.[40]

Table 3-2: Dräger Apollo® Anesthesia Machine Example HL7 Transaction.

```
MSH|^~\&|<Sending_App>|<Sending_Fac>|<Receiving_App>|Receiving_
Fac>|20131001113233|
|ORU^R01|0101:01:0000034E|P|2.3
PID|||
PV1||||^^
OBR|1|||||20131001113233
OBX|1|NM|COMP||23.9|L-1
OBX|2|NM|HAL-CONS||0|mL
OBX|3|NM|ENF-CONS||0|mL
OBX|4|NM|ISO-CONS||0|mL
OBX|5|NM|DES-CONS||0|mL
OBX|6|NM|SEV-CONS||1|mL
OBX|7|NM|ISO-P-IN||0|kPa
OBX|8|NM|ISO-P-EX||0|kPa
OBX|9|NM|SEV-P-IN||1.1|kPa
OBX|10|NM|SEV-P-EX||0.8|kPa
OBX|11|NM|AGNT1-P-IN||1.1|kPa
OBX|12|NM|AGNT1-P-EX||0.8|kPa
OBX|13|NM|AGNT2-P-IN||0.6|kPa
OBX|14|NM|AGNT2-P-EX||0.4|kPa
OBX|15|NM|O2-UPTAKE||270|L/min
OBX|16|NM|BARO-MBAR||1000|mbar
OBX|17|NM|AWP||4|mbar
OBX|18|NM|PPLAT||16|mbar
OBX|19|NM|PEEP||0|mbar
OBX|20|NM|PIP||16|mbar
OBX|21|NM|TV||358|mL
OBX|22|NM|TV-IN||365|mL
OBX|23|NM|MAC-IN||0.6|kPa
OBX|24|NM|MAC-EC||0.4|kPa
OBX|25|NM|SEV-IN||1.1|%
ORX|26|NM|SFV-FX||0.8|%
OBX|27|NM|LEAKAGE||13|mL/min
OBX|28|NM|P-RR||1.7|/min
OBX|29|NM|MV||6.1|L/min
OBX|30|NM|APN-T||0|s
OBX|31|NM|O2-DELTA||4|%
OBX|32|NM|CO2-RR||17|/min
OBX|33|NM|RR||17|/min
OBX|34|NM|D-RR||17|/min
OBX|35|NM|CO2-IN||0|%
OBX|36|NM|CO2-EX||3.6|%
OBX|37|NM|FGF-N2O||0|L/min
OBX|38|NM|FGF-AIR||0|L/min
OBX|39|NM|FGF-O2||2.4|L/min
OBX|40|NM|CO2-P-EX||3.6|kPa
OBX|41|NM|CO2-PHG-IN||0|mmHg
OBX|42|NM|CO2-PHG-EX||27|mmHg
OBX|43|NM|AGNT1-IN||1.1|%
OBX|44|NM|AGNT1-EX||0.8|%
OBX|45|NM|AGNT2-IN||0.6|%
OBX|46|NM|AGNT2-EX||0.4|%
OBX|47|NM|O2-EX||92|%
```

Table 3-2: Dräger Apollo® Anesthesia Machine Example HL7 Transaction. (cont.)

```
OBX|48|NM|O2-IN||96|%
OBX|49|NM|ISO-IN||0|%
OBX|50|NM|ISO-EX||0|%
OBX|51|NM|N20-IN||0|%
OBX|52|NM|N20-EX||0|%
OBX|53|NM|CO2-P-IN||0|kPa
OBX|54|NM|SET-TV||370|mL
OBX|55|NM|SET-TI||1.2|s
OBX|56|NM|SET-IPPV||17|/min
OBX|57|NM|SET-PEEP||0|mbar
OBX|58|NM|SET-HI-AWP||40|mbar
OBX|59|NM|SET-INSP-PR||10|%
OBX|60|NM|SET-RAMP||0|s
OBX|61|NM|SET-AGE||66|
OBX|62|NM|SET-WEIGHT||53|kg
OBX|63|ST|DEV-MODEL||Apollo|
OBX|64|ST|DEV-CODE||8057|
OBX|65|ST|DEV-PROT||MEDIBUS|
OBX|66|ST|DEV-PROT-VER||04.03|
OBX|67|ST|DEV-VER||04.11|
OBX|68|ST|DEV-TXT-TS||11:33:0001-OKT-13|
OBX|69|TS|DEV-TS||20130101113300|
OBX|70|ST|DEV-MODE||Carrier Gas AIR\No 2nd anesthesia gas\Volume
Mode|
```

The time stamp of the network time server is 11:32:33 and that of the anesthesia machine is 11:33:00. Therefore, the anesthesia machine time is ahead of the network time server by 27 seconds.

It is important to verify with the clinical and IT staff during the MDI rollout process as to which time stamps are to be used for health IT system patient charting. It is imperative that a common time stamp be used to the exclusion of local or medical device specific time stamps, as there are serious clinical implications to entering time stamps incorrectly in the clinical record.

Validating Medical Device Data in the Health IT System Patient Chart

The process of validating medical device data prior to going live on the MDI solution begins with an evaluation of the medical devices in use within the enterprise and their data as recorded in the patient chart. Medical device drivers from vendors should be certified by the vendors in a testing environment on-site at the healthcare enterprise, and designated members of the MDI project team should review the results of this testing prior to allowing the MDI solution go-live within the clinical environment.

Using the several medical devices to follow as examples, the process of validation should proceed with each medical device using data normally collected during normal use in clinical practice. The physiologic monitor shown in Figure 3-8 is an example of one that might be used in an OR or a CCU.

Validation of the data begins by applying an emulator or using a live test subject as the source for data collection through the physiologic monitor (for example, use of ECG leads, pulse oximetry cuff, blood pressure cuff, etc.).

Some physiologic monitors (like that shown) possess an internal simulator function that provides the capability to create test data for display on the monitor. An example of the monitor set in this internal simulation mode is shown in Figure 3-9.

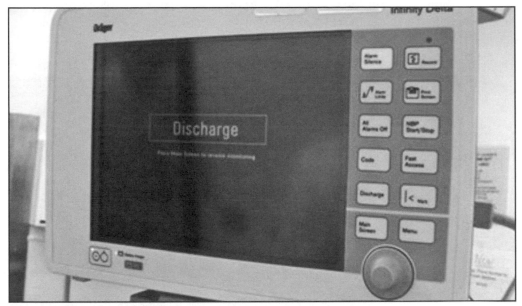

Figure 3-8: Dräger Infinity® Delta Physiologic Monitor.

(Photo by Author)

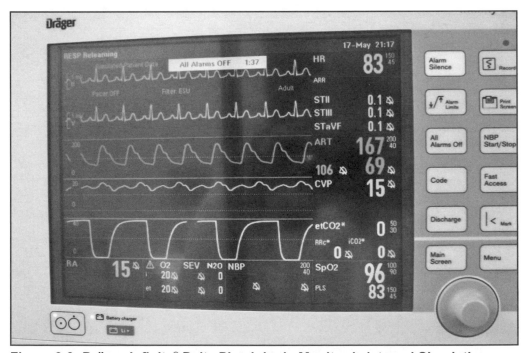

Figure 3-9: Dräger Infinity® Delta Physiologic Monitor in Internal Simulation Mode Displaying Waveform and Discrete Physiologic Data.

(Photo by Author)

Testing of the medical devices should occur using connectivity hardware that is intended for live use. Figure 3-10 illustrates the serial attachment for the Dräger Infinity® Delta monitor shown in the previous two figures. All physical connectivity hardware should be of the quality intended for proximal use with patients. Testing or engineering mock-ups of the connectivity hardware (i.e., test cables and adapters) should not be employed since the testing environment should approximate the live production environment as closely as possible.

Figure 3-10: Serial Medical Device Connector for the Dräger Infinity® Delta Physiologic Monitor.

Once the physical environment is configured and data are available, a clinical end user (e.g., in the OR, this should be an anesthesiologist or a certified registered nurse anesthetist, CRNA; in critical care, a nurse or respiratory therapist) should create a test patient within the AIMS or create a sample or test patient and participate in the following steps:

- As data are displayed on the medical device, each value on the user interface of the medical device should be compared with the data being obtained from the medical device itself via the MDI solution.
- It is not yet necessary to compare the data with that shown in the EHR or clinical record itself. At this point, validating that the information displayed on the user interface of the medical device compares with each data element extracted from the medical device via the MDI solution provider prior to communication to the health IT system serves as verification that the medical device driver is operating properly.
- Next, data within the health IT system patient chart should be reviewed. In the OR, AIMS access is typically available through workstations that are either attached to or adjacent to the anesthesia machines. While data are being collected, the anesthesiologist or CRNA should review the chart and validate (i) values are being posted; and, (ii) UOMs are correct.

- While the anesthesiologist continues to review the patient chart, various settings, changes in operation and changes in values should be made to the anesthesia machine and physiologic monitor. The end user should validate that the changes (i.e., settings, measurements, etc.) are displayed in the patient chart and are displayed in a timely manner (that is, within the reporting interval for data reporting from the MDI solution). In other words, if data updates within the patient chart are set to occur each minute, changes in medical device settings should be reflected within that chart within one minute of the change on the medical device.

The results of the testing should be recorded by the IT team, inclusive of photographs of the medical devices, their displays, and the values of the settings. Furthermore, screen snapshots of the raw data as measured through the MDI solution, as well as HL7 messages should be taken and included as part of the testing documentation. Table 3-3 provides an example of one of these HL7 messages that would be included within a testing report. A review of the HL7 segments within the HL7 message should be compared with photographs of the medical device display to provide verification of those values and a permanent testing artifact to validate compliance of the medical device driver, validation of the mapping to the health IT system, and validation of the HL7 transaction.

A careful inspection of the results from each device should be conducted in this way so that positive confirmation of the actual results can be made and recorded. This

Table 3-3: Infinity® Delta Output Translated into HL7 Format.

```
MSH|^~\&|<Sending_App>|<Sending_Fac>|<Receiving_App>|Receiving_Fac>
|20140517214113||ORU^R01|0014:1384ACB9
:052|P|2.3
PID|||
PV1|||<CR>
OBR|1||||||20140517214113<CR>
OBX|1|NM|HR||83|/min<CR>
OBX|2|NM|ARR-STAT||0|/min<CR>
OBX|3|NM|PVC||0|/min<CR>
OBX|4|NM|ST-I||0|mm<CR>
OBX|5|NM|ST-II||0.1|mm<CR>
OBX|6|NM|ST-III||0.1|mm<CR>
OBX|7|NM|ST-AVR||0|mm<CR>
OBX|8|NM|ST-AVF||0.1|mm<CR>
OBX|9|NM|ST-V1||0|mm<CR>
OBX|10|NM|ST-V2||0|mm<CR>
OBX|11|NM|ST-V3||0|mm<CR>
OBX|12|NM|ST-V4||0|mm<CR>
OBX|13|NM|ST-V5||0|mm<CR>
OBX|14|NM|ST-V6||0|mm<CR>
OBX|15|NM|ST-VM||0|mm<CR>
OBX|16|NM|ST-VCM||0|mm<CR>
OBX|17|NM|ABP-S||167|mmHg<CR>
OBX|18|NM|ABP-D||69|mmHg<CR>
OBX|19|NM|ABP-M||106|mmHg<CR>
OBX|20|NM|PA-S||33|mmHg<CR>
OBX|21|NM|PA-D||14|mmHg<CR>
OBX|22|NM|PA-M||21|mmHg<CR>
```

Table 3-3: Infinity® Delta Output Translated into HL7 Format. (cont.)

```
OBX|23|NM|PAW||0|mmHg<CR>
OBX|24|NM|RAP||15|mmHg<CR>
OBX|25|NM|CVP||15|mmHg<CR>
OBX|26|NM|RR||20|/min<CR>
OBX|27|NM|SPO2||97|%<CR>
OBX|28|NM|SPO2-HR||82|/min<CR>
OBX|29|NM|CO2-P-EX||0|mmHg<CR>
OBX|30|NM|CO2-P-IN||0|mmHg<CR>
OBX|31|NM|PC-RR||0|/min<CR>
OBX|32|NM|SET-O2||20|%<CR>
OBX|33|NM|O2-EX||20|%<CR>
OBX|34|NM|N20-IN||0|%<CR>
OBX|35|NM|N20-EX||0|%<CR>
OBX|36|NM|SEV-IN||0|%<CR>
OBX|37|NM|SEV-EX||0|%<CR>
OBX|38|NM|PA-M||0|mmHg<CR>
OBX|39|NM|SVO2||75|%<CR>
OBX|40|NM|CCCO||5|L/min<CR>
OBX|41|NM|INTCCO||15|L/min<CR>
OBX|42|NM|CSVR||770|mL*cmH2O-1<CR>
OBX|43|NM|SAO2||97|%<CR>
OBX|44|NM|BT||36|cel<CR>
OBX|45|NM|CCCI||3|cmH2O*L-1*s<CR>
OBX|46|NM|INTCCI||3|cmH2O*L-1*s<CR>
OBX|47|NM|CSVRI||1155|mL*cmH2O-1<CR>
OBX|48|NM|DO2||775|<CR>
OBX|49|NM|VO2||230|<CR>
OBX|50|NM|PIP||60|cmH2O<CR>
OBX|51|NM|AWP||20|cmH2O<CR>
OBX|52|NM|INSPP||75|%<CR>
OBX|53|NM|IE-I||1|<CR>
OBX|54|NM|IE-E||5|<CR>
OBX|55|NM|MVEX||0|L/min<CR>
OBX|56|NM|TVEX||15|mL<CR>
OBX|57|NM|TVIN||15|mL<CR>
OBX|58|NM|VNT-RR20|/min<CR>
OBX|59|NM|MVIN||3|L/min<CR>
OBX|60|NM|O2-IN||100|%<CR>
OBX|61|NM|PPLAT||60|cmH2O<CR>
OBX|62|NM|BIS||8|<CR>
OBX|63|NM|BISSQI||1|%<CR>
OBX|64|NM|BISEMG||2|<CR>
OBX|65|NM|BISSR||3|%<CR>
OBX|66|NM|BISSEF||0|Hz<CR>
OBX|67|NM|BISTPOW||5|%<CR>
OBX|68|NM|RVP-S||60|mmHg<CR>
OBX|69|NM|RVP-D||0|mmHg<CR>
OBX|70|NM|RVP||0|mmHg<CR>
OBX|71|NM|LVP-S||100|mmHg<CR>
OBX|72|NM|CCP||0|mmHg<CR>
OBX|73|NM|IBP5-S||0|mmHg<CR>
OBX|74|NM|IBP5-D||25|mmHg<CR><1C><CR>
```

provides the necessary first step prior to validating results in the clinical record and serves to assert that the medical device driver is operating correctly.

Validating the data from mechanical ventilators can be more tedious in that the various modes of mechanical ventilation should be verified with clinical staff present to ensure that all parameters are reliably reported. Figure 3-11 is a photograph of an anesthesia ventilator typical of those that might be used in ORs or cardiac catheterization labs. This particular unit requires physical connectivity to a DCA to facilitate data communication. Figure 3-12 shows the reverse side of the anesthesia machine illustrating the serial communication ports. Figure 3-13 provides an alternate view of the serial communication port with an RS 232 adapter attached.

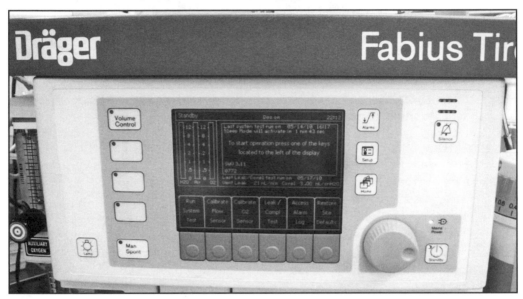

Figure 3-11: Dräger Fabius® Tiro® Anesthesia Machine.

(Photo by Author)

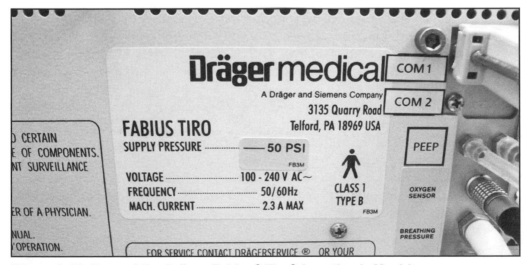

Figure 3-12: Rear of the Dräger Fabius® Tiro® Anesthesia Machine.

Note: Serial Ports Shown Top Right of Photograph. (Photo by Author)

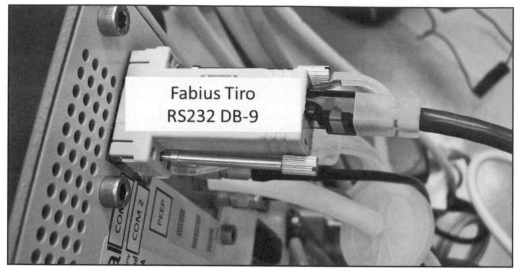

Figure 3-13: RS 232 Serial Port Adapter Attached to the Dräger Fabius® Tiro® Anesthesia Machine. (Photo by Author)

Table 3-4 summarizes an example HL7 output vector from the Dräger Fabius® Tiro.® In a manner similar to that of the physiologic monitors, the mechanical ventilator parameters should be compared with those displayed within the medical device user interface. As stated earlier, mechanical ventilators should be run through the various modes of ventilation to ensure all parameters are communicated. Obtaining results using spontaneous modes of mechanical ventilation can be approximated using an artificial lung and via user interaction with the lung (e.g., squeezing to cause the emulation of variability not related to set respiratory rates). This validation and verification ascertains that the medical device drivers are valid and operational.

Preparation for Go-Live Checklist

The following checklist is offered in preparation for going live on the MDI solution, as pertains to data mapping and semantic integration of medical device data:

- Create clinical validation teams, consisting of a minimum of one clinical staff member or stakeholder associated with each clinical area for which the MDI solution is being implemented, one IT staff member and one clinical engineering staff member. A technical project manager or equivalent from the MDI solution provider is also required as part of this team. A clinical validation team should be created for each department within which an MDI solution is to be deployed. These teams will be responsible for completing and validating the steps as outlined following.
- For each clinical environment, a clinical validation team charged with developing the desired health IT system patient record chart template should be tasked with identifying the standard flow sheet or charting summary for each clinical environment (i.e., OR, ICU, PACU, etc.).
- Create lists of validated parameters for each medical device associated with a particular unit or department in the form similar to Table 3-5 and Table 3-6, respectively. In the case of medical devices that vary their output with device

mode, create sub-lists associated with each mode of the particular medical device. The tables shown next provide examples that list the names of the parameters, UOMs, a common definition, desired mapping within the clinical record, and the desired periodicity or interval timing of the finding in the record.

Table 3-4: Dräger Fabius® Tiro® HL7 Example Output.

```
MSH|^~\&|<Sending_App>|<Sending_Fac>|<Receiving_App>|Receiving_Fac>|
20140517223806||ORU^R01|0014:1384BA0E
:631|P|2.3
PID|||
PV1|||
OBR|1||||||20140517223806
OBX|1|NM|AWP||13|mbar
OBX|2|NM|PPLAT||34|mbar
OBX|3|NM|PEEP||2|mbar
OBX|4|NM|PIP||42|mbar
OBX|5|NM|TV||0|mL
OBX|6|NM|MV||0|L/min
OBX|7|NM|RR||10|/min
OBX|8|NM|FGF-N2O||2.088|L/min
OBX|9|NM|FGF-AIR||6.712|L/min
OBX|10|NM|FGF-O2||3.102|L/min
OBX|11|NM|O2-IN||37|%
OBX|12|NM|SET-TV||600|mL
OBX|13|NM|SET-IEI||1|
OBX|14|NM|SET-IEE||2|
OBX|15|NM|SET-RR||10|/min
OBX|16|NM|SET-PEEP||0|mbar
OBX|17|NM|SET-HI-PEEP||40|mbar
OBX|18|NM|SET-INSP-PR||10|%
OBX|19|ST|IE||1:2|
```

Table 3-5: Example Physiologic Monitoring Parameter Mapping Validation Worksheet.

Device Parameter (Unified Code)	Unit of Measure	Definition	Map To Unified Code in EHR	Timing or Periodicity
HR (HR)	/min	Heart rate or pulse	HR	Periodic (30 seconds)
NBP-Systolic (NBP-S)	mmHg	Non-invasive Blood Pressure – Systolic Component	NBP-S	Aperiodic/ Episodic
NBP-Diastolic (NBP-D)	mmHg	Non-invasive Blood Pressure – Diastolic Component	NBP-D	Aperiodic/ Episodic
NBP-Mean (NBP-M)	mmHg	Non-invasive Blood Pressure – Mean	NBP-M	Aperiodic/ Episodic
ST-II	Mm	ECG Segment II	ST-II	Periodic (30 seconds)
Temperature (T)	C	Body Temperature	T-Cel	Periodic (30 seconds)
PVC (PVC)	--	Pre-ventricular contractions	PVC	Periodic (30 seconds)
O2 Saturation (SpO2)	%	Oxygen saturation derived from pulse oximetry	SpO2	Periodic (30 seconds)
Cardiac Output (CO)	L/min	Cardiac output derived from pulmonary catheter measurement	CO	Aperiodic/ Episodic
…	…	…	…	…

Table 3-6: Example Mechanical Ventilation Parameter Mapping Validation Worksheet.

Mode of Operation	Device Parameter (Unified Code)	Unit of Measure	Definition	Map To Unified Code in EHR	Timing or Periodicity
Continuous Mandatory Ventilation (CMV)	Mandatory respiratory rate (SET-RR)	/min	Set or mandatory respiratory rate	SET-RR	Periodic (30 seconds)
	Mandatory tidal volume (SET-TV)	milliliters	Set or mandatory tidal volume	SET-TV	Periodic (30 seconds)
	Mandatory or set positive end-expiratory pressure (SET-PEEP)	cmH2O	Set or mandatory PEEP value	SET-PEEP	Periodic (30 seconds)
	Peak Inspiratory Pressure (PIP)	cmH2O	Peak Inspiratory pressure value	PIP	Periodic (30 seconds)

Table 3-6: Example Mechanical Ventilation Parameter Mapping Validation Worksheet. (cont.)

Mode of Operation	Device Parameter (Unified Code)	Unit of Measure	Definition	Map To Unified Code in EHR	Timing or Periodicity
	Airway pressure (AWP)	cmH2O	Airway Pressure value	AWP	Periodic (30 seconds)
	Set I:E ratio (SET-I:E)	--	Mandatory I:E ratio, either as text ratio or as normalized expiratory component	SET-I:E or SET-I:E-E	Periodic (30 seconds)
	Total minute volume (MV-T)	L/min	Total value derived from product of tidal volume and respiratory rate	MV-T	Periodic (30 seconds)
Synchronous Intermittent Mandatory Ventilation (SIMV) (Note: all mandatory parameters previously shown, plus the following spontaneous values)	Spontaneous respiratory rate (RR or SPO-RR)	/min	Spontaneous or patient-measured value	RR	Periodic (30 seconds)
	Spontaneous tidal volume (SPO-TV)	milliters	Spontaneous or patient-measured value	TV	Periodic (30 seconds)
	Spontaneous minute volume (SPO-MV)	L/min	Spontaneous or patient-derived value	MV	Periodic (30 seconds)
	I:E ratio patient value (I:E)	--	Text value of patient-measured I:E ratio or expiratory component normalized to inspiratory component	I:E or I:E-E	Periodic (30 seconds)
Continuous Positive Airway Pressure (CPAP)	...	...	...	...	...

- Each clinical validation team works to verify the mapping of the output from the medical devices to those parameters contained within the health IT system patient record template. Once validated, a validation record inclusive of the validation checklists should be signed by the team members and retained by the MDI solution vendor and the healthcare enterprise MDI project team.

SUMMARY

This chapter covered semantic and temporal data interoperability with specific examples of aligning parameters collected from medical devices with those receiving fields within the health IT system patient chart. Emphasis was also placed on synchronizing data from medical devices to common reporting times. The concept of time synchronization also was discussed with respect to the local and network time bases to draw the distinction between a local medical device timestamp versus use of a common, enterprise timestamp derived using a network time server. Specific approaches to validating medical device data and the use of checklists and clinical teams to assist in the validation of data collected from medical devices into the charting system were discussed and examples of best practices were presented.

CHAPTER 4

Standards Surrounding Medical Device Integration to Health IT Systems

In a 2012 article in Healthcare IT News, Michelle McNickle, quoting Shahid Shah, reported on reasons why medical device data are essential to EHR systems.[42] Of these, reason number 3, "Medical device data [are] the least error prone" is one of the key reasons. Structured data, being quantifiable and devoid of subjective inference, tells a story of the patient over time.

However, to ensure communication of these medical device data to the health IT system, it is necessary to translate the format from something proprietary—at the device level—to something more standardized and common to the health IT system.

In this chapter, we discuss the use of standards, the most common being HL7, and the forms most often used to communicate medical device data.

MEDICAL DEVICE STANDARDS SPECIFIC TO DATA INTEGRATION

Many standards have been developed to which medical device manufacturers adhere, partially out of regulatory requirements and partially out of industry and business requirements. The use of standard application-layer communication is becoming more the standard among medical devices. In the medical device integration space, those standards most specifically applicable to communicating data from medical devices to electronic storage systems (e.g., EHRs, data warehouses, information systems) are these:

- ISO/IEEE 11073™ Medical/Health Device Communication Standards
- IHE Patient Care Device (PCD) Technical Framework (TF)
- HL7

These are not mutually exclusive. The 11073™ standards have been formally recognized by the FDA.[43] The collection of standards comprising the 11073 suite is summarized in Table 4-1.

Table 4-1: List of Key IEEE 11073™ Standards Recognized by FDA for Medical Device Connectivity.

#	Standard Identifier	Standard Title
1	11073-10101™	Health informatics—Point-of-care medical device communication—Part 10101: Nomenclature
2	11073-10201™	Health informatics—Point-of-care medical device communication—Domain information model
3	11073-20101™	Health informatics—Point-of-care medical device communication—Application Profile—Base Standard
4	11073-20601™	Health informatics—Personal health device communication—Part 20601: Application profile—Optimized exchange protocol
5	11-73-20601a-2010™	Health informatics—Personal health device communication—Part 20601: Application profile—Optimized exchange protocol
6	11073-10408™	Health informatics—Personal health device communication—Part 10408: Device specialization—Thermometer
7	11073-10415™	Health informatics—Personal health device communication—Part 10415: Device specialization—Weighing scale
8	11073-10404™	Health informatics—Personal health device communication—Part 10404: Device specialization—Pulse oximeter
9	11073-10421-2010™	Health informatics—Personal health device communication—Part 10421: Device specialization—Peak expiratory flow monitor (peak flow)
10	11073-10406-2011™	Health informatics—Personal health device communication—Part 10406: Device specialization—Basic electrocardiograph (ECG) (1- to 3-lead ECG)
11	11073-10407™	IEEE ISO/IEEE Health informatics—Personal health device communication—Part 10407: Device specialization—Blood pressure monitor
12	110703-10417™	IEEE ISO/IEEE Health informatics—Personal health device communication—Part 10417: Device specialization—Glucose meter

Health Level Seven (HL7) Standards Developing Organization

With the creation, rollout, and adoption of EHRs and with medical instrumentation that communicates data for the management, diagnosis, and treatment of patients, methods for communicating those clinical and financial data associated with enterprise patient care management has matured over time. Standards for data communication have evolved principally through standards developing organizations (SDOs). The creation of new SDOs associated with specialty data communication have sprung up as well. These have been focused on promoting more standardized communication from medical devices at the POC to the EHR systems and other clinical information management systems, as well as data warehouses used for clinical treatment within the patient care environment. Perhaps the most well-known of the SDOs is HL7, which was founded in 1987 as a not-for-profit entity for developing

> *"a comprehensive framework and related standards for the exchange, integration, sharing, and retrieval of electronic health information that supports clinical practice and the management, delivery and evaluation of health services."*[44]

The focus of HL7 is on application-level data communication, which is reflected in their name owing to the level of the International Organization for Standardization (ISO) 7-layer communication model, with the seventh layer being the application layer. The data communication from application to application is the principal focus of the organization, and standards for data communication surrounding the interchange of medical data (both clinical and financial) have been codified in standards that are in wide use internationally.

Medical data that are typically derived from and communicated throughout the healthcare enterprise include laboratory information, medication, patient demographics and registration, radiographic imagery and notes, clinical notes produced by physicians and nurses, billing records and other financial information, private insurance information, diagnoses, and many other forms. Each of these categories is rendered into a standardized format of communication as messages that can be transmitted and interpreted by disparate systems that employ as part of the interchange of these data, templates for creating, receiving and parsing the information in accord with one of any number of HL7 standards formats or radiographic formats.

Yet, as we have seen, many medical devices still communicate using the more proprietary methods, often via serial ports and using data formats that are non-standard across medical device manufacturers and even across medical devices developed by some manufacturers. The data standardization and communications process for medical devices is analogous to the early days of railroading in the United States, during which railroads of differing gauges travelled across spurs that were isolated from one another. Further complicating travel in those days was also the fact that railroads often used their own and un-synchronized timetables, making planning and translating schedules across systems difficult, if not impossible.

In current day practice, medical devices span the gamut of possible application layer communication. Some manufacturers (particularly physiologic monitors used in ICUs) will provide a standardized mechanism using HL7 from device aggregators, sometimes referred to as gateways. Gateways provide for the data aggregation and conduct the data from the bedside physiologic monitors to the aggregation point from which a single data connection may be made with an interacting system. For instance, a physiologic monitoring gateway may interface directly with an EHR system so as to provide a single point of entry and data communication of the vital signs data to the receiving system.

Institute of Electrical and Electronics Engineers (IEEE) 11073™ Medical/Personal Health Device

IEEE announced in 2013 that it had received notification by the FDA that the IEEE 11073™ family of standards, supportive of medical device communication and interoperability, had been formally recognized.[45] The standards encompassed risk-management for connected and networked environments; interoperability standards surrounding nomenclature and medical device communication; and cyber-security standards. The standards recognized are listed in Table 4-1.

Many of these device standards cover the personal health device (PHD) domain. While the 11073 standards have been around for awhile and have been applied to many high acuity settings, such as ORs and ICUs, they were more recently adopted through the IEEE 11073 PHD Working Group (WG) to support the PHD domain.[46] The benefits of using 11073 families of standards is that the "syntax and semantics are fully defined,"[46] thus facilitating interoperable communication. Nonetheless, most interoperability at the medical device level from many of today's medical device vendors adhere to the physical layer interfaces of the 11073 requirements but in terms of the semantics and data interoperability, MDI solutions are required to support or provide the capability to translate the more proprietary data into more acceptable or usable formats, such as HL7.

HL7 Observation Reporting

HL7 was founded in 1987 for the purpose of developing, providing, and maintaining an ANSI-accredited standards framework for the exchange of information related to clinical, financial, and practice management data.[47] The definition of the organization's beginnings and the root of its name are all common knowledge and a perusal of the organization's website will give more details along these lines. The key item of importance is that HL7.org is a SDO that principally operates in the healthcare domain. As such, HL7.org has created a series of standards that pertain to information exchange to, from, and between various systems within the healthcare enterprise. Examples include laboratory data, pharmacy, imaging, insurance, registration, ordering, et al. Table 4-2 is a list of approved data standards from HL7.[48] All of these standards contain published revisions and are backwards compatible.

Table 4-2: Listing of Health Level Seven Version 2 Approved Standards.

HL7 Version	Name
HL7 Version 2.2	An application Protocol for Electronic Data Exchange in Healthcare Environments Designation: ANSI/HL7 v2.2-1996 Date Approved: 2/8/1996
HL7 Standard Version 2.3	An application Protocol for Electronic Data Exchange in Healthcare Environments Designation: ANSI/HL7 v2.3 1997 Date Approved: 5/13/1997. Note: Revision of ANSI / HL7 v2.2-1996
HL7 Standard Version 2.3.1	An application Protocol for Electronic Data Exchange in Healthcare Environments Designation: ANSI / HL7 v2.3.1-1999 Date Approved: 4/14/1999 Note: Revision of ANSI / HL7 v2.3-1997
HL7 Standard Version 2.4	An application Protocol for Electronic Data Exchange in Healthcare Environments Designation: ANSI / HL7 v2.4-2000 Date Approved: 10/16/2000 Note: revision of ANSI / HL7 v2.3.1-1999
HL7 Version 3.0 Standard	Clinical Document Architecture, Release 1 Designation: ANSI / HL7 CDA, R1-2000 Date Approved: 10/24/2000

Table 4-2: Listing of Health Level Seven Version 2 Approved Standards. (cont.)

HL7 Version	Name
HL7 Standard Version 2.5	An application Protocol for Electronic Data Exchange in Health-care Environments Designation: ANSI / HL7 v2.5-2003 Date Approved: 6/26/2003 Note: revision of ANSI / HL7 v2.4-2000
HL7 Version 3.0 Standard	Implantable Device Cardiac – Follow-up Device Summary, Release 1 Designation: ANSI / HL7 v3 IDC, R1-2006 Date Approved: 11/2/2006
HL7 Standard Version 2.6	An application Protocol for Electronic Data Exchange in Healthcare Environments Designation: ANSI / HL7 2.6-2007 Date Approved: 10/12/2007 Note: revision of ANSI / HL7 v2.5.1-2007
HL7 Standard Version 2.7	An application Protocol for Electronic Data Exchange in Health-care Environments Designation: ANSI / HL7 v2.7-2011 Date Approved: 1/28/2011 Note: revision of ANSI / HL7 v2.6-2007
HL7 Standard Version 2.7.1	An application Protocol for Electronic Data Exchange in Health-care Environments Designation: ANSI / HL7 v2.7.1-2012 Date Approved: 7/9/2012 Note: revision of ANSI / HL7 v2.7-2011

While data transmission to health IT systems need not follow the HL7 standard (that is, healthcare enterprises and health IT system vendors may offer their own proprietary method for data communication), by far, the most common means for data communication to the EHR is through the Unsolicited Observation Message, or Observational report—Unsolicited (ORU), identified as the R01 Event.[49] These, together with ADT messages, are normally transmitted in combination with acknowledgements (ACK) messages, as illustrated in Figure 4-1. The transmitted message contains the observations (data) from the MDI system. The acknowledgement provides confirmation of receipt of the ORU message.

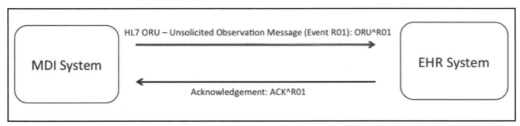

Figure 4-1: Unsolicited Observation Message Transmission from MDI System to the Health IT System, with Acknowledgement Message Response to Confirm Receipt.

For those unfamiliar with the specific syntax of the HL7 ORU or the acknowledgement message, details are provided within the context of the HL7 specification, available from http://www.hl7.org. Chapter 7 of the v2.6 specification details the content of the message and example uses of the standard to build or recreate such messages for testing purposes, as well as education on the use of the ORU.

The HL7 standard surrounding unsolicited observation reporting provides considerable flexibility in terms of the specific structure of the messaging.

From the perspective of observations or results communicated from an MDI solution, the key focus will be placed on the unimpeded communication of data from these systems at some predefined rate. This is a good assumption, as many EHRs simply listen for the incoming results and then process them for interactive display for the clinical end user in a chart-type format.

To facilitate an understanding of the use of the ORU, we will present a high level version of the message along with several examples. Table 4-3 lists the commonly used segments when communicating observations from medical devices through an MDI to an EHR. Table 4-4 lists the commonly used segments contained within the acknowledgement message transmitted in response to the ORU message.

Table 4-3: Commonly Used Form of the Unsolicited Observation Message: ORU^R01^ORU_R01.

Message Segment	Description
MSH	Message Header
PID	Patient Identification
PV1	Patient Visit
OBR	Observations Request
OBX	Observation related to OBR

Table 4-4: Acknowledgement Message: ACK^R01^ACK.

Message Segment	Description
MSH	Message Header
MSA	Message Acknowledgement

The example HL7 message provided in Table 4-5 shows an ORU communicated from an anesthesia machine together with its accompanying acknowledgement message. The SENDING_APP = sending application and SENDING_FAC = sending facility are the source application and facility of the message, respectively. Each message is encapsulated by framing characters. Framing characters for the message are usually the vertical tab, the file separator, and the carriage return, defined next.

Table 4-5: Sample HL7 ORU Message with Acknowledgement.

```
MSH|^~\&|<Sending_App>|<Sending_Fac>|<Receiving_App>|Receiving_Fac>|
20140115093417||ORU^R01|0099:01:00832E34|P|2.x
PID|||123148||Public^John||YYYYMMDD|M
PV1||I|^^Bed2&0&0
OBR|1|||||20140115093411
OBX|1|NM|AWP||6|mbar
OBX|2|NM|PPLAT||14|mbar
OBX|3|NM|PEEP||2|mbar
OBX|4|NM|PIP||16|mbar
OBX|5|NM|TV||100|mL
OBX|6|NM|MV||0.2|L/min
OBX|7|NM|VNT-RR||16|/min
OBX|8|NM|FGF-N2O||0|L/min
OBX|9|NM|FGF-AIR||0|L/min
OBX|10|NM|FGF-O2||9.999|L/min
OBX|11|NM|O2-IN||92|%
OBX|12|ST|DEV-MODEL||Fabius GS Premium|
OBX|13|ST|DEV-PROT||MEDIBUS|
OBX|14|ST|DEV-PROT-VER||04.00|
OBX|15|ST|DEV-TXT-TS||9:32:2815:JAN:14|
OBX|16|TS|DEV-TS||20140115093228|
ACK:
MSH|^~\&||||SENDING_APP|SENDING_FAC|201401150934||ACK|0099:01:00832E
34|P|2.3
MSA|AA|0099:01:00832E34
```

Examples of framing characters typically used with ORU messages:

Vertical Tab	<VT> =	013 (octal)	0B (hexadecimal)	11 (decimal)
File Separator	<FS> =	034 (octal)	1C (hexadecimal)	28 (decimal)
Carriage Return	<CR> =	015 (octal)	0D (hexadecimal)	13 (decimal)

The major messaging component for each segment is readily available through http://www.hl7.org. However, many healthcare enterprises already have individuals dedicated to mapping of HL7 messaging and, therefore, have experts well-versed in the particulars of HL7 results communications.

The message ACK may be received if specified as part of the interface negotiation between the sending and receiving systems. If the receiving system (EHR) does not specify or provide an ACK, then this response message may be omitted from the transaction. The ACK message contains the header segment (MSH) and the acknowledgement segment (MSA). If an error were to occur in interpretation or receipt of the message, the receiving system would specify an error in the MSA. If the message is received properly, the acknowledgement message code "AA" will appear in the MSA segment, as shown in Table 4-5. Otherwise, if there is an error in the receipt, the acknowledgement message code "AE" will appear, together with the specific error (optionally) following the message code (message code appears after the acknowledgement message code in the MSA message).

The messages that are communicated in the HL7 format to the health IT system either directly to the EHR or through an Interface Engine—an intermediary that receives the messages and forwards to the EHR system—carry some level of tailoring in terms of the content. Examples of this tailoring can be

    a. Unified code names (that is, the parameter names of the individual observations)

    b. Unit of measure changes (that is, the units of the individual observations)

    c. Content of the patient identifying information (that is, identifiers of various types and other patient information)

    d. Patient location information and variations in locations identity (that is, the names of individual rooms, their formats, bed identifiers)

    e. Communication of persistent parameters versus transmission of single or aperiodic observations only one time (that is, communicate aperiodic measurements such as non-invasive blood pressure only at the time of the measurement)

Other variations exist, as well. This means that it is likely that some tailoring of the HL7 messaging is required to ensure that the messages are not met with a negative acknowledgement, a "NACK" or error associated with the receiving system not responding to or not properly acknowledging the message transmission.

Solicited Observations, or observations resulting from queries, are also described within the HL7 specification, adapted from the HL7 2.6 specification, and shown in Table 4-6 and Table 4-7, respectively.[50,51] Per the HL7 specification, the MSA segment consists of an acknowledgement code and a message control ID to link the message acknowledgement back to the original message.

Table 4-6: Query/Response Transactions (QRF / QRF).

QUERY:
1.   MSH (message header)
2.   QRD (query definition segment)
3.   [QRF] query filter (optional)

RESPONSE:
4.   MSH (message header)
5.   MSA (message acknowledgement; contains an acknowledgement code and the corresponding message control ID, along with an error string in case of an error)
6.   QRD
7.   [QRF] (if specified in query)
8.   PID The PID segment contains the patient ID and name
9.   OBR(segment contains the timestamp in ISO format of the OBX parameters that follow)
10. OBX(1)…OBX(n)(contains the result for the timestamp specified in the preceding OBR segment)

The example <query> and <response> transaction pairing, which mimics the QRY/QRF example in the HL7 specification, provides a unique coupling between the data being requested and on which patient and the resulting data or observations. This pairing provides assurance that the data are not incorrectly associated between the data source and identification of whom the data correspond so that when transmitted to an EHR system, they can be properly parsed and booked to the correct patient through the associated identifiers.

Note that, in these transactions, the message header segment contains message type and message control ID fields, which are echoed back in the query filter (QRF) message. In the message contained within Table 4-7, the following definitions apply:

The message header (MSH) segment:

MSH-2	Encoding Characters:	^~\&
MSH-3	Sending Application:	<Sending_App>
MSH-4	Sending Facility:	<Sending_Fac>
MSH-5	Receiving Application:	<Receiving_App>
MSH-6	Receiving Facility:	<Receiving_Fac>
MSH-7	Message Date/Time:	YYYYMMDDhhmm
MSH-8	Security:	<security> Details not specified
MSH-9	Message Type:	QRY^R02 (message type, trigger event, message structure ID).
MSH-10	Message Control ID:	ABC12345 (unique message identifier)
MSH-11	Processing ID:	'P'
MSH-12	Version ID:	2.6 (release 2.6, July 2007)

The Query Definition (QRD) segment follows:

QRD-1	Query Date/Time:	YYYYMMDDhhmm
QRD-2	Query Format Code:	'R' (D=respond in display format; R=response in record-oriented format; T=response in tabular format)
QRD-3	Query Priority:	'I' (D=deferred; I=immediate)
QRD-4	Query ID:	Q1234
QRD-5	Deferred Response Type:	[empty] (B=before the time specified; L=later than the date/time specified-optional)
QRD-6	Deferred Response Date/Time:	[empty] (optional)
QRD-7	Quantity-Limited Request:	10RD (<quantity^<units>, CH=characters; LI=lines; PG=pages; RD=records; ZO=locally-defined)
QRD-8	Who Subject Filter:	<Patient_ID> (optional)
QRD-9	What Subject Filter:	"RES" (RES=result—optional field)
QRD-10	What Department Data Code:	QRF

QRD-11   What Data Code Value Qual: EKG (optional field)

QRD-12   Query Results Level: 'T' (O=order plus order status; R=results without bulk text; S=status only; T=full results—optional field)

Table 4-7: Example Query/Response Transaction for a Query from an ECG (EKG) System for Data on a Particular Patient.

```
QUERY:
MSH|^~\&|<Sending_App>|<Sending_Fac>|<Receiving_App>|Receiving_Fac>|
YYYYMMDDhhmm|<security>|QRY^R02|ABC12345|P|2.6
QRD|YYYYMMDDhhmm|R|I|Q1234|||10^RD|<Patient_ID>|RES|
QRF|EKG|T
RESPONSE:
MSH|^~\&|<Receiving_App>|Receiving_Fac>|<Sending_App>|<Sending_Fac>|
YYYYMMDDhhmm|<security>|ORF^R04|XYZ98765|P|2.6
MSA|AA|ABC12345|P| QRD|YYYYMMDDhhmm|R|I|Q4412|||10^RD|<Patient_
ID>|RES| QRF|EKG|T
PID|1||<Patient_ID>||FAMILY_NAME^GIVEN_NAME^MI|||||||||
OBR|1|43215^OE|98765^EKG|93000^EKG REPORT||||YYYYMMDDhhmmOBX|1
|ST|8897-1^QRS COMPLEX^LN||91|/MIN|60-100|||||F| OBX|2|ST|8894-8^P
WAVE^LN||92|/MIN|60-100|||||F| OBX|3|ST|8625-6^P-R INTERVAL^LN||0|/
MSEC|1.06-.10|||||F| OBX|4|ST|8633-0^QRS DURATION^LN||.368|/
MSEC|.18-.22|||||F|
```

In the response, the QRD and QRF segments are listed, followed by the patient identifier segment, the OBR segment and then the OBX segments. Each OBX segment lists the parameter (e.g.,QRS, P Wave, P-R interval, QRS duration) with the related values, UOMs and the range of normal values (e.g. 0.18-0.22 seconds, or 180–220 milliseconds for QRS duration). The specific timeframe for the retrieved data is not specified (i.e., for historical data). However, this may be done and specified as part of the QRY.

Conditioning and Translating Connected Medical Device Data for IT System Consumption

Once data are received from the medical device, they are converted into some version of the HL7 standard. However, this normalization is usually insufficient to complete the process for data communication to the EHR.

For example, Figure 4-2 illustrates a simple case in which a medical device produces several values including pulse rate (HR-SPO2) derived from pulse oximetry measurement, oxygen saturation (SpO2), non-invasive blood pressure and pulse rate (HR-NIBP) derived from the non-invasive blood pressure cuff. This example was chosen to illustrate the case of a medical device that produces overlapping or redundant measurements from different sensors, or redundant measurements are produced from different medical devices that are associated with the same patient. Frequently, medical devices of differing types used in the same setting and on the same patient will produce such overlapping measurements. In some cases, redundant measurements may be rejected or ignored by clinical staff based on the required workflow or policy or clinical relevance of the data. In other cases, redundant measurements are both welcome and necessary to provide corroborating evidence of measured values, particularly if the measurements are taken from competing or uncorrelated sources. Environments in which this can be experienced are OR and ICU. Certain clinicians may wish to have these competing or corroborating measurements posted separately into the EHR system or anesthesia information management system. To illustrate this using Figure 4-2, the two measurements of pulse from the bedside are measured via pulse oximetry and NIBP cuff, respectively. The measurements may both be received by the translating or aggregating function with the parameter name (or encoding) of HR. However, lacking any further conditioning on the data, they might both be reported as HR, although their context is different.

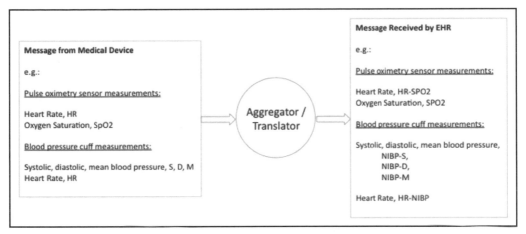

Figure 4-2: Example of Data Conditioning to Meet Inbound Requirements for Clinical Staff and Health IT System.

On the face of it, this may not be a problem. However, the heart rate being derived from two different sources may report somewhat different values and at differing times. These variations may cause confusion. Furthermore, it may be important for the clinical end user (e.g., anesthesiologist, attending physician, or nurse) to understand the context of the measurement. For instance, a measurement of pulse from the oxygen saturation cuff and the measurement of pulse from the NIBP cuff, being taken from different locations, can provide corroborating evidence as to the accuracy of the measurement. If a cuff is misapplied, it may be that the measurements are inaccurate. By receiving redundant measurements from different devices, this may serve in the eyes of the clinician as a method for ensuring the likelihood that the values obtained are valid.

But, to capture these corroborating values within the clinical record as distinct, it is necessary to translate their parameter names (sometimes referred to as unified codes or encodings) so that they may be received as unique. In the previous figure, this is accomplished by translating the pulse values from their medical device encodings of HR into HR-SPO2 and HR-NIBP, respectively. It should be noted that mapping these distinctive pulse rates will only be possible if the source monitor distinguishes them by encoding or containment. While this may seem trivial, identifying their differences will be necessary during the process of configuring anesthesia information management systems or the health IT systems. This is where it becomes necessary to have a complete understanding of the types of data that can be issued by medical devices and an understanding of how these data can and should be used for clinical consumption.

This conditioning of the medical device data for the EHR or anesthesia information management system is closely related to the following aspects of the data being received:

1. Having a full understanding of the definition of the medical device parameter values and their context (that is, their meaning relative to modes of operation)
2. Validating that these data are indeed a true representation of those values displayed on the medical device(s) and their consumption within the EHR are interpreted correctly
3. Verifying that the data are correctly mapped to the labels within the EHR system, anesthesia information management system or other clinical information system prior to going live on such systems with patients.[2]

The conditioning and translating of the output data from medical devices is distinct from the validation of the MDI vendor-based device driver development. MDI solution vendors will validate that data derived or queried from the medical device are accurately translated from the source at the bedside to the aggregator and end point recipient of the data (i.e., health IT system). However, the process of validating the data mapping from the raw medical device data to the clinical labels and fields used within the health IT system must be validated by the clinical end users of the system. There can be no substitute for this step, and ample time must be allocated for this validation process prior to system go-live. Just how much time is allocated varies by the extent of the devices, their complexity, and the type and amount of data that must be collected. However, to establish a rule-of-thumb estimate for this process, the following validation steps related to data conditioning should be considered:

- Validation of all modes of mechanical ventilation from anesthesia machines should be performed in concert with the MDI vendor
- The enterprise IT team responsible for the anesthesia information management system mappings, with the aid of an anesthesiologist or a CRNA on each anesthesia machine contained within the enterprise OR environments, must validate the data displayed on those devices and their accurate rendering within the EHR system including UOM
- All modes of mechanical ventilation normally employed during each type of typically performed procedure should be evaluated, and the mapping of parameters obtained from the connected anesthesia machine(s) should be validated in the chart together with UOMs
- The measured or set values on the anesthesia machine should be validated with those displayed in the anesthesia information management system, to include a measurement of the time from display on the device to the actual availability for viewing within the anesthesia information management system.

Performing this process on a single anesthesia machine, particularly if this is the first time being conducted, can take several hours on the part of all involved. Therefore, in terms of planning, the time allocation of the clinician, as well as the IT staff, must be carefully assessed and a time in the ORs must be determined, usually after hours, during which free access to the equipment is possible. It should be noted that in many enterprises, the time of the clinician is billable. Hence, making the most use of time available to support this validation process must be heeded.

In practice, the validation process usually involves several revisits and re-attempts. Parameter mappings at the outset, particularly if this is a first-time MDI attempt within an enterprise health system, are fraught with issues, such as unmapped parameters within the enterprise health record or parameter mappings that are incorrect, missing, or incomplete. Therefore, planning for the completion of this activity should take a certain level of pragmatism into account in realizing that this process may need to be frequently revisited to ensure alignment and correctness. This is the normal process of testing and validation.

Each validation session should also be considered an opportunity to educate and inform the clinical staff as to what is actually available from the connected medical device. The ability to pull medical device data into the end point information system brings a level of accuracy and precision that some may not be used to: the regularity of the timing of the data; the values associated with the particular measurements; attention given to response time of the medical device with respect to the values displayed in the chart, etc. may provide insight that was not previously understood. For instance, adjusting the gas levels on the anesthesia machine may, visually, indicate rapid or instantaneous changes in settings on the device. However, in terms of the measured data, the output displayed in the chart may show a more gradual increase over time. This type of behavior does not necessarily indicate an error or problem in the MDI solution provider's system, but merely represents the realistic and actual reporting behavior of the medical device.

Furthermore, certain values that appear in the end point information system may be displayed in units that are either real-valued (i.e., having decimal places) or integer-valued. The end point information system must be able to interpret these correctly and provide proper rounding of values where appropriate, or the MDI solution provider must be able to provide rounding as required. For instance, a flow rate display on the anesthesia machine may indicate visually 3.0 liters per minute. This may be displayed as a visual reading of an analog gauge on the anesthesia machine itself or through an electronic display. However, in terms of the data issued by the anesthesia machine, the actual value may appear as 2.999 or 3.001 liters per minute. As part of the validation process, it must be determined as whether acceptable that what the clinician validates (e.g., 3.0 L/min) is principally the same as what is displayed in the flow sheet (e.g., 2.999 L/min). If this poses a problem clinically, then steps must be taken to provide proper rounding or limiting of the decimal places to ensure that what is viewed on the machine is the same as that displayed within the information management system.

Related to conditioning of the data is the output frequency to the EHR or anesthesia information management system.

Consider the illustration in Figure 4-3 depicting the display of data in a generic charting window. The arrival of data are shown in relationship to processing of those data, with the ultimate display within the chart indicating a processing delay between arrival at the interface to the EHR or information system and the time required to display within the columnar format. Note that the non-invasive blood pressure (NIBP) measurements are not continuously measured but appear at discrete intervals (that is, they are measured ad-hoc). This is consistent with the approach to NIBP measurement in that they are not normally measured continuously (unless the source monitor is set to perform regular measurements). Here, the measurements of NIBP are performed discretely at irregular intervals. The NIBP can be measured automatically at regular intervals of, say, one minute, five minutes, etc. This is prescribed clinically. The key point is that NIBP measurements are distinguished from measurements of, say, pulse rate or oxygen saturation in that the latter are reported at much higher frequency than NIBP measurements and are collected automatically. The NIBP measurements require that the NIBP cuff be inflated (on a patient's arm or leg), and this consumes time such that most NIBP measurements cannot be taken more rapidly than once every few minutes. More continuous measurements can be collected through invasive means (e.g., arterial blood pressure measurements).

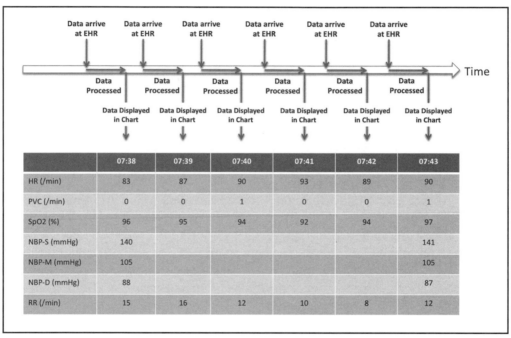

Figure 4-3: Sample Chart Display Showing Juxtaposition of the Arrival of Data to the EHR System and the Display of Those Data in the Chart.

Figure 4-4 shows the same figure but with the time intervals between the arrivals of each measurement depicted. This time interval, which can vary by measurement (although is most often a fixed interval), is given by Δt_i, Δt_{i+1}, etc., and denotes an interval or period within which each transaction arrives. Noting that the sample chart displays a value each minute (such as is common with anesthesia information management system charting), this would imply that the interval, Δt_i, must be less than 60 seconds. Understanding the requirement on charting interval based upon the end user clinical needs is key to defining the update frequency of data required for the clinical record, and ultimately will dictate how frequently the data must arrive at the interface of the health IT system (i.e., how frequently the MDI system must deliver data to the interface).

When the inter-arrival time of data into the information system is too large, the example of Figure 4-5 may be the result: missed data intervals and empty columns of data due to the fact that the data do not arrive in time to post in the chart. Hence, the inter-arrival times associated with the charting requirements must be tuned to the needs of the clinical end user and the departments being supported.

The health IT system's patient charting in ORs, and specifically AIMS, mandates a relatively high frequency of data collection. Similarly, ICUs have relatively high data throughput requirements, yet the charting requirements are not typically as stringent as those in the OR. However, the process of validating the display requirements in intensive care is similar to those in the OR, and the appropriate clinical individuals must be part of this validation process. This means that respiratory therapy (for mechanical ventilators) and nursing staff are normally the clinical end users who are participating in this validation process. As described earlier for validating data from anesthesia machines, validating data from mechanical ventilators should proceed with an assessment of each machine mode and a comparison between the visible data and the reported data through the information system.

Validation of data from physiologic monitors and ancillary devices (e.g., bi-spectral index monitors, end-tidal CO_2 monitors, intra-aortic balloon pumps, etc.) should follow the same procedure as for mechanical ventilators; most of these devices are either unimodal or have a reduced number of modes through which the medical devices can operate, thereby simplifying the clinical workflow in terms of charting.

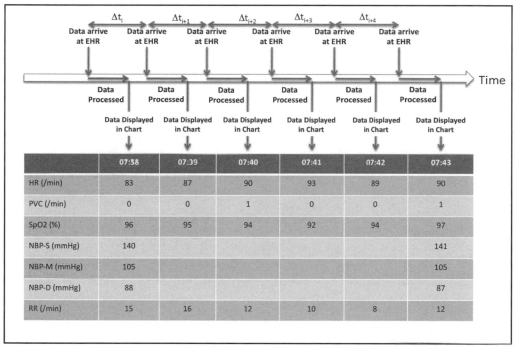

	07:38	07:39	07:40	07:41	07:42	07:43
HR (/min)	83	87	90	93	89	90
PVC (/min)	0	0	1	0	0	1
SpO2 (%)	96	95	94	92	94	97
NBP-S (mmHg)	140					141
NBP-M (mmHg)	105					105
NBP-D (mmHg)	88					87
RR (/min)	15	16	12	10	8	12

Figure 4-4: Chart Display with Time Intervals Between Vitals Data Entries Shown.

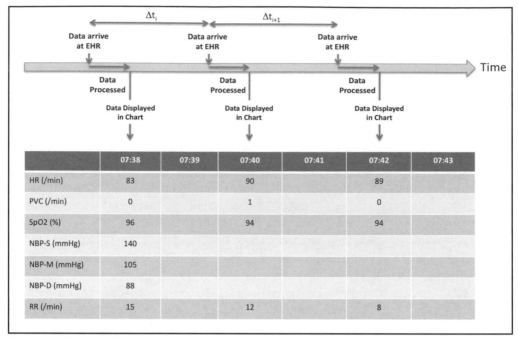

	07:38	07:39	07:40	07:41	07:42	07:43
HR (/min)	83		90		89	
PVC (/min)	0		1		0	
SpO2 (%)	96		94		94	
NBP-S (mmHg)	140					
NBP-M (mmHg)	105					
NBP-D (mmHg)	88					
RR (/min)	15		12		8	

Figure 4-5: Data Posting in the EHR When Time Interval Between Data Arrivals Is Too Large, Resulting in Missed Data Intervals and Spotty Data.

The validation process can consume a significant amount of time—perhaps several weeks of overall effort, depending on the availability of clinical staff and other participants and stakeholders. Hence, adequate time allocation must be given to the planning process to ensure that the project takes this scheduling into account so as to meet overall project timeline.

Patient Administration

The demographic and administrative information relating to patient identification, insurance, location, and payment are managed through patient administration messaging referred to as admission-discharge-transfer (ADT) HL7 transactions.

There are more than 50 ADT message event types. Some of the most commonly used event types include the following:

A01 – Patient admit

A02 – Patient transfer

A03 – Patient discharge

A08 – Patient information update

A11 – Cancel patient admit

A12 – Cancel patient transfer

A13 – Cancel patient discharge

A18 – Merge patient information

As shown in Table 4-8, the HL7 version 2.6 standard lists the following ADT events:[52]

Table 4-8: Listing of HL7 ADT Event Transactions from the Version 2.6 Final Specification.

ADT Message Event	Definition
A01	Admit/Visit Notification
A02	Transfer a patient
A03	Discharge/End Visit
A04	Register a patient
A05	Pre-admit a patient
A06	Change an outpatient to an inpatient
A07	Change an inpatient to an outpatient
A08	Update patient information
A09	Patient departing – tracking
A10	Patient arriving – tracking
A11	Cancel admit/visit notification
A12	Cancel transfer
A13	Cancel discharge
A14	Pending admit
A15	Pending transfer
A16	Pending discharge
A17	Swap patients
A18	Merge patient information
A19	Patient query
A20	Bed status update
A21	Patient goes on a leave of absence
A22	Patient returns from a leave of absence
A23	Delete a patient record
A24	Link patient information
A25	Cancel pending discharge
A26	Cancel pending transfer
A27	Cancel pending admit
A28	Add person or patient information
A29	Delete person information
A30	Merge person information
A31	Update person information
A32	Cancel patient arriving – tracking

Table 4-8: Listing of HL7 ADT Event Transactions from the Version 2.6 Final Specification. (cont.)

ADT Message Event	Definition
A33	Cancel patient departing – tracking
A34	Merge patient information – patient ID only
A35	Merge patient information – account number only
A36	Merge patient information – patient ID & account number
A37	Uplink patient information
A38	Cancel pre-admit
A39	Merge person – patient ID
A40	Merge patient – patient identifier list
A41	Merge account – patient account number
A42	Merge visit – visit number
A43	Move patient information – patient identifier list
A44	Move account information – patient account number
A45	Move visit information – visit number
A46	Change patient ID
A47	Change patient identifier list
A48	Change patient alternate ID
A49	Change patient account number
A50	Change visit number
A51	Change alternate visit ID
A52	Cancel leave of absence for a patient
A53	Cancel patient returns from a leave of absence
A54	Change attending doctor
A55	Cancel change attending doctor
A60	Update adverse reaction information
A61	Change consulting doctor
A62	Cancel change consulting doctor

An example of an ADT-A01 transaction is provided in Table 4-9. This transaction represents the admission message associated with a fabricated patient. This message contains patient identifier, date of birth, hospital identifier, patient address, spouse information, gender, location and attending physician name and identifier.

Table 4-9: Example ADT-A01 Patient Administration Message for Admitting a Patient.

```
MSH|^~\&|ADT1|GOOD HEALTH HOSPITAL|GHH LAB, INC.|GOOD HEALTH HOSPITA
L|201407221957|SECURITY|ADT^A01^ADT_A01|MSG00001|P|2.6|
EVN|A01|201407221957||
PID|1||567196345^5^M11^ADT1^MR^GOOD HEALTH HOSPITA
L~123456789^^^USSSA^SS||Last^First^M^||19560412|F
||C|1111 HOME STREET^^GREENSBORO^NC^27401-1020|GL|(555)
555-2004|(555)555-2004||S||960156^2^M10^ADT1^AN^A|444333333|987654
^NC|
NK1|1|Last^First^M|SPO^SPOUSE||||NK^NEXT OF KIN
PV1|1|I|SICU^BED^02|||||004777^ATTEND^PhysLast^PhysFirst|||SUR||||AD
M|A0|
```

A Few Words About HL7 Fast Healthcare Interoperability

HL7 introduced a new specification and standards framework (under development), termed Fast Healthcare Interoperability Resources (FHIR®), which leverages the existing standards work, as well as incorporating more information exchange best practices, particularly WEB standards, with an increased focus on facilitating implementation.[53] Key features advertised by the HL7 FHIR resources site include the following:[53]

a. Faster, simpler implementation

b. Implementation libraries with examples to assist in development

c. No cost and no restrictions on use

d. Evolutionary in that can build upon existing Version 2 and Version 3 HL7 products

e. Foundation in Web standards, particularly XML, JSON, HTTP, Atom, OAuth et al.

f. Supports RESTful* architecture and interfaces

g. Simplified, concise, and human readable specifications with formalized ontologies

*Representational State Transfer (REST): RESTful architectural style and services are characterized by the following principles: (1) statelessness (i.e., do not depend on prior or subsequent requests); (2) uniqueness and context-free interaction (i.e., that each request for data are entirely self-contained and all information necessary to interpret the request are provided within the request); (3) uniformity in the representation of a resource, particularly between a client and a server (i.e., HTTP methods for create, read, update, delete); (4) uniform representations of the resources are safe and idempotent (i.e., requests do not change server state and re-execution of the same operation produces the same result as a single execution). Services are examples of REST architechture.

Integrating the Healthcare Enterprise® (IHE)

As described in the section beginning this chapter, standards development organizations, such as HL7, are distinct from implementation frameworks. Perhaps the most well-known of these is the implementation framework established by the IHE Patient Care Device Technical Framework.

IHE (http://www.ihe.net) was established as an initiative to improve the manner in which healthcare information systems interact and share information.[54] Through IHE, a number of open profiles for integration implementation have been created. One such profile for interoperability among connected medical devices and the information systems that receive their data is the Patient Care Device, or PCD profile.

The IHE Patient Care Device Technical Framework, dated October 11, 2013, comprises three volumes:[55]

Vol. 1 (PCD TF-1): Integration Profiles

Vol. 2 (PCD TF-2): Transactions

Vol. 3 (PCD TF-3): Semantic Content

The volumes include specifications surrounding Alert Communication Management (ACM), Device Enterprise Communication (DEC), Implantable Device – Cardiac Observation (IDCO), Point-of-care Infusion Verification (PIV), and Rosetta Terminology Mapping (RTM).

In terms of the relationship between the IHE PCD TF to standard, including HL7, IEEE, DICOM and others, Volume 1 states:

> *"The IHE Technical Framework identifies functional components of a distributed healthcare environment (referred to as IHE actors), solely from the point of view of their interactions in the healthcare enterprise... IHE does not introduce technical choices that contradict conformance to these standards... IHE is therefore an implementation framework, not a standard."*[56]

Contained within the PCD-TF are transaction profiles specified that describe mechanisms by which data are communicated, responses are issued, and individual actors are to respond. Of particular import to EHR interaction is the DEC profile, which:

> *"...describes mechanisms to communicate [patient care device] data to enterprise information systems. The typical PCD data includes periodic physiologic data (heat rate, invasive blood pressure, respiration rate, etc.), aperiodic physiologic data (non-invasive blood pressure, patient weight, cardiac output, etc.), and CLIA waived (equivalent international waiver) point-of-care laboratory tests (i.e., home blood glucose, etc.). The data may also include contextual information such as the patient ID, caregiver identification, and patient care device configuration information."*[57]

Other profiles include the IDCO, focused on cardiac device discrete data reporting, ACM communication of alerts from medical devices to alert management systems, and the RTM, which is a set of established nomenclature elements intended to relate proprietary medical device-specific terminology and information encodings to standard representation "using the ISO/IEEE 11073 semantics and UCUM units of measurement."[58]

The IHE hosts a yearly event in January, called Connectathon, in which developers of healthcare IT systems and medical device vendors get together to test use cases related to interoperability among these systems. Examples indicate data communication from connected medical devices to EHR systems, medical device alarms communication to nurse call systems, receipt of inbound data from EHR systems (e.g., admission, discharge and transfer transactions), communication among EHR CPOE systems, pharmacy, and infusion systems, and other related profiles that seek to improve the workflow and communication offerings among information technology systems and connected medical devices. To illustrate the IHE TF implementation, let's consider an example IHE PCD-01 transaction for medical device data communication from an anesthesia machine. One such transaction is shown in Table 4-10. The PCD-01 transaction is used by a Device Observation Reporter (DOR) to communicate PCD data to either a Device Observation Consumer (DOC) or a Device Observation Filter (DOF). In the IHE PCD Technical Framework, these are actors, which link to abstract functions versus physical devices.[59]

The DOR may be a free-standing system such as a physiologic monitoring system together with the monitoring system concentrator or gateway. Alternatively, the DOR may be implemented as part of the patient care device itself, such as a physiologic monitor that can communicate a PCD-01 transaction.

The DOC could be represented by the health IT system. The DOF could be part of a health IT system, a standalone commercial or proprietary HL7 integration engine. The DOF serves in the role of echoing and further filtering transactions received from the DOR.

The PCD-01 transaction contains specific fields that are used to identify the source device (OBX-4), known as the containment tree within the structure of IEEE 11073.[60] The observation structure of the IHE PCD implementation is similar to that of the standard HL7 solicited or unsolicited observation (ORU). Yet, there are specific aspects of the OBX – Observation/Result segment that are unique to the PCD-01 transaction and that differ from the standard HL7 ORU message.

Table 4-11 lists the individual OBX segments that are used within the standard PCD-01 message implementation. Some key observations related to the OBX message segments:

OBX-3 Observation Identifier: This field identifies the type of device that is collecting the measurements.

OBX-4 Observation Sub-ID: This field identifies and distinguishes among multiple OBX segments within an OBR. The key to this field is the use of

> "an unambiguous mapping from observation contained in the OBX segment to the IEEE 11073 containment tree for the Medical Device System sourcing the observation. For device-related data, this field is used to group devices hierarchically."[61]

For medical device-related observation data, the OBX-4 is used to group medical device hierarchically. The origin of this distinction is from the HL7 standard itself:[62]

> "The use of the sub ID to distinguish repeating OBXs for the same observation ID is really a special case of using the sub ID to group... a particular species of observation... the sub ID would be associated with each corresponding OBX."

Table 4-10: Example IHE PCD-01 Message Containing the Medical Device Data from an Anesthesia Machine.

```
MSH|^~\&|ANESTHE_A-SERIES^00A0370029000033^EUI-64|NEW TOWN|||201
20912194537+0800||ORU^R01^ORU_R01|57|P|2.6|||NE|AL||UNICODE UTF-
8|||IHE_PCD_001^IHE PCD^1.3.6.1.4.1.19376.1.6.1.1.1^ISO
PID|||3423^^^NEW TOWN^PI||Last^First11^^^^^M||19500912|
PV1||I|ICU^3A^10^NEW TOWN
OBR|1|57^ANESTHE_A-SERIES^00A0370029000033^EUI-64|57^ANESTHE_A-
SERIES^00A0370029000033^EUI-64|70040^MDC_DEV_SYS_ANESTH^
MDC|||20120912194537+0800|
OBX|1|CWE|268422^MDC_EVT_STAT_DEV^MDC|1.1.1.268422|268438^MDC_
EVT_STAT_RUNNING^MDC|262656^MDC_DIM_DIMLESS^MDC|||
||F|||20120912194537+0800|
OBX|2|CWE|30002^ANESTH_EVT_STAT_MODE_DEV^99ANEST|1.1.1.30002|30003
^ANESTH_EVT_STAT_MODE_NORMAL^99ANEST|262656^MDC_DIM_DIMLESS^MDC|||
||F|||20120912194537+0800|
OBX|3|CWE|30005^ANESTH_EVT_PATIENT_TYPE^99ANEST|1.1.1.30005|268424
^MDC_EVT_STAT_DEV_MODE_PEDIATRIC^MDC|262656^MDC_DIM_DIMLESS^MDC|||
||F|||20120912194537+0800|
OBX|4|CWE|30007^ANESTH_EVT_STAT_WARMER_ON_BOOL^99ANEST|1.3.1
.30007|30000^MDC_TRUE^99ANEST|262656^MDC_DIM_DIMLESS^MDC|||
||F|||20120912194537+0800|
OBX|5|CWE|184352^MDC_VENT_MODE^MDC|1.3.1.184352|50005^AN
ESTH_VENT_MODE_VCV^99ANEST|262656^MDC_DIM_DIMLESS^MDC|||
||F|||20120912194537+0800|
OBX|6|NM|151868^MDC_VOL_AWAY_TIDAL_SETTING^MDC|1.3.2.151868|300|263
762^MDC_DIM_MILLI_L^MDC|||||F|||20120912194537+0800|
OBX|7|NM|151586^MDC_VENT_RESP_RATE_SETTING^MDC|1.3.2.151586|30|2649
28^MDC_DIM_RESP_PER_MIN^MDC|||||F|||20120912194537+0800|
OBX|8|SN|20000^MDC_RATIO_IE_SETTING^99ANEST|1.3.2.20000|^1^:^2|2626
56^MDC_DIM_DIMLESS^MDC|||||F|||20120912194537+0800|
OBX|9|NM|20007^ANESTH_VENT_PAUSE_TIME_PERCENT_SETTING^99ANEST|1.3.2
.20007|0|262688^MDC_DIM_PERCENT^MDC|||||F|||20120912194537+0800|
OBX|10|NM|151976^MDC_PRESS_AWAY_END_EXP_POS_SETTING^MDC|1.3.2.15197
6|0|266048^MDC_DIM_CM_H2O^MDC|||||F|||20120912194537+0800|
OBX|11|NM|20013^ANESTH_VENT_PRESS_LIMIT_SETTING^99ANEST|1.3.2.20013
|45|266048^MDC_DIM_CM_H2O^MDC|||||F|||20120912194537+0800|
OBX|12|NM|113^MDC_FLOW_O2_FG^99ANEST|1.3.3.113|3.7|265216^
MDC_DIM_L_PER_MIN^MDC|||||R|||20120912194537+0800|
OBX|13|NM|114^MDC_FLOW_N2O_FG^99ANEST|1.3.3.114|0.00|265216^
MDC_DIM_L_PER_MIN^MDC|||||R|||20120912194537+0800|
OBX|14|NM|115^MDC_FLOW_AIR_FG^99ANEST|1.3.3.115|1.9|265216^
MDC_DIM_L_PER_MIN^MDC|||||R|||20120912194537+0800|
OBX|15|NM|151957^MDC_VENT_PRESS_MAX^MDC|1.3.2.151957|11|266048^
MDC_DIM_CM_H2O^MDC||||||R|||20120912194537+0800|
OBX|16|NM|151819^MDC_PRESS_AWAY_INSP_MEAN^MDC|1.3.2.151819|6|266048
^MDC_DIM_CM_H2O^MDC|||||R|||20120912194537+0800|
OBX|17|NM|151784^MDC_PRESS_RESP_PLAT^MDC|1.3.2.151784|10|266048^
MDC_DIM_CM_H2O^MDC||||||R|||20120912194537+0800|
OBX|18|NM|151976^MDC_PRESS_AWAY_END_EXP_POS^MDC|1.3.2.151976|3|2660
48^MDC_DIM_CM_H2O^MDC|||||R|||20120912194537+0800|
OBX|19|NM|151880^MDC_VOL_MINUTE_AWAY^MDC|1.3.2.151880|2.2|265216^
MDC_DIM_L_PER_MIN^MDC|||||R|||20120912194537+0800|
```

Table 4-10: Example IHE PCD-01 Message Containing the Medical Device Data from an Anesthesia Machine. (cont.)

```
OBX|20|NM|151868^MDC_VOL_AWAY_TIDAL^MDC|1.3.2.151868|67|263762^
MDC_DIM_MILLI_L^MDC|||||R|||20120912194537+0800|
OBX|21|NM|151586^MDC_VENT_RESP_RATE^MDC|1.3.2.151586|31|264928^
MDC_DIM_RESP_PER_MIN^MDC|||||R|||20120912194537+0800|
OBX|22|SN|151832^MDC_RATIO_IE^MDC|1.3.2.151832|^4.5^:^1|262656^
MDC_DIM_DIMLESS^MDC|||||R|||20120912194537+0800|
OBX|23|NM|151840^MDC_RES_AWAY^MDC|1.3.2.151840|2|268064^
MDC_DIM_CM_H2O_PER_L_PER_SEC^MDC|||||R|||20120912194537+0800|
OBX|24|NM|151688^MDC_COMPL_LUNG^MDC|1.3.2.151688|8|268050^
MDC_DIM_MILLI_L_PER_CM_H2O^MDC|||||R|||20120912194537+0800|
OBX|25|NM|152196^MDC_CONC_AWAY_O2_INSP^MDC|1.4.1.152196|23|262688^
MDC_DIM_PERCENT^MDC|||||R|||20120912194537+0800|
OBX|26|NM|188736^MDC_MASS_BODY_ACTUAL^MDC|1.2.1.188736|55.0|263875^
MDC_DIM_KILO_G^MDC|||||F|||20120912194537+0800|
OBX|27|NM|151708^MDC_CONC_AWAY_CO2_ET^MDC|1.4.1.151708|12|266016^
MDC_DIM_MMHG^MDC|||||R|||20120912194537+0800|
OBX|28|NM|151716^MDC_CONC_AWAY_CO2_INSP^MDC|1.4.1.151716|9|266016^
MDC_DIM_MMHG^MDC|||||R|||20120912194537+0800|
OBX|29|NM|152440^MDC_CONC_AWAY_O2_ET^MDC|1.4.1.152440|20|262688^
MDC_DIM_PERCENT^MDC|||||R|||20120912194537+0800|
OBX|30|NM|152108^MDC_CONC_AWAY_N2O_ET^MDC|1.4.1.152108|0|262688^M
DC_DIM_PERCENT^MDC|||||R|||20120912194537+0800|
OBX|31|NM|152192^MDC_CONC_AWAY_N2O_INSP^MDC|1.4.1.152192|0|262688^
MDC_DIM_PERCENT^MDC|||||R|||20120912194537+0800|
OBX|32|NM|119^MDC_CONC_MAC^99ANEST|1.4.1.119|0.0|262656^MDC_DIM_DIM
LESS^MDC|||||R|||20120912194537+0800|
OBX|33|NM|152088^MDC_CONC_AWAY_ENFL_ET^MDC|1.4.1.152088|0.7|262688^
MDC_DIM_PERCENT^MDC|||||R|||20120912194537+0800|
OBX|34|NM|152172^MDC_CONC_AWAY_ENFL_INSP^MDC|1.4.1.152172|1.0|26268
8^MDC_DIM_PERCENT^MDC|||||R|||20120912194537+0800|
OBX|35|NM|152084^MDC_CONC_AWAY_DESFL_ET^MDC|1.4.1.152084|0.4|262688
^MDC_DIM_PERCENT^MDC|||||R|||20120912194537+0800|
OBX|36|NM|152168^MDC_CONC_AWAY_DESFL_INSP^MDC|1.4.1.152168|0.6|2626
88^MDC_DIM_PERCENT^MDC|||||R|||20120912194537+0800|
OBX|37|NM|126^MDC_VOL_DELIV_HALOTH_LIQUID_CASE^99ANEST|1.4.1.126|0.
00|263762^MDC_DIM_MILLI_L^MDC|||||R|||20120912194537+0800|
OBX|38|NM|127^MDC_VOL_DELIV_ENFL_LIQUID_CASE^99ANEST|1.4.1.127|0.00
|263762^MDC_DIM_MILLI_L^MDC|||||R|||20120912194537+0800|
OBX|39|NM|128^MDC_VOL_DELIV_ISOFL_LIQUID_CASE^99ANEST|1.4.1.128|0.0
0|263762^MDC_DIM_MILLI_L^MDC|||||R|||20120912194537+0800|
OBX|40|NM|129^MDC_VOL_DELIV_SEVOFL_LIQUID_CASE^99ANEST|1.4.1.129|0.
00|263762^MDC_DIM_MILLI_L^MDC|||||R|||20120912194537+0800|
OBX|41|NM|130^MDC_VOL_DELIV_DESFL_LIQUID_CASE^99ANEST|1.4.1.130|0.0
0|263762^MDC_DIM_MILLI_L^MDC|||||R|||20120912194537+0800|
```

Table 4-11: OBX Segments Field Identifiers Used in HL7 ORU and PCD-01 Messages.

Sequence	Element Name
1	Set ID – OBX
2	Value Type
3	Observation Identifier
4	Observation Sub-ID
5	Observation Value
6	Units
7	References Range
8	Abnormal Flags
9	Probability
10	Nature of Abnormal Test
11	Observation Result Status
12	Effective Data of Reference Range
13	User Defined Access Checks
14	Date/Time of the Observation
15	Producer's ID
16	Responsible Observer
17	Observation Method
18	Equipment Instance Identifier
19	Observation Site

The notation employed in the OBX-4, OBX-5, and OBX-6 rely on two definitions:

- VMD: Virtual Medical Device, or a subsystem of a Medical Device System (based on ISO/IEEE 11073 representation)
- MDS: A total Medical Device System

The containment tree employed in the OBX-4 field associated with the item expressed in OBX-3 is accomplished by defining an n-tuple node hierarchy of the following form:

<MDS><VMD><CHAN><METRIC>. In this way, "each of the OBX-3 [fields] is expressed unambiguously with respect to...OBX-4."[63]

Volume 2 of the Technical Framework provides detailed examples on the creation of these Containment Tree Hierarchies. A simple example will be included here to illustrate, and the discussion surrounding is carried out with the aid of Table 4-12.

The corresponding OBX-4 field for <VS Mon> <Pulse Ox> <Ptach> <PR> would be represented by 1.1.2.2 (using dot notation). In this way, the PCD may be dynamically valued and changed. This dot notation is employed in the sample PCD-01 transaction of Table 4-10, and serves to provide this dynamic mapping. A much more thorough treatment of the IHE PCD Technical Framework is available for download and review from the IHE site.

Table 4-12: Example of a Mapping Containment to OBX-4 per the IHE PCD Technical Framework.[64]

1	Virtual (Medical)	<VS Mon>	<Pulse Ox>	<Oxim>	<SpO2>
	Ordinal	1	1	1	1
2	Virtual (Medical)	<VS Mon>	<Pulse Ox>	<Ptach>	<PR>
	Ordinal	1	1	2	2
3	Virtual (Medical)	<VS Mon>	<ECG>	<Ctach>	<HR>
	Ordinal	1	2	1	3

Other Medical Device Integration-Related Standards

- The ASTM F2761-09 is an international standard entitled "Medical Devices and Medical Systems—Essential safety requirements for equipment comprising the patient-centric integrated clinical environment (ICE)." The purpose of the ASTM standard is to promote a framework for plug-and-play interoperability among medical devices (that is, communication to support interactive workflow) in order to improve patient safety. Information about the ASTM standard and the Integrated Clinical Environment initiative may be found at http://www.mdpnp.org.
- The ISO/IEC 80001-1:2010 standard, "Application of risk management for IT-networks incorporating medical devices" seeks to set forth specific principles for improving quality and minimizing risk in the use of enterprise networks to communicate data taken from connected medical devices.
- Continua Alliance, http://www.continuaalliance.org, seeks to bring together medical device technology vendors with the clinical industry to improve the management of chronic disease. Management of chronic ailments is normally managed between the healthcare enterprise and the home, which brings in the integration of connected medical devices within the ambulatory space. Many of the medical devices of note in this category include home weight scales, blood pressure cuffs, pulse oximetry, glucometry, thermometry, and medication tracking, as well as wellness-related devices such as pedometers.
- The Personal Connected Health Alliance (PCHA)—www.pchalliance.org, is a collaboration between Continua, mHealth Summit and HIMSS, …"focused on engaging consumers with their health via personalized health solutions designed for user-friendly connectivity (interoperability) that meet their lifestyle needs."[65] The PCHA mission is to "facilitate the development and adoption of personal health solutions that foster independence and empower people to better manage their health and wellness from anywhere, at any time"[65] by delivering on three specific elements of that mission: (i) promoting plug-and-play personal health technology and solutions and unifying all stakeholders (consumers, technology and healthcare providers, purchasers and policymakers) around the delivery of an integrated personal health solution; (ii) increasing focus and awareness on personal connected health technology through education, advocacy, and the leadership capabilities of its umbrella partners; and, (iii) standardizing around connectivity, privacy and security aspects of connected health devices and the systems with which they communicate using Continua's

interoperability standards to promote plug-and-play connectivity. The overall objective of PCHA is to promote better management of personal health maintenance and management with increased interoperability through the use of standards-based integration, realized by the participation of vendors through their adherence to accepted interoperability standards; through purchasers and providers via increased awareness of the role of improved interoperability in achieving better patient care management, and thus their support for the standards; and through public policy achieved through increased awareness with improved interoperability and healthcare delivery, management, safety and reduced inefficiencies in managing patients both inside and outside of the healthcare enterprise.

- AAMI/UL 2800: AAMI announced in early 2013, joint development of a family of standards with underwriter's laboratories (UL) around medical device interoperability.[66] The focus of this family of standards will be around safety: "BSR UL 2800, Standard for safety of interoperable medical devices interface standards (IMDIS) and guidelines…would define the safety and related specifications of medical device interfaces required when a device is declared an interoperable medical device… [and] will address … available medical device interface characteristics needed to operate under safe interoperable conditions. The standard will focus on the safety and risks mitigation associated with the interoperability of the medical device interface within an ICE implementation."[67]

SUMMARY

The objective of this chapter was to present the principal standards surrounding medical device integration data communication. The HL7 standard remains the principal by which data are communicated within the healthcare enterprise. Implementation frameworks developed in recent years, particularly by IHE, have served to align and codify data communication from the point of care to the health IT system. The development of implementation frameworks has also elevated the visibility of medical device communication and brought many stakeholders together to accelerate the process of enabling standardized data communication from POC medical devices to the health IT system, not just within the hospital but also within the ambulatory space focused on chronic disease management in the home.

CHAPTER 5

Notifications, Alerts and Clinical Uses of Medical Device Data

This chapter is focused on specialty areas related to MDI systems, to include notifications, alerts associated with technical and clinical medical device data and clinical uses of real-time medical device data. Also discussed are the differences between aperiodic and periodic data collection and the implication of these differences on HL7 messages.

INTERFACE HEALTH AND STATUS NOTIFICATION AND TECHNICAL ALERTS

The interface between the MDI and health IT systems represents a handshake whereby messages are sent outbound by the MDI (and, in the case of query/response, whereby the health IT system requests data of the MDI system via solicited transactions), followed by an acknowledgement message or confirmation of delivery, or payload, to the health IT system. In certain instances, this communication may experience aberrant or abnormal behavior. That is, for an unsolicited observation, as illustrated in Figure 5-1, there is a normal, operational message transfer and there are abnormal or aberrant transfers or modes that are possible during this message communication.

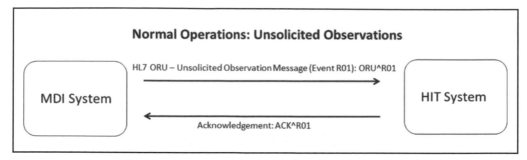

Figure 5-1: Examples of Normal Communication and Response between MDI and Health IT System.

One aberrant or abnormal mode of behavior may be the situation in which the payload of an unsolicited observation result is transmitted, but no acknowledgement is received from the recipient system. One possibility, illustrated in Figure 5-2, is that no acknowledgement is transmitted in response to the sent message. This can be the result of an error in the receiving system in terms of processing the result transaction; a network issue; or a problem in the sending system not configured to receive an acknowledgement or an error in processing the acknowledgement.

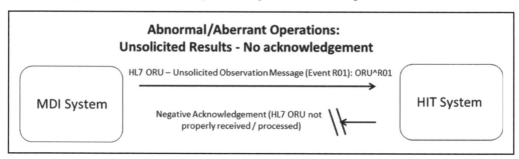

Figure 5-2: Unsolicited Observation Result—No Acknowledgement Received.

This type of issue extends to the scenario illustrated in Figure 5-3, in which the receiving system (health IT) simply issues no acknowledgement. If the sending system (MDI) is expecting an acknowledgement, the result could cause a backup of further transactions or an error condition on the sending side whereby the sending system will either not transmit additional messages until an acknowledgement is received or the sending system will continuously transmit the same message in an effort to cause the receiving system to respond, under the assumption that the receiving system has not received the payload. Causes of this problem can range from the receiving system not configured to transmit an acknowledgement to network issues between the sender and receiver.

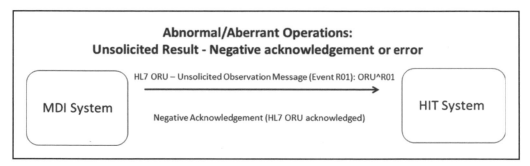

Figure 5-3: Unsolicited Observation Result—No Acknowledgement Transmitted by Receiving System.

Other aberrant conditions are expressed in the scenario of Figure 5-4, in which the message cannot be transmitted or is simply not received by the receiving system. Such would be the situation if the network was down, the receiving system was offline, or the interface communication was unattainable or blocked to the receiving system.

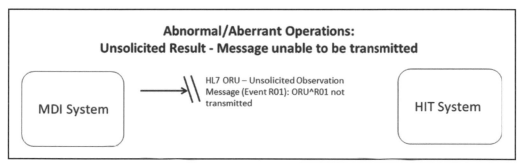

Figure 5-4: Unsolicited Observation Result—Message Unable to be Transmitted.

In all of these situations, it is important to be able to communicate the health and status of the interface connection between the MDI and the health IT systems. Similar behavior may be experienced in situations involving a solicited query/response action. Figure 5-5 illustrates this query, initiated by the receiving system to the sending system, resulting in an observational report back to the receiving system. In this messaging interchange, an acknowledgement MSA message can be integrated into the observational report (ORF) message.

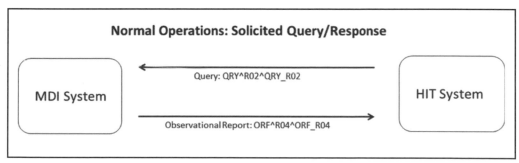

Figure 5-5: QRY/ORF Normal Operational Response.

Two modes of interface "failure" can occur in operation. One is illustrated in Figure 5-6, in which the response to the QRY message is not received. The second is illustrated in Figure 5-7, which indicates the original QRY message cannot or is not transmitted to the sending system by the receiving system.

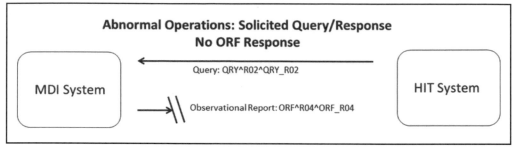

Figure 5-6: Example of QRY/ORF Messaging Failure: Failure to Receive an Observational Report.

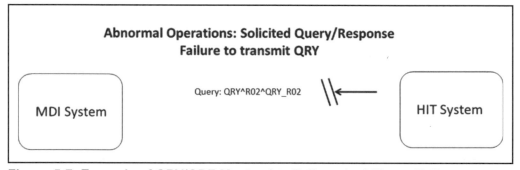

Figure 5-7: Example of QRY/ORF Messaging Failure: Inability or Failure to Transmit QRY Message.

In each of these cases, it is of great utility and value to both the healthcare enterprise and to the MDI solution provider to understand if and when these interfaces experience aberrant behavior. From the clinical perspective, a failure of these interfaces will result in no data appearing in the health IT system. From the support perspective, as an aid to clinicians, being informed of the failure of these interfaces or the dropout of messaging as soon as possible can assist the enterprise support team in remedying issues causing the failures. Simply having the information that the interfaces are down is cause to act in many situations, particularly in high-acuity settings.

Some MDI solutions support notifications, including email alerts that can be directed to the healthcare enterprise and MDI solution provider support personnel when interfaces fail. On the enterprise side, certain health IT systems provide similar types of alerts. Those enterprises, which employ an integration engine or messaging intermediary, often provide native alert mechanisms for communicating when their interfaces are down.

Regardless of which method or which source is used (i.e., alerting on receiving, sending side, or through messaging intermediary), maintenance of the interfaces is part of the support program that should be in place relative to the MDI implementation.

The interfaces between the MDI and health IT systems usually fall under the purview of the IT department because they are specific to the data and interfaces to the health IT system. Yet, another set of interfaces—those associated with the communication between the MDI system and the medical device(s), can also pose challenges in terms of broken or aberrant connectivity, and also merit notification in the event a medical device goes offline unexpectedly or the interface to the medical device stops working.

Figure 5-8 illustrates a hypothetical case of the query/response handshake between the medical device and the MDI system. Depending on the degree of sophistication and capability, the MDI system may have the ability to detect certain conditions associated with the medical device connection(s). Some medical devices can communicate their health and status over the connection between themselves and the MDI system (i.e., for either serial- or network-based medical devices). Examples of some medical devices that do communicate state information, and alarm information, in addition to the measured parameters associated with patient data include the following:

- Physiologic monitors (e.g., model numbers, mode, firmware versions, time stamps; alarms, sensor status)
- Anesthesia machines and mechanical ventilators (e.g., model numbers, modes, firmware versions, time stamps; alarms, tubing status, leaks)
- Certain specialty monitors such as certain brands of end-tidal CO_2 monitors (e.g., model numbers, modes, alarms, health and status, pump status, sensor status)

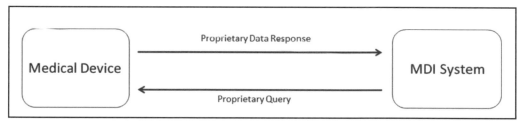

Figure 5-8: Interface Handshake Between MDI System and Medical Device.

In such instances, responses from the medical devices (or lack thereof) can be used to assess the health and status of the physical connections between the MDI system and the medical device.

The ability to communicate the connection or lack of connection can be of great use, particularly to the clinical or biomedical engineering staff. Should medical devices cease to communicate, particularly during cases such as OR sessions, then expedited knowledge of this can save not only irritation but also lost information on a patient. It may not be known immediately that medical device connections are lost until minutes after the occurrence. In extreme cases, this can pose a patient safety concern if the data stop populating the patient record and the clinician requires knowledge of a value to make a clinical decision. In such instances, migration to manual or paper recording is usually the approach taken to mitigate the impact of data loss. Nevertheless, the sooner that data interruption can be detected, the sooner a plan can be implemented (i.e., manual charting) to mitigate the potential negative clinical effects of the situation.

This idea can be illustrated through the diagram of Figure 5-9. In this figure, the MDI system is shown to trigger an alert notification (sometimes referred to as a technical alert) in the event of a failure to receive data from a medical device, or in the event of the detection of a connection failure (e.g., broken cable, broken serial adapter, etc.). The alert notification could be transmitted via email or pager (for instance) to clinical or biomedical engineering staff, indicating an off-nominal or aberrant occurrence at the point of data collection.

The enterprise, in purchasing an MDI system, should query the vendor as to its ability to provide such technical alerts in the instance of a medical device connectivity failure or equivalent that would cause interruption of data collection at the POC.

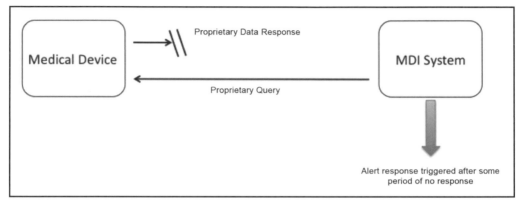

Figure 5-9: Alert Notification Triggered Upon Failure to Receive Data from a Medical Device, or Based Upon the Failure to Detect a Connection to a Medical Device.

Clinical Alerts and Notifications

Medical device data are used for manifold purposes, including the following:
- Charting vital signs
- Validating patient condition prior to writing clinical orders
- Assessing and corroborating patient response as a result of prescribed medication
- Evaluating the onset of conditions
- Trending state over time to determine condition improvement or decline, etc.

In summary, patient care data derived from medical devices are used for assessing status of patients (primarily cardiovascular and pulmonary/respiratory state)—the key bodily functions most associated with maintaining existence.

As we have seen in Chapter 1 and Chapter 3 and as will be seen in Table 5-1, the types of medical device data can vary by department and by clinical need. The frequency of data collection is also setting-dependent. This is captured qualitatively in Table 5-1. The collection frequency of data is driven by workflow in these clinical settings, which, in turn, drives the clinical use of the data. In higher acuity settings, the need for rapid and continuous communication of vital signs and other, non-medical device-based data is necessary to assess the status of the patient from moment to moment. Related to this is the communication of aberrant information, such as alarms and notifications. For example, in emergency departments, patients who arrive complaining of chest pain are monitored closely in terms of vital signs while assessments are made (e.g., laboratory, imaging). Patient heart function is monitored to determine whether they have experienced signs of cardiovascular problems (e.g., heart attack, stroke). For instance, some of the non-invasive and invasive diagnostic tests performed to confirm or rule out the existence of a heart attack include ECG (electrocardiogram), repeated blood tests such as troponin, CK or CK-MB and myoglobin, and coronary angiography.[68]

Table 5-1: Typical Medical Device Data Collection Intervals by Department.

Unit	Function Measured	Frequency of Measurement	Time Duration
Emergency Department	Heart (e.g., pulse, ST segments); Perfusion (e.g., O2 saturation); Temperature	Continuous	Hours
Surgery	Heart (e.g., pulse, ST segments); Perfusion (e.g., O2 saturation, end-tidal CO2); Pulmonary (e.g., breath rate, tidal volume); Temperature; Drug administration	Continuous	Hours
Cardiac Catheterization	Heart (e.g., pulse, ST segments); Perfusion (e.g., O2 saturation)	Ad hoc	Hours
Intensive Care	Heart (e.g., pulse, ST segments, cardiac output, ejection fraction); Perfusion (e.g., O2 saturation, end-tidal CO2); Pulmonary (e.g., breath rate, tidal volume); Temperature; laboratory measurements; Drug administration; Outputs	Continuous	Hours Days Weeks
Medical/ Surgical	Heart (e.g., pulse); Perfusion (e.g., O2 saturation); Temperature	Ad hoc	Days Weeks
Radiology	Heart (e.g., pulse); Perfusion (e.g., O2 saturation)	Ad hoc	Hours

In Table 5-1, measurements of ECG are continuous, and variations in heart rhythm, as well as the shape and character of the ECG PQRST complexes (or wave forms) are used to diagnose various conditions of the heart and cardiovascular system. Detection of specific issues or ailments or impending problems can be made through ECG 12-lead monitoring or through continuous measurement using a physiologic monitor, although normally with a reduced number of leads (usually three or five).

Physiologic monitors contain algorithms designed to detect abnormal rhythms and behaviors and issue alerts in the form of transactions that can be communicated to the health IT charting system or to central monitoring stations, where remote monitoring staff can provide notifications in the event of detection of dangerous ECG events. An example of such an alert transaction from a Philips Intellivue physiologic monitor is shown in Table 5-2.[69]

Table 5-2: Example of an Alarm Message Issued by a Philips Physiologic Monitoring System in the Form of an HL7 Transaction.

```
MSH|^~\&|||||||ORU^R01|HP138999681041|D|2.3|||||||8859/1
PID|||""||""^""||""|U
PV1||I|LOCATION
OBR|||||||20140117141330
OBX||TX|2^Yellow Alarm^MDIL-ALERT|2|**ABPs140 > 120||||||F
OBX||TX|1^Red Alarm^MDIL-ALERT|1|***BRADY 40 < 60||||||F
```

The example transaction contains OBX messages indicating, respectively, that the systolic component of arterial blood pressure (ABPs) 120mmHg is above the limit of 90 mmHg and the heart rate of 40 beats/min falls below the bradycardia threshold of 60/min.

Alert and notification messages may be issued by many types of connected medical devices, including physiologic monitors, mechanical ventilators, anesthesia machines, and specialty devices such as intra-aortic balloon pumps, end-tidal CO2 monitors, and ad-hoc spot vital signs monitors. The key is how to use the information that is issued through the MDI system.

Aperiodic Versus Periodic Data Collection

Periodic data are those findings and observations that are transmitted at a predefined interval. Transmission of periodic data is not dependent on any particular action associated with the medical device or the clinical workflow associated with collecting the measurement, other than the sensors must be applied to collect the data. Example elements of periodic data include heart rate (HR), respiratory rate (RR), and oxygen saturation derived from pulse oximetry (SpO2).

Aperiodic data are those findings that are valid at a specific time and based upon the event that a specific measurement has been taken at that specific time. Examples of aperiodic data include non-invasive blood pressure (NIBP), cardiac output (CO), and pulmonary artery wedge pressure (PAWP).

Figure 5-10 illustrates qualitatively the concept behind periodic versus aperiodic measurements. Periodic measurements appear regularly in the output stream of data from the MDI system, as demonstrated through the shorter arrows. The longer arrows are shown at irregular intervals and are intended to occur only when the particular aperiodic parameter is measured.

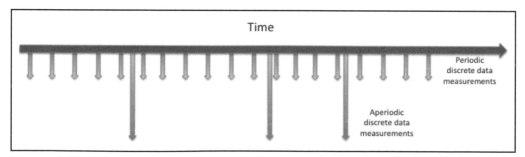

Figure 5-10: Periodic Versus Aperiodic Measurement Timeline.

An example of an HL7 transaction showing the aperiodic communication of NIBP is illustrated in Table 5-3. Aperiodic data elements are normally only communicated when measured. For example, NIBP may be collected every 5, 10, or 15 minutes. The values of these measurements are, therefore, only valid at the time of their measurement. Therefore, they are not continuous measurements.

Table 5-3: HL7 Transaction Illustrating Aperiodic Non-Invasive Blood Pressure Measurement Reported at the Time Blood Pressure is First Measured.

Note: Blood pressure measurements contain time stamps in OBX segment OBX.14 for each of the blood pressure measurements (NBP-S, -D, -M) indicating the time of validity of these measurements.

```
MSH|^~\&|<Sending_App>|<Sending_Fac>|<Receiving_App>|Receiving_Fac>|
20140221232307||ORU^R01|0532:01:000006E1|P|2.3
PID|SICU^^B103&01&1||456789||Surname^Forename
PV1||||^SICU^^B103&01&1
OBR|1|||||||20140221232307
OBX|1|ST|RHYSTA||Sinus Rhythm|
OBX|2|NM|SPO2||98|%
OBX|3|NM|RR||9|/min
OBX|4|NM|PNN50||0.47|%
OBX|5|NM|HR||107|/min
OBX|6|NM|PVC||0|/min
OBX|7|NM|PULSE||107|/min
OBX|8|NM|ST-I||0|mm
OBX|9|NM|ST-II||-0.3|mm
OBX|10|NM|ST-III||0|mm
OBX|11|NM|ST-aVR||0|mm
OBX|12|NM|ST-aVL||-0.1|mm
OBX|13|NM|ST-aVF||-0.2|mm
OBX|14|NM|ST-V||0.1|mm
OBX|15|NM|ART-S||170|mmHg
OBX|16|NM|ART-D||55|mmHg
OBX|17|NM|ART-M||93|mmHg
OBX|18|NM|CVP-M||8|mmHg
OBX|19|NM|NBP-S||105|mmHg|||||||20140221232307
OBX|20|NM|NBP-D||76|mmHg|||||||20140221232307
OBX|21|NM|NBP-M||85|mmHg|||||||20140221232307
OBX|22|NM|TCORE||101.1|F
OBX|23|NM|ICP||17|mmHg
OBX|24|TS|NBP-TS||20120221232307|
```

The MDI system should be able to communicate both periodic and aperiodic messages and provide the capability to distinguish among these types of measurements. Firstly, the time stamp associated with the aperiodic element should be displayed and provided as either a separate transaction (e.g., NBP-TS) or in the same OBX segment as the aperiodic message itself (e.g., within the OBX.14 segment).

When aperiodic measurements are not taken (that is, between measurements), the HL7 transaction should omit the time stamp associated with the measurement, indicating the measurement is not current, as shown in Table 5-4. Alternatively, the measurement can be omitted from the HL7 transaction altogether, as shown in Table 5-5.

Table 5-4: HL7 Transaction Illustrating Aperiodic Non-Invasive Blood Pressure Message After the Blood Pressure Is Measured.

Note: Blood pressure measurements do not have time stamps associated with them, implying they are not current values.

```
MSH|^~\&|<Sending_App>|<Sending_Fac>|<Receiving_App>|Receiving_Fac>|
20140221232317||ORU^R01|0532:01:000006E1|P|2.3
PID|SICU^^B103&01&1||456789||Lastname^Firstname
PV1|||^SICU^^B103&01&1
OBR|1|||||20140221232317
OBX|1|ST|RHYSTA||Sinus Rhythm|
OBX|2|NM|SPO2||98|%
OBX|3|NM|RR||9|/min
OBX|4|NM|PNN50||0.47|%
OBX|5|NM|HR||107|/min
OBX|6|NM|PVC||0|/min
OBX|7|NM|PULSE||107|/min
OBX|8|NM|ST-I||0|mm
OBX|9|NM|ST-II||-0.3|mm
OBX|10|NM|ST-III||0|mm
OBX|11|NM|ST-aVR||0|mm
OBX|12|NM|ST-aVL||-0.1|mm
OBX|13|NM|ST-aVF||-0.2|mm
OBX|14|NM|ST-V||0.1|mm
OBX|15|NM|ART-S||170|mmHg
OBX|16|NM|ART-D||55|mmHg
OBX|17|NM|ART-M||93|mmHg
OBX|18|NM|CVP-M||8|mmHg
OBX|19|NM|NBP-S||105|mmHg
OBX|20|NM|NBP-D||76|mmHg
OBX|21|NM|NBP-M||85|mmHg
OBX|22|NM|TCORE||101.1|F
OBX|23|NM|ICP||17|mmHg
OBX|24|TS|NBP-TS||20140221232307|
```

Clinical Uses of Medical Device Data

Data are at the heart of clinical decision making, and data from connected medical devices are unique in that they can be obtained regularly and are not prone to interpretive error. For these reasons, they can serve as a key tool in clinical decision support (CDS) applications and functions. The following examples serve to illustrate how data that are collected at the POC can assist in mitigating adverse clinical events. Perhaps the highest acuity environments (i.e., ICUs and ORs) provide the best examples of the benefits brought to the clinical workspace associated with obtaining medical device data, because it is in these environments that patients are most often dependent upon medical devices for existence.

In ICUs, many patients are mechanically ventilated. Mechanically ventilated patients run the risk of higher occurrences of hospital-acquired infections (HAIs), and, in particular, sepsis (or septicemia) and ventilator acquired or associated pneumonia (VAP):[70]

Table 5-5: HL7 Transaction Illustrating Aperiodic Non-Invasive Blood Pressure Message After the Measurement Has Been Taken.

Note: Blood pressure elements no longer appear in the HL7 transaction.

```
MSH|^~\&|<Sending_App>|<Sending_Fac>|<Receiving_App>|Receiving_Fac>|
20140221232317||ORU^R01|0532:01:000006E1|P|2.3
PID|SICU^^B103&01&1|||456789|||Surname^Forename
PV1||||^SICU^^B103&01&1
OBR|1|||||||20140221232317
OBX|1|ST|RHYSTA^^170-2||Sinus Rhythm|
OBX|2|NM|SPO2||98|%
OBX|3|NM|RR||9|/min
OBX|4|NM|PNN50||0.47|%
OBX|5|NM|HR||107|/min
OBX|6|NM|PVC||0|/min
OBX|7|NM|PULSE||107|/min
OBX|8|NM|ST-I||0|mm
OBX|9|NM|ST-II||-0.3|mm
OBX|10|NM|ST-III||0|mm
OBX|11|NM|ST-aVR||0|mm
OBX|12|NM|ST-aVL||-0.1|mm
OBX|13|NM|ST-aVF||-0.2|mm
OBX|14|NM|ST-V||0.1|mm
OBX|15|NM|ART-S||170|mmHg
OBX|16|NM|ART-D||55|mmHg
OBX|17|NM|ART-M||93|mmHg
OBX|18|NM|CVP-M||8|mmHg
OBX|19|NM|TCORE||101.1|F
OBX|20|NM|ICP||17|mmHg
```

"Ventilator-associated pneumonia (VAP) is common in the intensive care unit (ICU), affecting 8% to 20% of ICU patients and up to 27% of mechanically ventilated patient%s... Several risk factors have been reported to be associated with VAP, [are] duration of mechanical ventilation ... Mortality rates in patients with VAP range from 20% to 50% and may reach more than 70% when the infection is caused by multi-resistant and invasive pathogens."

An HAI, in particular, septicemia, is a blood infection that has the potential to impact all patients, particularly in the ICU. Two classes of patients—the old and the very young—are most susceptible:[71]

"Sepsis is the 10th most common cause of death in the United States and its management has been estimated to cost 17 billion dollars annually. Seventeen percent of all patients who develop sepsis have a malignancy as an underlying co-morbidity."

"...as many as 10% of all cancer deaths (46,729 annual deaths) are attributable to sepsis..."

Late onset neonatal sepsis (LONS) is also of critical concern:[72]

"Earlier detection and treatment of LONS offers the best opportunity to improve outcomes. To date, the approach has been to use biomarker screen-

ing or empiric antibiotic therapy for every patient with subtle non-specific symptoms. Neither of these strategies is satisfactory due to insufficient diagnostic accuracy of biomarkers and complications associated with overuse of antibiotics. A new technology, continuous monitoring of neonatal heart rate characteristics, has been developed for earlier diagnosis and treatment of LONS in NICU patients."

The use of data obtained from regularly collected vitals has had encouraging results in terms of early detection of sepsis in ICU patients. Measurement of heart rate and respiratory rate variability has been linked to early sepsis onset:[73]

"Heart rate and respiratory rate variability, when measured continuously, provide non-invasive metrics for detecting the early onset of sepsis ...the presence of at least two of four clinical signs, including abnormalities in heart rate, temperature, respiratory rate and white blood cell count or its differential count, herald the onset of sepsis and that these conditions manifest many hours before the actual diagnosis..."

Examples of parameters that can be readily measured in ICU include heart rate or pulse, respiratory rate, temperature, and white blood cell count. Study findings also relate particular value thresholds that have been found consistent with detection of sepsis onset:[73]

- Heart rate >90 beats per minute
- Respiratory rate >20 breaths per minute or $PaCO_2$ <32 mmHg
- Temperature >38.0°C or <36.0°C
- White blood cell count >12,000 cells/mL, <4,000 cells/mL, or >10% bands

SUMMARY

The following observations are intended as takeaways for this chapter:

- Technical and clinical alerts are an important aspect of MDI system support and maintenance workflow, and methods for communicating technical and clinical alerts should be addressed by the MDI implementation team as part of project planning for support.
  - □ Technical alerts represent those notifications related to the operational health and status of the MDI system and its interactions with the medical device at the POC, and can be separated into two areas:
  - □ Notifications of health and status associated with the collection of medical device data from the devices at the POC
  - □ Notifications of health and status of the HL7 connection between the MDI system and the health IT system. This corresponds to the status of the HL7 interconnection between the data aggregator (i.e., gateway) that receives the medical device data from the POC data collection appliance, and the health IT system. These transactions are as described in the preceding sub-section on Interface Health and Status Notification and Technical Alerts.
- Notifications associated with technical alerts should be able to be directed to the appropriate groups of individuals (i.e., clinical engineering, IT staff) depending on the type of technical alert.

- The healthcare enterprise MDI implementation team should determine whether the MDI system can support clinical alerts and alarms associated with medical device settings and measured parameters, as issued by the medical devices themselves.
- As per the previous bullet point, the healthcare enterprise MDI implementation team should also verify that all possible data may be retrieved from the connected medical device(s) as per medical device specifications.
- Clarification of the reporting of aperiodic measurements is necessary to ensure there are no ambiguities.
  - Examples include posting of non-invasive blood pressure (NIBP, cardiac output (CO), and PAWP.
  - Communication of clear understanding to the MDI solution provider and the IT integration team should be made as to whether these and other aperiodic data elements are to be displayed at all times in HL7 messages or only when the measurements are newly taken. Certain health IT systems do not possess the logic to exclude data when it is "stale" (i.e., when the measurements are not current). Hence, the MDI solution is often called upon to handle this logic and exclude data elements when they are not current.
- Data from connected medical devices provide important input to methods that can be used to clinically evaluate the likelihood of onset of specific conditions, such as sepsis and HAIs.

CHAPTER 6

Patient Identification and Medical Device Association

In 2007, the World Health Organization (WHO) in concert with The Joint Commission identifies that "…the failure to correctly identify patients continues to result in medication errors, transfusion errors, testing errors, wrong person procedures, and the discharge of infants to the wrong families."[74] Approaches to solving the medical device-related patient identification issues in healthcare environments have principally evolved around patient wrist bracelets imprinted with barcodes or with radio frequency identification chips (RFID) for detection and identification using bar code scanners or RFID scanners.

METHODS FOR PATIENT IDENTIFICATION

In the medical device-to-patient association area, several approaches are in use and can vary by department and by enterprise policy. The basic approaches include the following:

- Fixed-location medical device association, wherein medical devices are permanently associated or located within a patient room. In this case, the medical device is associated with the patient through either manual association of the patient with the medical device, via a pick list within the patient clinical record, or a more automated approach, such as through an external means such as a barcode scanner or an RFID scanner reading a patient wrist bracelet.
- Mobile or non-fixed-location medical device association, wherein medical devices can be moved from patient to patient as required. The workflow then involves associating the medical device with the patient upon use of the device, typically associated with the beginning of the clinical encounter. In this case, too, either a manual or more automated approach may be employed.

In the former case, in which the fixed association methodology is employed, the workflow usually involves a permanent assignment of medical device equipment with a specific room and bed. The room and bed information, entered uniquely through the health IT system, is then available for association through the clinical information system to the patient. The patients may be selected from a census list, populated through inbound feed from the enterprise registration system, or may be manually entered through the keyboard on a computer, such as a WOW. In this case, too, an automated complement to the fixed medical device bedside approach can assist in selecting the patient by mitigating the need to manually enter patient information or manually select the patient through keyboard and mouse.

In the latter case of mobile association, the workflow usually entails attaching the medical device to the patient record, which, again, can be done via manual means or through the more automated approach previously outlined.

From an MDI system perspective, the important outcome in both the fixed-location and mobile (non-fixed) location approaches is to ensure that the medical device data associated with a particular patient are communicated from the patient to the correct patient record. This involves embedding or otherwise including patient-specific identifiers within the datafeed from the medical device to the patient with those enterprise-specific identification tags. This will ensure positive identification and posting of the medical device data transaction to the correct patient, and the least amount of ambiguity in the process.

The Joint Commission and WHO have published standards and best practices surrounding the positive identification of patients and the mechanisms that promote minimizing errors surrounding the patient identification process within the healthcare enterprise.

Table 6-1 lists patient identification elements, descriptions and examples, as identified by WHO and The Joint Commission.[74]

Bar Code and RFID

Most healthcare enterprise clinical staff (e.g., nursing, physicians) are familiar with bar code scanning as a means of identifying objects using bar code symbology. Anyone who has purchased an item from a commercial retailer has been exposed to bar code scanning devices, and the medical application of these devices differs very little from their retail counterparts.

An example of a bar code scanner, which has been used in healthcare settings is the Gryphon one-dimensional unit shown in Figure 6-1. Figure 6-2 compares an older but comparable RFID scanner with a standard bar code scanner. Figure 6-3 displays an example universal-product-code (UPC) symbol using the 128 ASCII character set encoding type.

Positive patient identification is integral to the "five rights" of patient medication administration. These include the right dose, right time, right route, right medication, and the right patient.[75] The key to the use of a bar code is employing an objective measure of positive identification using something the patient has—in this case, a wrist bracelet containing unique identifiers such as name, medical record number, visit identifier, account number or master patient identification index. Other information may also be present, such as date of birth, attending physician, height and weight. The point of using a bar code is to provide a rapid, relatively error-free mechanism for identifying the patient with respect to medications, clinical service providers, and equipment in the direct environs of the patient.

Technologies and specific mechanisms deployed for the purpose of patient identification abound. These include RFID, in which a programmed chip containing embedded patient information is read through an RFID reader versus the aforementioned bar code. A bar code optically reads or scans a UPC symbol containing a subset of the previously discussed examples of patient information. In the following subsections, a detailed review of the various types of association processes will be taken into account.

Table 6-1: Table of Patient Identification Elements and Examples.

Patient Identification Element	Background	Example
Policy	Healthcare providers assert primary responsibility for validating and verifying patient identity.	All care providers in the environment should be educated on the need for positive patient identification and should be familiar with the preferred approach for patient identification.
Admission	Prior to care administration, a minimum of two identifiers are required to verify a patient's identity, neither of which should be patient location such as room number.	Patient name and date of birth are often used as examples.
Patient Identifiers	Develop a consistent approach using specific identification nomenclature and markings around the enterprise. Examples can include name, external identifiers such as account number or medical record number and master patient identifiers. Develop objective mechanisms for uniquely identifying, which can include biometric schemes that apply to unconscious or comatose patients.	Use of barcode and wrist bracelet as the standardized approach for verifying a patient's identity, coupled with verbal response from the patient to validate. If the patient is comatose, then provide the capability to validate using objective means such as biometrics (e.g., fingerprint).
Intervention	Check details of patient identification for each encounter with a patient, even if care provider is familiar with the patient.	The healthcare provider must check each patient for each encounter such as a medication administration or collection of vital signs data.
Patient	Have patient validate and verify identification where possible.	Query patients to identify themselves and a second piece of information, such as date of birth, where possible.

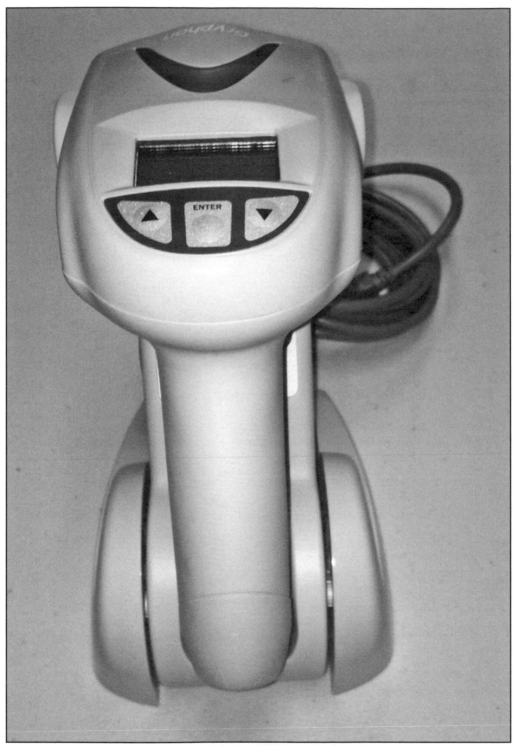

Figure 6-1: Example of a Healthcare-centric Barcode Scanner—a Gryphon Barcode Scanner Employing a Wireless Handheld Unit That Communicates via Bluetooth to a Charging Base Station.

Note: The base station, in turn, can communicate with a barcode application. (Photo by Author)

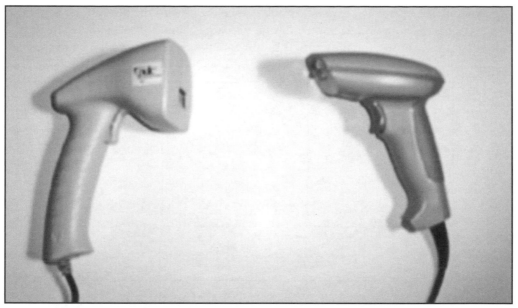

Figure 6-2: Comparison Between an RFID Scanner and a Barcode Scanner.

Note: Examples included in photograph are depictions of Precision Dynamics Corporation (PDC) RFID and an IT 3800 barcode reader (*right*). (Photo by Author)

Figure 6-3: Standard UPC Code Using 128 Encoding Type (i.e., 128 ASCII character set).

Medical Device Association Workflows

When discussing the association of medical devices to patients, there are two basic approaches, or methods, to performing such an association: fixed medical device and mobile medical device types. Figure 6-4 depicts qualitatively the difference between these two approaches at the physical level. In the first case, medical devices are affixed within the rooms of patients and are associated with a bedside of a particular patient. For example,

Room: 101 Bed: A (assuming a double room)
        Medical Device: Physiologic Monitor

Here, the room and bed uniquely establish the location of the medical devices, which in this case are a physiologic monitor and a mechanical ventilator. In the illustrative example shown, the physiologic monitor is attached to the wall next to the bed.

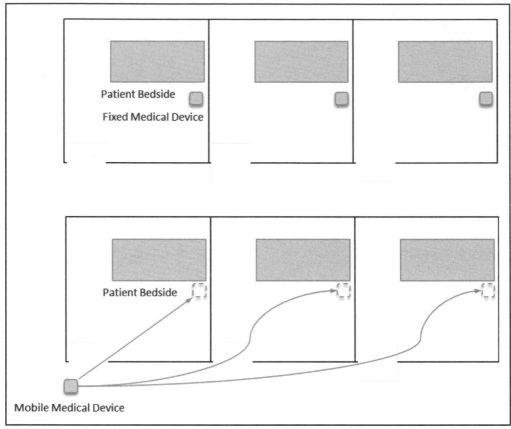

Figure 6-4: Bedside Association of Medical Devices Using Fixed and Mobile Approaches.

The patient who is admitted to the room is then associated with the room itself. For example,

Patient: John Q. Public
Room: 101 Bed: A

Hence, the physiologic monitor in Room 101 Bed A now is established as being associated with patient John Q. Public.

But, where does this actual association take place? In many of the clinical information systems available today, the software systems themselves provide the capability to either:

    a. Associate the patient with a fixed location using a census list (or pick list)
    b. Enter the patient information manually into the clinical record associated with a particular fixed location (e.g., Room 101 Bed A)

However, the process of manual association of patient information with a fixed bedside assumes that the patient information is available within the clinical information system, which usually is the case, but is linked to the registration system and made available locally through HL7 ADT messaging.

Hence, the display of patient information through the clinical information system is dependent upon the accuracy of the registration system, as well as the timely update of data associated with a patient. For example, location information for the patient derived through the registration system may lag behind the actual location of the patient. This may result in patients not being available within the census list of a particular clinical user, given the user's census is restricted to only those patients displayed within a particular department (possibly a restriction imposed based upon patient privacy policies and the Health Insurance Portability and Accountability Act, or HIPAA).

In Figure 6-5, the process of associating a fixed location medical device using the health IT census list is depicted. The preliminary step or requirement is that the medical device, through the MDI system, has a label that establishes its location within the location identification naming fields of the HL7 data transaction. In other words, the data arriving from the MDI system contains no specific patient identifying information—just the location identifiers of the medical device (e.g., Room 101 Bed A). Then, through linkage with the patient managed through the health IT system, when the health IT system receives any transaction containing the location identifiers, these data are automatically mapped to the record of the particular patient (e.g., John Q. Public).

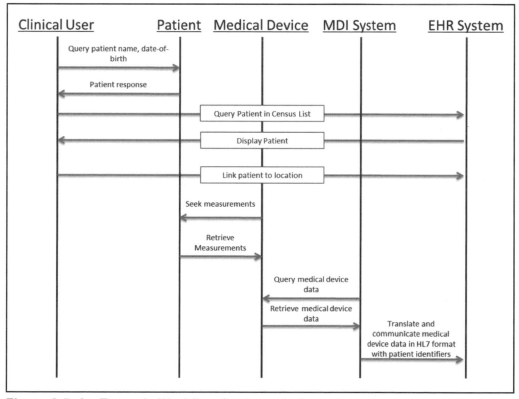

Figure 6-5: An Example Workflow for Associating a Patient with a Medical Device in a Fixed Location via the Clinical Information System or Health IT System.

The process begins with the querying of the patient at the bedside—this is a manual part of the nursing interaction with the patient to confirm the identity of the patient before proceeding with the medical device assignment. Next, in the steps shown in Figure 6-5, the user begins the process by querying the census list for the specific patient to be associated or linked with the medical device. The user, through the health IT or clinical information system, establishes this linkage. Meanwhile, independent of this, the MDI system is querying the medical device and transmitting these data to the health IT system.

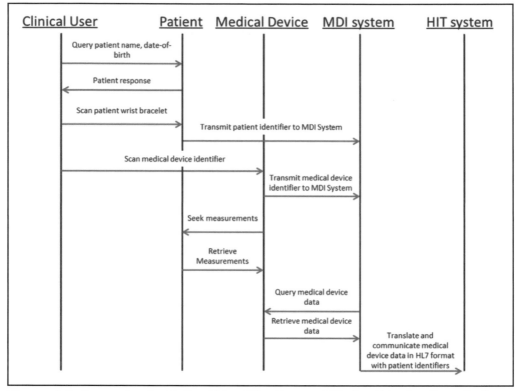

Figure 6-6: Example of a Patient Identification and Medical Device Data Collection Example Workflow.

In the case of using a barcode or RFID scanner to associate the medical device with the patient, Figure 6-6 shows an example workflow associated with identifying a patient and then communicating medical device data with patient identifiers to the health IT system.[76] The process also involves manual query and confirmation of the patient's identity, followed by scanning the patient wrist bracelet to retrieve the information associated with the patient, which is then transmitted to the MDI system for incorporation into the medical device datafeed.

However, in the case of some MDI solutions, an additional step may be necessary whereby the medical device (or the appliance associated with the medical device) is scanned to confirm its identity and provide that link to the MDI system, as well. In other cases, the medical device identity may already be established through the MDI system, thereby mitigating the need for this further step.

Once the patient identity, read locally from the wrist bracelet, and the medical device identity, also read through the barcode process, are communicated to the MDI system, the MDI system then links these elements with the medical device data queried from the medical device and then communicates these all together via HL7 transaction to the health IT system.

Table 6-2 depicts a sample HL7 transaction containing patient identifying as well as location information, to include patient identifiers in HL7 PID segment and location in PV1 segment. In the case of a fixed location with manual association of the patient to the medical device, the PID segment transmitted in the HL7 message from the MDI system to the health IT system would be blank and only the PV1 would be populated.

Table 6-2: Sample HL7 Transaction Containing Patient Identifier Segment.

```
MSH|^~\&|<Sending_App>|<Sending_Fac>|<Receiving_App>|Receiving_Fac>|
YYYYMMDDhhmm||ORU^R01|YYYYMMDDhhmmss|P|2.3|||||||||
PID|1||123456^^^^MRN~123456789^^^^ACN||Public^John
Q.|||||||||||||||CAN
PV1||I|101A
OBR|1||||||200403130304||||||||||||||||||||||||||||||||||||||||||
OBX|1|ST|Resp||20|/min|||||R||||||||
OBX|2|ST|Pulse||65|/min|||||R|||||||
OBX|3|ST|Pulse Location||Monitor||||||R|||||||
OBX|4|ST|Temp||29.3|°C|||||R|||||||
OBX|5|ST|Temp Site||Oral||||||R|||||||
OBX|6|ST|NIBP Systolic||122|mmHg|||||R|||||||
OBX|7|ST|NIBP Diastolic||80|mmHg|||||R|||||||
OBX|8|ST|NIBP Location||LeftArm|||||R|||||||
OBX|9|ST|NIBP Source||Monitor||||||R|||||||
OBX|10|ST|NIBP Position||Sitting||||||R|||||||
OBX|11|ST|Weight||52|kg|||||R|||||||
OBX|12|ST|Scale Type||Bed||||||R||||||||
OBX|13|ST|Height||120|cm|||||R|||||||
OBX|14|ST|O2 device||Mask||||||R||||||||
OBX|15|ST|lpm||5|L/M|||||R|||||||
OBX|16|ST|O2Sat||98|%|||||R|||||||
OBX|17|ST|Pain Scale||2|||||||R|||||||
```

Example types of identifiers that may be used in combination to identify the patient uniquely are provided in Table 6-3. These do not represent the totality of identifiers and other identifiers may be substituted. The list displays those that have been seen in practice at healthcare enterprises to date.

Table 6-3: Table of Example Identifiers Typically Used in Patient Identification.

Identifier	Definition
Given Name	Patient first or given name
Last Name	Patient last or family name
MRN	Medical record number
CAN	Account number
VN	Visit number
DoB	Date of birth
Sex	Patient sex
Ht	Patient height
Wt	Patient weight
Location	Current patient location

SUMMARY

When implementing mechanisms for associating medical devices with patients, the enterprise should survey those departments within which the MDI system is to be deployed, the existing workflow for the medical device (patient association), and the desired future workflow. The ability to associate medical devices with patients using a more mobile scheme involving a barcode or RFID may be more desirable in those situations in which the medical devices are migrated to the patients and there is a one-to-many association of devices. For example, in medical-surgical units or step-down units in which spot vital signs checking is performed, the medical device may be rolled to each patient in succession. In this case, a mobile mechanism for assigning the medical device to the patient may be more desirable and more consistent with existing workflows.

In situations in which the medical device is affixed to the bedside, the barcode mechanism for associating the medical device to the patient may also be employed, but may also be inconsistent with existing nursing workflow. An example of this situation might be the ICU, in which nursing is familiar with and normally employs the process of selecting patient assignments to rooms using a census list approach. In this situation, assigning the patient to the room wherein the medical device(s) is (are) already located may be simplest and most consistent with the workflow in which the clinical staff are most familiar.

The key in this situation is having the option and understanding of knowing that the MDI system can meet the workflow demands and requirements of the various departments within the enterprise. Flexibility is very important, and a one-size-fits-all approach is most likely not the best approach to solving the assignment problem.

While assigning medical devices to patients is important, the enterprise should also familiarize itself with the approach for disassociating, or de-assigning medical devices to patients. The process should be straightforward, fit within the context of the existing workflow, and not introduce hazards such as the likelihood of disassociating a medical device with a patient during monitoring by accident.

The healthcare enterprise should request of the MDI solution vendor(s) flow diagrams and details associated with the aforementioned use cases, and should include clinical staff in review of these use cases to determine whether they meet the enterprise policy and workflow requirements and future state.

CHAPTER 7

Regulatory and Security Considerations of MDI

This chapter addresses the requirements surrounding MDI systems from a regulatory perspective, identifies terms and provides references to key regulations with which the enterprise and the MDI solution vendor should be aware and compliant. The chapter ends with a summary of key questions to be asked of the MDI solution provider to verify conformance and provide the healthcare enterprise with confidence that any deployed MDI system will be compliant with federal regulations.

MEDICAL DEVICE DATA SYSTEMS (MDDS)

MDI systems, in communicating with and translating information from regulated medical devices, fall into the class of a federally regulated category of an MDDS.[77] As defined by the FDA:

> *"Medical Device Data Systems (MDDS) are hardware or software products that transfer, store, convert formats, and display medical device data. An MDDS does not modify the data or modify the display of the data, and it does not by itself control the functions or parameters of any other medical device. MDDS are not intended to be used for active patient monitoring...*
>
> *Examples of MDDS include:*
> * *software that stores patient data such as blood pressure readings for review at a later time;*
> * *software that converts digital data generated by a pulse oximeter into a format that can be printed; and*
> * *software that displays a previously stored electrocardiogram for a particular patient.*

The quality and continued reliable performance of MDDS are essential for the safety and effectiveness of health care delivery. Inadequate quality and design, unreliable performance, or incorrect functioning of MDDS can have a critical impact on public health."

The most prevalent example of MDDS are MDI solutions of today that communicate with health IT system patient charting; alert and alarm management are excluded and only discrete data communication for the purpose of populating the patient clinical record is the objective.

The Federal Register provides guidance on identification of an MDDS, per section 880.6310:

§ 880.6310 Medical device data system. -- (a) Identification:[78]

> *"1. A medical device data system (MDDS) is a device that is intended to provide one or more of the following uses, without controlling or altering the functions or parameters of any connected medical devices:*
>
> > *i. The electronic transfer of medical device data;*
> >
> > *ii. The electronic storage of medical device data;*
> >
> > *iii. The electronic conversion of medical device data from one format to another format in accordance with a preset specification; or*
> >
> > *iv. The electronic display of medical device data.*
>
> *2. An MDDS may include software, electronic or electrical hardware such as a physical communications medium (including wireless hardware), modems, interfaces, and a communications protocol. This identification does not include devices intended to be used in connection with active patient monitoring."*

The following sections provide guidance on working with MDI solution vendors regarding regulatory classification and management of regulated systems.

REGULATORY CLASSIFICATION AND IDENTIFICATION OF RISK

In 2011, the FDA produced guidance on software and hardware that are used with medical devices for the purpose of translating data from medical devices to clinical information systems:[79]

> *"... the FDA announced a final rule that provides a less-burdensome path to market for certain hardware and software products used with medical devices. The rule classifies these products, known as Medical Device Data Systems or MDDS, as Class I or low-risk devices, making them exempt from premarket review but still subject to quality standards."*

The FDA further provided guidance on what is not considered to be an MDDS:[80]

> *"General-purpose IT infrastructure used in health care facilities ... not altered or reconfigured outside of its manufactured specifications.*

Components with the following functions by themselves are NOT considered MDDS if they are used as part of general IT infrastructure even though they may transfer, store, display or convert medical device data, in addition to other information:

- *The electronic transfer of medical device data (e.g., Network Router, Network Hub, Wireless access point)*

- *The electronic storage of medical device data (e.g., Network Attached Storage, Storage area network);*

- *The electronic conversion of medical device data from one format to another in accordance with a preset specification (e.g., Virtualization System such as VM Ware, PDF software);*

- *The electronic display of medical device data (e.g., Computer Monitor, Big screen display);*

- *Networks used to maintain medical devices to see which systems are running or malfunctioning, or other similar uses that do not meet the definition of medical device under 201(h) of the FD&C Act;*

- *Standard IT software that is not specifically sold by the manufacturer as a MDDS, which may have MDDS functionality such as reading serial numbers, barcodes, UDI or other data from a medical device, but is not used in providing patient care; and,*

- *Off the shelf passive network sniffing software that is generally used to monitor any network performance by reading TCP/IP packets on a network if this software is not intended to connect directly to a medical device."*

Recently, the FDA decided to reduce its oversight of MDDS:[81]

"The FDA says the following devices would be exempt from regulatory compliance:

MDDS subject to 21 CFR 880.6310,

Medical image storage devices subject to 21 CFR 892.2010, and Medical image communications devices subject to 21 CFR 892.2020.

If a device fits into any of the above classifications, the agency says it does not intend to enforce compliance with regulatory controls, including registration and listing, premarket review, postmarket reporting, and quality system regulation for manufacturers…"

In Feburary 2015, the FDA issued its final guidance regarding MDDS.[82] This guidance is applied to MDDS, which are not intended to alter the function of patient care devices. The intended use of the MDDS must adhere to the following:

- *"Facilitate electronic transfer or exchange of medical device data;*

- *Store and retrieve medical device information…;*

- *Convert medical device data from one format to another; and,*

- *Display medical device information."*

However, regardless of this recent decision, when considering whether any medical device or system must be considered to be regulated hardware and software, the key questions surrounding resolution are intended use and risk.[83] When data from the connected medical devices are to be used for intervention, and/or decision making, or data are transformed, these functions would then fall outside of the MDDS rule and would need to be considered for regulatory filing per either premarket notification (class II) or premarket approval (class III).

The FDA has established three classes of controls governing the development, management, monitoring, marketing, and sale of medical devices. A complete treatment of the subject of MDI software as a medical device is provided both on the FDA's website and in references provided at the end of this book.[84] The general classes of controls are listed next and are covered under Title 21 of the Code of Federal Regulations (CFR) Part 820.

- Class I: general controls
- Class II: special controls
- Class III: pre-market approval

Classification of a medical device into one of these three categories does, to a large degree, depend on the risks and the potential to cause harm. The degree of harm that may result, along with the likelihood of the event that can cause the harm, together provide a measure of where on the scale in terms of general controls, special controls, and pre-market approval the system may fall. The risk-likelihood assessment weighs the likelihood of an event in the range from improbable to frequent along the vertical axis. On the horizontal axes, the risk of harm ranges from negligible to catastrophic (e.g., death).[85] A graphic depicting this relationship is shown in Figure 7-1. The risk likelihood-severity matrix can have multiple applications and can be used as a tool by the enterprise to assess risk and hazards. Typically, values of assigned severity and likelihood are discretized such that anything exceeding low risk requires risk mitigation steps, which can involve developmental, procedural, educational, or other changes.

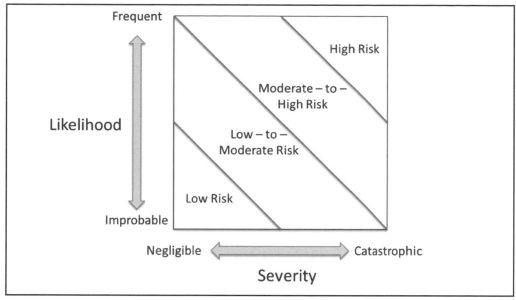

Figure 7-1: Likelihood-Severity Matrix to Derive Medical Device Risks and Hazards.

(Adapted from original reference)[86]

In the MDI solution space, examples of where a reevaluation of risks would be appropriate for the healthcare enterprise involve new applications of the MDI system and an assessment of the potential hazards and impact in terms of potential harm to a patient or an end user.

The FDA has identified on its website an MDDS rule.[87] Relative to possible risks associated with an MDDS , the FDA states:

> "Risks associated with MDDS include the potential for inaccurate, incomplete, or untimely data transfer, storage, conversion, or display of medical device data. In some cases, this can lead to incorrect patient diagnosis or treatment. Based on evaluation of these risks, the FDA has determined that general controls such as the Quality System Regulation (21 CFR part 820), will provide a reasonable assurance of safety and effectiveness. Therefore, special controls and premarket approval are not necessary."

Risk analysis and hazard assessment approaches have been codified, and a recommended approach is captured within the ISO 14971 standard.[88] Hazard mitigation tools as described in the ISO 14971 and elsewhere[89,90] provide a model for identifying potential hazards and risks, their relative importance and impact on patients and users, approaches for mitigation to reduce their impact, and verification of the mitigation techniques applied. The process of identifying, assessing, and improving risk follows a verification process similar to that of requirements analysis and verification of system performance against requirements, as described below. The basic process, as identified in ISO14 971:2009, involves assessing severity of an event versus probability of occurrence, as defined in Table 7-1.

Table 7-1: Hazard Severity versus Probability of Occurrence. Hazard = Severity x Probability of Occurrence.

		Severity				
		1-Negligible (no significant risk)	2-Minor (potential for minor injury)	3-Moderate (potential for moderate injury)	4-Critical (severe injury likely)	5-Catastrophic (death likely)
Probability of Occurrence	5-Frequent (daily or more often)	5	10	15	20	25
	4-Probable (weekly)	4	8	12	16	20
	3-Occasional (monthly)	3	6	9	12	15
	2-Remote (yearly)	2	4	6	8	10
	1-Improbable (once during lifecycle	1	2	3	4	5

Key: Unacceptable Risk: [░░░░░]   Investigate Risk Reduction: [░░░░]   Acceptable Risk: [   ]

Assessments are performed for each identified risk, prior to and post mitigation, with subjective as well as objective assessments made on severity and probability of occurrence (or, actual outcomes if data are available). The hazard assessment is made with the objective being to reduce the impact of each identified hazard to an acceptable risk level.

MEDICAL DEVICE SECURITY

Most medical devices as they exist today were not designed with sophisticated or robust data security infrastructures. Unlike modern operating systems, which can impose user-level authentication and layers of encrypted access, most medical devices do not support this level of sophistication. Access to key functions or settings on many medical devices is restricted to nothing more than a simple fixed password. In terms of data security, most medical devices do not provide any means for encrypting or otherwise protecting the data they issue through their serial or network ports. Sometimes MDI solution providers, through their systems, can provide a level of encryption on top of the MDD to ensure that before the data hit the enterprise network, they are protected. In this way no patient-identifying information will be transmitted in the clear on the enterprise network.

Recently, HIMSS, together with the National Electrical Manufacturers Association (NEMA), published Standard HN 1-2013.[91] This document, referred to as MDS^2 or the Manufacturer Disclosure Statement for Medical Device Security, is intended to be a reporting form for medical device manufacturers for use by health provider organizations. The intent:

"...is to supply healthcare providers with important information to assist them in assessing the vulnerability and risks associated with protecting private data transmitted or maintained by medical devices and systems. Because security risk assessment spans an entire organization, this document focuses on only those elements of the security risk assessment process associated with medical devices that maintain or transmit private data..."

The forms accompanying the standard are to be completed by the medical device manufacturer and the content of which will assist provider organizations in assessing potential security risks associated with their online medical device environment vis-a-vis the enterprise health IT system. This form offers provider organizations with an objective measure of assessing security risk during the medical device procurement process and beyond so as to enable quantification and mitigation of risks imposed by disclosure of private information. Specifically, the information concerning medical device manufacturers in their responses to provider organizations include the following:[92]

- The type of data maintained/transmitted medical device
- How data are managed and transmitted by the manufacturer's medical device
- Any available security-related features incorporated natively into the manufacturer's medical device

A copy of the manufacturer worksheet can be downloaded from the NEMA website at http://www.nema.org.

IEC 80001

An increasing number of medical devices communicate with and are becoming embedded within the enterprise networking infrastructure of healthcare enterprises. Due to this fact as it relates to medical device security and vulnerabilities on the enterprise network, an effort was undertaken by ISO and the International Electrotechnical Commission (IEC) to develop a framework around IT systems that communicate with medical devices to address key aspects of data communication, including security, throughput and other requirements unique to medical device data and interaction with enterprise IT networks.

The main standard, *"IEC 80001-1:2010 Application of risk management for IT-networks incorporating Medical Devices – Part 1: roles, responsibilities and activities,"*[93] comprises a set of requirements developed jointly by consensus with members of healthcare provider organizations and medical device manufacturers. The specification, developed in several parts (listed in Table 7-2) provides general requirements surrounding essential properties inclusive of safety, interoperability, and security.

The original IEC document together with four technical information reports (TIRs) are listed in Table 7-2. Documents may be purchased at AAMI at the following site: http://www.aami.org/publications/standards/80001.html.

Table 7-2: Listing of 80001-Related Documents.

ANSI/AAMI/IEC 80001-1:2010	Application of risk management for IT-networks incorporating Medical Devices – Part 1: roles, responsibilities and activities
ANSI/AAMI/IEC TIR 80001-2-1:2012	Application of risk management for IT-networks incorporating medical devices—Part 2-1: Step-by-step risk management of medical IT-networks; Practical application and examples
ANSI/AAMI/IEC TIR 80001-2-2:2012	Application of risk management for IT-networks incorporating medical devices—Part 2-2: Guidance for the communication of medical device security needs, risks and controls
ANSI/AAMI/IEC TIR 80001-2-3:2012	Application of risk management for IT-networks incorporating medical devices—Part 2-3: Guidance for wireless networks
ANSI/AAMI/IEC TIR 80001-2-4:2012	Application of risk management for IT-networks incorporating medical devices—Part 2-4: Application guidance—General implementation guidance

Software Development Methodologies

Software development requires adherence to a disciplined, organized, repeatable and independently verifiable approach ensuring that products deployed for use with patients have been demonstrated to minimize hazards to both patients and clinical end users. Many approaches to software development and managing the software development life cycle (SDLC) have been published and applied over the years. Many forms and approaches to managing software development have, likewise, been published.[94,95,96] There have been both proponents and opponents of the traditional "V" model approach to software development. Focus on different types of project management (e.g., Agile Project Management[97]), which involves more iterative development, has frequently supplanted the more traditional "V" model development processes.

Nonetheless, an example of a model employed by the author for software development, testing and rollout is illustrated in Figure 7-2.

The model provided in Figure 7-2 deviates somewhat from more traditional "V" models that are represented by the "purist" documentation on SDLC. However, the objective in presenting this information here is to expose readers to the concept in the interest of pursuing further independent study. Using the previously presented model, the reader can be walked through from the top left to the top right.

The development of the Mission Requirements Specification and Use Cases is akin to capturing the wishes of the end users and business reasons for engaging in the project. This is intended to be a high-level document that establishes the business case and the problem being solved, the key stakeholder requests (i.e., the objectives of the client or clients) and the reason why the end product needs to be developed or the project needs to be undertaken. A document or artifact accompanies this process exercise from which more detailed requirements are to be developed. For instance, the objective of developing a system to collect and communicate physiologic data from a bedside vital signs monitor for use by nursing staff during regular rounds in medical/surgical environments represents a high-level business objective. The Mission Requirements Specification associated with this would lay out the detailed operational use case(s) to be solved or addressed.

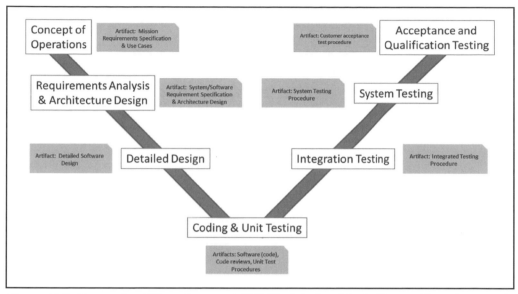

Figure 7-2: Example of Development "V" Model Used in Software Development and Testing.

Subsequent to development of the Mission Requirements Specification and Use Cases, the process of Requirements Analysis is undertaken. Requirements Analysis seeks to decompose the Mission Requirements, Use Cases and Stakeholder Requests into specific and individually measurable and testable requirements. Hence, the specific requirements describing features of the product, as outlined in the Mission Requirements Specification, would be captured in an artifact such as a System/Software Requirement Specification. This specification does not specify the how of the solution, merely the what.

The how of developing the solution begins to be addressed through the creation of the architecture, which focuses on how the product will look once created, at least at a high level. A rendering of the design is captured during this process in an architecture design artifact (Architecture Design Document) and elaborated on down to the software level in a Detailed Software Design Document.

The process of developing the design is normally a highly iterative one, developed through initial elicitation and analysis of the requirements and then refined based on improving and maturing knowledge. The documentation results in a specification that yields the actual software to be coded.

The software development process proceeds, which involves software development, unit testing, creation of unit testing procedures, and validation of the software versus the system and software requirements. The software are developed and evaluated against functional and non-functional (e.g., performance) requirements decomposed from the system-level requirements developed earlier. Adherence to these functional and non-functional requirements is assessed to validate compliance and debug. This is a highly iterative process. Unit testing is normally of the bench variety: testing against canned use cases or simulation, or fixed testing against laboratory-based instrumentation; for example, testing medical device drivers against medical devices in a laboratory environment using simulators or canned settings on the medical devices.

The unit testing is expanded upon through Integration Testing, in which end-to-end evaluations of the software are assessed, still possibly in the laboratory setting, but with all software modules involved in the overall product operating in concert with one another. An example of this is evaluating whether medical device drivers produce the correct data and that these data are correctly translated through several modules comprising the overall product into the correct format.

Integration testing procedures are developed and evaluated, and the resulting artifact(s) document the performance against testing procedures. Non-compliance or failures during testing at this stage can cause the process to revert back to software development for further refinement, unit testing, and then new rounds of integration testing. Once satisfactory performance is achieved through integration testing, integration testing can then evolve into full system testing, exercising all modules, and possibly occurring in a live or near-live environment with outside influences involved. System testing and acceptance and qualification testing may have blurred lines in terms of overlap: System and qualification testing may occur in clinical trials or in a controlled environment at a client site (for instance) and may involve a controlled trial period (a beta, for instance) whereby the performance and operation are monitored with a complete exercising of system functionality performed.

Aberrations or errors are fed back into all of the preceding phases. Yet, most notably, detailed design and coding may need to be revisited to correct logic issues or issues in basic design (e.g., design flaws or flawed logic or both). In some instances, live results may impact the initial assumptions gathered during the mission requirements and the use case development phase of the lifecycle. Hence, subsequent requirements will be impacted, leading to design and development. Examples of areas where basic operational requirements may be impacted involve user interface testing and clinical or end-user workflow. Flaws or issues discovered in workflow assumptions or user interfaces can result in the need for changes that may not have been discovered during initial design and coding. This is another important reason to have the appropriate stakeholders present during the entire development process to ensure feedback along the way.

Testing at each phase seeks to validate written requirements in addition to workflow. A useful tool associated with the design and development phases is to measure the performance in testing against each requirement, through a tool such as a requirements traceability matrix (RTM). The RTM provides a linkage of each decomposed and testable requirement to a specific validation and verification procedure with accompanying results. In this way, every measured requirement (non-functional and functional) that can be quantified has an associated measure through which adherence to compliance can be assessed.

The process of developing a complete RTM can be, admittedly, a tedious and difficult one. Yet, it cannot be overemphasized just how important the measurement of product performance is relative to requirements. This also applies to hazard and risk assessments. That is, hazard analysis and mitigation should be treated as any requirement, with validation and verification applied to show compliance with a risk mitigation approach, as described in the Regulatory Classification and Identification of Risk section of this chapter.

SUMMARY

The MDI solution provider should be familiar with the regulations governing FDA classification and should be able to answer questions regarding:

- Whether their MDI solution has received FDA clearance
- The intended use of their MDI solution
- Whether their level of FDA clearance meets with the intended use cases within the healthcare enterprise

If the MDI solution is cleared as a class II medical device, the MDI solution provider should be able to point to their clearance letter, intended use, and FDA K Number. If the MDI solution in question is cleared based upon premarket notification under 510k approval, a summary of their clearance letter should be available, as well as any corrective action reports or other disciplinary action undertaken based upon noncompliance of the MDI solution or other issues that may have occurred in the past.

The MDI solution providers normally are developing and adapting medical device drivers that allow their systems to communicate with an ever-increasing array of medical devices. The MDI solution provider should be queried as to their approach for creating new medical device drivers and their procedures for rolling out these new drivers with respect to their MDI solutions. Some suggested questions to ask the MDI solution provider:

- Is there a need for an augmented FDA filing with each new medical device driver or is a letter- or memorandum-to-file sufficient?
- What testing is performed to certify upgrades to medical device firmware, when an existing driver may have been developed under a previous version of medical device firmware? (Note: Evaluation of the potential risks of using an older driver with newer medical device firmware is an example application of the Severity-Likelihood matrix derived earlier).
- Given the MDI solution provider is adhering to good manufacturing processes (GMP) associated with the development or modification of the new device driver, what does this translate into in terms of the normal development time for new or upgraded drivers?

Understanding the specific questions that should be asked of an MDI solution provider will aid the healthcare enterprise in assessing the maturity of the product, potential impacts to development timelines, and the rigor or level of adherence to FDA compliance and GMP. This will also facilitate understanding of potential impacts requested changes will have on the MDI solution provider's ability to meet new stakeholder requests, and the potential impact requests may have on the overall rollout and implementation of an MDI solution within the healthcare enterprise. For instance, if the MDI solution provider must develop a certain quantity of medical device drivers to meet the needs of the enterprise in preparation for a new MDI rollout, then this translates into time and the need for proper testing within the healthcare environment. Such development timelines must be accommodated into the overall project schedule or else the likelihood of overrunning that schedule will be highly likely.

Appendix 1:
Medical Device Quantity Planning Table

As an aid in the planning and communication of MDI needs, both internally to the healthcare enterprise and externally to MDI solution providers (perhaps as part of an RFI or RFP), Table A1-1 is included as a planning guide.

Table A1-1 lists the following: hospital department (i.e., specific location for certain medical devices), phase of the project in which the particular MDI deployment is to take place, medical device types to be used and their quantity, a statement as to whether connectivity will be achieved through network or serial protocols, specific medical device brand and model, specific data communication protocols or firmware versions (if available), and a query as to whether the bidding MDI solution provider has a driver for the stated medical device (if not, how long they would estimate to build a driver for the requested unit).

It is worthwhile for the healthcare enterprise (clinical engineering department, principally) to maintain such a table for its own management purposes. Yet, this also provides a clear and succinct summary of the current medical devices contained within the enterprise and their ability to communicate.

Table A1-1: Example MDI Solution Provider Costing and Quantity Planning Tool.

Department	Medical Device Types	Deployment Timeline	Quantities of particular medical devices	Serial or network connectivity? If Serial, Adapter Type?	Device Model (if known)	Current Data Communication Protocol (if known)	MDI Solution Vendor Has Driver?	If Driver Development Required, Estimated Time to Completion
<Unit or department location>	<Types of medical devices used in Department>	<Rollout schedule anticipated or project phase>	<Counts of particular medical devices to be used in this location>	<Type of physical connectivity offered by medical devices>	<Specific brands and models of medical devices>	<Firmware version and/ or specification for data communication, if known>	<Response from MDI solution provider as to capability to communicate with this device>	<If MDI solution provider currently does not possess a medical device driver for this device, what is the time required by the MDI solution provider for medical device driver development>

Appendix 2:
Testing Tools

Healthcare enterprises will no doubt have many testing tools for HL7 communication for their EHR traffic, interface engines and port monitoring that the author has periodically used. While many more tools exist, these have become part of the author's regular toolkit.

EXAMPLES OF HL7 AND NETWORK TESTING TOOLS

HL7 GForge provides a number of tools, schema, documentation, and data publishing for HL7 unsolicited observation results. Gforge is a site within the larger http://www.hl7.org that provides access to a number of resources for those involved in the development, use, testing, and analysis of HL7 messaging transactions.

http://gforge.hl7.org/gf/

QuickViewHL7 and an HL7 message viewer and editor are available through SourceForge.net. As with most tools available through SourceForge, this application is available under the Academic Free License (AFL).

http://sourceforge.net/projects/quickviewhl7/

7Edit is a paid tool that provides for a free download trial run for several weeks. As of this writing, 7Edit Professional costs $249, which provides the ability to browse, compare, validate, create, modify, customize, send and receive HL7 messages via TCP/IP or serial connections. Support for HL7 versions 2.1-2.7.1 is available using this tool. The author has used the professional version and can attest to it, particularly for results and ADT testing. The less expensive "Viewer" version of the tool allows for browsing, comparison, and validation of HL7 messages but does not provide the send/receive functions. The send/receive functions are essential, in this author's opinion, and the ease of use combined with the fairly intuitive user interface make this worth it.

http://www.7edit.com/home/index.php

For those who prefer to build their own application programming interfaces (APIs), the SourceForge Hapi project may be for you. Hapi (pronounced happy) is an open-source HL7 parser for Java.

http://hl7api.sourceforge.net/

Mirth™ Connect provides an interface/integration engine for tailoring HL7 transactions to end-point recipient systems and is a good tool to cut teeth on the use of interface engines. Integration engines provide the means for transforming and translating various types of HL7 transactions from one proprietary format to another, as well as providing the capability to aggregate, monitor, and re-transmit streams of data from a sender to a recipient. There are many different brands of integration engines out in the market (for example, Rhapsody Integration Engine by Orion Health, OpenLink™ by Siemens, and MD Link by MDI Solutions). Mirth Connect is an open source product. However, there is a subscription pricing service for various levels of subscription service, related to both training and support. These levels, from Silver, Gold and Platinum, range in price from $5,000 to $30,000, with the Silver level limited to healthcare providers, only.

   http://www.mirthcorp.com/products/mirth-connect

Wireshark is a network analyzer that allows an end user to capture packet level traffic across an enterprise switch. The tool allows capture of TCP and UDP traffic across a LAN or WAN and features a graphical user interface together with logging and data capture tools. This tool is essential to diagnosing issues in networks and has saved this author on more than one occasion in terms of diagnosing deep and intractable problems that were simply not obvious. The tool also enables capture of network traffic which, particularly for medical devices that only communicate on networks, gives a record of the query/response data available on the network. This tool provides deep details into network data and is the equivalent of the serial port monitor (next) in terms of insight and usability for network protocol analysis.

   http://www.wireshark.org/

Free Serial Port Monitor, from HHD Software, provides a very convenient tool for monitoring query-response through serial ports. The tool installs on multiple platforms, including Windows 7, and provides the capability to intercept queries and responses by sniffing the serial port (or a USB-to-serial mapped port). A convenient transmit-receive console provides a display of what is being sent, as well as what is received. The tool provides a number of features, including logging, configuration export and import, and data time stamping.

   http://www.serial-port-monitor.com/

Appendix 3:
HL7 Testing Simulator

While many excellent tools exist on the market—both paid and freeware/shareware, there is always room for specialty tools that perform very specific functions that fill gaps. Such is the case with the following simulator, which was developed by the author, for the specific purpose of creating medical device traffic from physiologic monitors (e.g., Philips or GE, but can be applied to other brands).

Simulator

The simulator, called simMain, is written in Java due to the author's preference for this language in terms of graphical user interfaces and memory management. The simulator comprises a main class (simMain.java) and a supporting worker class (simulator. java).

Compilation

The simulator is compiled using a standard Java SDK (version 1.8 is downloadable from the Oracle website here: http://www.oracle.com/technetwork/java/javase/downloads/jdk8-downloads-2133151.html).

Once the JDK is installed on target computer and the environment variables for JAVA_HOME, CLASS and BIN are entered, the source files are compiled as follows:

```
Javac simMain.java simulator.java
```
Execution of the resulting class file is accomplished as follows:
```
Java simMain
```

Simulator User Interface

The simulator user interface presents two windows: a management window and a simulator parameter window. These are displayed in Figure A3-1 and Figure A3-2. The simulator uses a default "patient" (fabricated, not pertaining to a real individual).

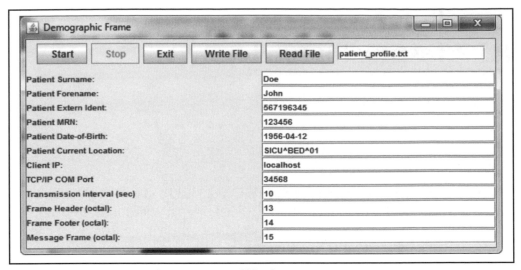

Figure A3-1: Simulator Management Window.

The simulator management window features include Start, Stop and Exit; Write and Read "patient_profile.txt" file; and fields associated with patient demographics. The default values are shown. The operator may create a tailored preference file— "patient_profile.txt"—whose name can be changed as the text field containing the text "patient_profile.txt" is editable. Pressing the Write File button will store the update. Entering a file name into the file name text field and pressing the Read File button will retrieve data from the saved file. Communication port is set to a default of 34568 and the default transmission interval for data is set to 10 seconds.

Select (0/1)	Unified Codes	UOMs	Minimum	Maximum	(I)nt/(D)ec?	(A)periodic/(P)eriodic
1	SpO2||	%	80	100	i	p
1	HR||	/min	40	160	i	p
1	Tblood||	C	34.7	37.0	d	p
1	TV||	l	100.0	1000.0	d	p
1	ABPs||	mmHg	110	160	i	b
1	ABPd||	mmHg	60	100	i	
1	ABPm||	mmHg			i	
1	CO||	l/min	3.0	5.5	d	a
1	CVPm||	mmHg	3.0	5.5	d	p
1	ST-II||	mm	-0.2	0.6	d	p
1	ST-II||	mm	-0.2	1.5	d	p
1	RR||	/min	6.0	35.0	i	p
1	PIP||	cmH2O	0.0	35.0	d	p
1	PEEP||	cmH2O	0.0	15.0	d	p
1	RR-SET||	/min	0.0	10.0	i	p
1	TV-set||	l	0.0	1.0	d	p
1	pH||		7.36	7.44	d	a
1	HCO3||		22	26	i	a
1	NA||	mmol/l	135	137	i	a
1	K||	mmol/l	3.5	5.0	d	a
1	GLU||	mg/dL	70	200	i	a
1	I:E-E||	sec	1.0	3.0	d	p
1	NBPs||	mmHg	120	160	i	b
1	NBPd||	mmHg	100	60	i	
1	NBPm||	mmHg			i	
1	BUN||	mg/dL	8	24	i	a
1	SEVO||	%	1.4	3.3	d	p
1	N2O||	%	10	20	i	p
1	TROP||	ng/ml	0.0	0.1	d	p
1	Hb||	g/dl	11.7	17.4	d	a
1	etCO2||	mmHg	0.0	65.0	d	p
1	Weight||	lb	180.0	180.0	d	p
1	Height||	in	69.0	69.0	d	p

Figure A3-2: Simulator Parameter Window Featuring a Default List of 33 Patient Care Device and Laboratory Parameters for Modeling Patient Measurements.

The key aspect of this window is the use of a formatting typical of HL7 encoding. Parameters are generated using random number generators between minimum and maximum values specified. Operator may change these values prior to launching simulator. Simulated values may be output as integer or decimal (column 6) and values may be periodic or aperiodic. If aperiodic, then values are transmitted with time stamps in the OBX.14 segments.

The Simulator Management Window, as shown in Figure A3-1, provides the features noted in Table A3-1.

Table A3-1: simMain User Interface Features.

Start Button	This initiates the writing of data through the TCP/IP port identified in the **TCP/IP COM Port** field.
Stop Button	Stops the simulation.
Exit Button	Closes the simulation windows and terminates all operation.
Write File	Writes the content of the text fields to a settings file provided in the text field to the right of the **Read File** button. The default name of this settings file profile.txt. However, the user can name the file to be anything and thereby maintain a library of settings files that can be used to run the simulator in parallel on many patients, as desired.
Read File	Reads the settings file created per the **Write File** button.
Profile Name Text Box	Contains the default name of the parameter file. Can be overwritten. In practice, upon first execution, a default profile is displayed. The user can modify the name of the profile and any field within the simulator and save as a new profile by pressing the "Write" button. This new profile can be read at execution time by entering the name of the profile in this text field and pressing the "Read" button.
Patient Surname	Patient last name.
Patient Forename	Patient given name.
Patient Extern Ident	This is an external identifier to be used in the PID.3 field of the HL7 results transaction.
Patient MRN	Patient medical record number, used to augment the external identifier in PID.3 as required depending on the recipient EHR system.
Patient Date-of-Birth	Date-of-birth field for HL7 PID segment.
Patient Current Location	Location per HL7 results transaction PV1 segment.
Client IP	TCP/IP address of recipient client.
TCP/IP COM Port	Communications port for TCP/IP network communication.
Transmission Interval	Time between HL7 transmissions, seconds.
Frame Header, Footer, Message Frame	The octal framing characters as illustrated in chapter 4. Those shown are a default set and can be changed based on the requirements of the receiving client.

The second user interface screen is depicted in Figure A3-2. This interface is tailored to the use of HL7 v2.3. However, this can be changed by modifying the Unified Code entries within the user interface window. The fields displayed on this user interface carry the meanings as defined in Table A3-2.

Table A3-2: Definitions of *simMain* Parameter Display Fields.

Select (0/1)	Unified Codes	UOMs	Minimum	Maximum	(I)nt / (D)ec	(A)periodic/ (P)eriodic
0=do not use this parameter; 1=use this parameter	parameter unified code	parameter unit of measure	Sample values are created using a Gaussian or normally-distributed random variate (i.e., a random number generated from a normally- or uniformly- distributed random number generator) with a mean computed as the average of the Minimum and Maximum value. Each iteration or time a value is transmitted, it is first calculated and then the HL7 transaction is created using the newly created value. If the user does not want any deviation or change in values, the Minimum and Maximum may be set to the same value.		I=transmit as integer; D=transmit as decimal	A=transmit with time stamps indicating the valid time of the measurement (typically in the HL7 and OBX.14 field of the results transaction); P=send periodically every time the HL7 transaction is created and issued.

In operation, the user can create a new profile beyond the existing default that is displayed when first executed by typing a new filename or altering the existing filename within the Profile Name Text Box and then pressing the Write button. This will save the profile to the local directory (e.g., normally the c:\simulators directory). The profile can be read at startup time by entering the name into the Profile Name Text Box and pressing the Read button.

The content of both the simulator Demographic Frame and Parameter Frame may be altered at will prior to executing the simulation, saved as part of a profile, and re-read at any time subsequently. Changes may be made to the Unified Codes and units of measure (UOMs), as well, to match with the requirements for these parameter elements. An example output HL7 message is provided in Table A3-3. Note that the sending application, facility and receiving application, facility are hard-coded. If the user desires, these could be made into fields that are input using an approach similar to the approach for other fields previously discussed.

Table A3-3: Example HL7 Output from Simulator.

```
13MSH|^~\&|src_app|src_fac|rx_app|rx_fac|20150207014713|||ORU^R01|HP1
2966768805249|P|2.3|||||||8859/1
PID|||23456789^123456||Doe^John|||1956-04-12|M
PV1|||I|SICU^BED^01
OBR|||||||20150207014713
OBX||NM|SpO2||80|%|||||F
OBX||NM|HR||73|/min|||||F
OBX||NM|Tblood||35.37|C|||||F
OBX||NM|TV||309.86|l|||||F
OBX||NM|ABPs||136|mmHg|||||F||APERIODIC|20150207014713
OBX||NM|ABPd||71|mmHg|||||F||APERIODIC|20150207014713
OBX||NM|ABPm||92|mmHg|||||F||APERIODIC|20150207014713
OBX||NM|CO||3.62|l/min|||||F
OBX||NM|CVPm||3.01|mmHg|||||F
OBX||NM|ST-II||0.22|mm|||||F
OBX||NM|ST-II||0.61|mm|||||F
OBX||NM|RR||26|/min|||||F
OBX||NM|PIP||26.82|cmH2O|||||F
OBX||NM|PEEP||3.69|cmH2O|||||F
OBX||NM|RR-SET||1|/min|||||F
OBX||NM|TV-set||0.68|l|||||F
OBX||NM|pH||7.43|||||F
OBX||NM|HCO3||24|||||F||APERIODIC|20150207014713
OBX||NM|NA||137|mmol/l|||||F||APERIODIC|20150207014713
OBX||NM|K||3.96|mmol/l|||||F
OBX||NM|GLU||107|mg/dL|||||F||APERIODIC|20150207014713
OBX||NM|I:E-E||2.89|sec|||||F
OBX||NM|NBPs||133|mmHg|||||F||APERIODIC|20150207014713
OBX||NM|NBPd||83|mmHg|||||F||APERIODIC|20150207014713
OBX||NM|NBPm||100|mmHg|||||F||APERIODIC|20150207014713
OBX||NM|BUN||12|mg/dL|||||F||APERIODIC|20150207014713
OBX||NM|SEVO||1.87|%|||||F
OBX||NM|N2O||11|%|||||F
OBX||NM|TROP||0.06|ng/ml|||||F
OBX||NM|Hb||14.04|g/dl|||||F
OBX||NM|etCO2||20.44|mmHg|||||F
OBX||NM|Weight||180|lb|||||F
OBX||NM|Height||69|in|||||F
```

Simulator Preference File Content

The preference file contains the demographic data saved from a selected simulation run plus the particular data associated with that patient (i.e., settings and preferences). An example listing of a saved preferences file is provided in Table A3-4.

Table A3-4: Saved Preferences File ("patient_profile.txt") Containing Simulated Patient Demographic Data and Parameter Settings Data.

Note: File may be updated and read by the simulator.

```
Doe              l/min            d                1
John             3.0             p                BUN||
123456789        5.5             1                mg/dL
123456           d               pH||             8
1956-04-12       a               7.36             24
SICU^BED^01      1               7.44             i
localhost        CVPm||          d                a
11003            mmHg            a                1
5                3.0             1                SEVO||
13               5.5             HCO3||           %
14               d               22               1.4
15               p               26               3.3
1                1               i                d
SpO2||           ST-II||         a                p
%                mm              1                1
80               -0.2            NA||             N2O||
100              0.6             mmol/l           %
i                d               135              10
p                p               137              20
1                1               i                i
HR||             ST-II||         a                p
/min             mm              1                1
40               -0.2            K||              TROP||
160              1.5             mmol/l           ng/ml
i                d               3.5              0.0
p                p               5.0              0.1
1                1               d                d
Tblood||         RR||            a                p
C                /min            1                1
34.7             6.0            GLU||             Hb||
37.0             35.0            mg/dL            g/dl
d                i               70               11.7
p                p               200              17.4
1                1               i                d
TV||             PIP||           a                a
l                cmH2O           1                1
100.0            0.0            I:E-E||          CO∠-EX||
1000.0           35.0            sec              mmHg
d                d               1.0              0.0
p                p               3.0              65.0
1                1               d                d
ABPs||           PEEP||          p                p
mmHg             cmH2O           1                1
110              0.0            NBPs||           Weight||
160              15.0            mmHg             lb
i                d               120              180.0
b                p               160              180.0
1                1               i                d
ABPd||           RR-SET||        b                p
mmHg             /min            1                1
60               0.0            NBPd||           Height||
100              10.0            mmHg             in
i                i               100              69.0
1                p               60               69.0
ABPm||           1               i                d
mmHg             TV-set||        1                p
i                l               NBPm||
1                0.0             mmHg
CO||             1.0             i
```

Source Files

The following source files for the simulator are available through this book's product detail page at www.himss.org/store.

- Source Code Listing for simMain.java.
- Source Code Listing for simulator.java.

References

1. 2012 Medical Device Integration Study. CapSite. http://capsite.com/news/press-releases/54-of-u-s-hospitals-plan-to-purchase-new-medical-device-integration-mdi-solutions/. Accessed Feb 2015.

2. JR Zaleski. Medical device integration: an implementation perspective successfully integrating data from medical devices into existing electronic health record systems requires close collaboration with vendors and informed decision-making. 24X7 Mag. http://24x7.com. Accessed Jul 2013. p. 16-18.

3. Quantifying the business value of medical device connectivity. Black Box SME. Black Box SME. Mesa Arizona. p. 1.

4. Ibid. p. 4.

5. AAMI White Paper 2012: Medical Device Interoperability. © The Association for the Advancement of Medical Instrumentation (AAMI). 4301 N. Fairfax Drive, Suite 301; Arlington, VA 22203-1633. p. 6.

6. JR Zaleski. Integrating Device Data into the Electronic Medical Record: A Developer's Guide to Design and Practitioner's Guide to Application. Publicis KommunikationsAgentur GmbH, GWA, Erlangen; 2009: pp 235-275.

7. West Health Institute. The value of medical device interoperability. http://www.westhealth.org. Mar 2013.

8. K Terry. Medical device integration software surges in hospitals. InformationWeek Healthcare. http://www.informationweek.com/healthcare/electronic-medical-records/medical-device-integration-software-surg/240005592. Accessed Aug 15, 2012.

9. G Perna. Hospitals looking at EHR integration. Healthc Inform. http://www.healthcare-informatics.com/news-item/report-hospitals-looking-ehr-integration. Accessed Aug 9, 2012.

10. AAMI White Paper 2012: Medical Device Interoperability: A Safer Path Forward. Priority Issues from the AAMI-FDA Interoperability Summit. © 2012 AAMI. p 3

11. Ibid. p. 3.

12. Ibid. p. 41.

13. http://www.fda.gov/MedicalDevices/DeviceRegulationandGuidance/PostmarketRequirements/QualitySystemsRegulations/Accessed Dec 2014.

14. http://www.klasresearch.com/segment/193. Accessed Dec 2014.

15. KLAS Research, http://www.klasresearch.com/segment/193. Accessed Feb 6, 2015.

16. The ECRI Institute, https://www.ecri.org/topics/pages/TopicLanding.aspx?k=*&Page=3&PageSize=10&Sort=relevance&mo=false&rf=ECRItopics:equals(%27Medical%20Device%20Integration%27)&topicid=634b31d69a01476888b109186225ca2e. Accessed Feb 6, 2015.

17. UL 60601-1: Medical Electrical Equipment, Part 1: General Requirements for Safety. http://ulstandards.ul.com/standard/?id=60601-1&edition=1&doctype=uliec. Accessed Dec 2014.

18. Examples are the Puritan Bennett™ 7200 and 7200ae mechanical ventilators and the much later Puritan Bennett™ 840 mechanical ventilator, use a similar proprietary query communication language to facilitate data retrieval from the mechanical ventilators.

19. JR Zaleski, Medical Device Connectivity. IEEE Smart Tech. Baltimore Metro Area Workshop. Baltimore, MD; Nov 3, 2012. pp. 30-34.

20. HL7 Parameter Data Interface Programmer's Guide. Philips Healthcare. Part Number 4535 641 03281 U.S.A. January 2009 Edition 1. Koninklijke Philips Electronics N.V. p. 1-1.

21. Nuvon HL7 Unified Codes. Version 1.05.27. 14. Oct 2013. Nuvon, Inc.

22. ECG Cards 2nd ed. Springhouse Corporation. Springhouse, Pennsylvania.

23. Normal hemodynamic parameters – adult. Edwards Life Sciences LLC. http://www.edwards.com. Accessed Dec 2014.

24. PL Marino. The ICU Book. 2nd ed. Williams & Wilkins. Baltimore MD;1998. p. 872.

25. Aspect Medical Systems BIS™ Monitor Serial Port Technical Specification. Covidien. Aspect Medical Systems, Inc. Norwood, MA;2010. p. B-1.

26. "BIS VISTA™ Monitoring System Bilateral Monitoring Addendum." Aspect Medical Systems, Inc. Aspect Medical Systems International B.V. One Upland Road Rijnzathe 7d2 Norwood, MA 02062 3454 PV De Meern U.S.A. © Copyright, 2010, Aspect Medical Systems, Inc. All rights reserved.

27. 840 Ventilator System Technical Reference (TR). 4-070088-00 Rev F (10/06). P. TR19-1 – TR19-7.

28. Medibus for Drager Intensive Care Devices. Instructions for Use. 13th ed. 90 28 329 – GA 5664.380 en. Dräger Medical AG & Co. Jul 2008.

29. K Deden. Ventilation modes in intensive care. Dragerwerk AG & Co. KGaA; Moislinger Allee 53-55; 23558 Lubeck, Germany. © 2010 Drägerwerk AG & Co. KGaA .

30. 840 Ventilator System Operator's and Technical Reference Manual. Part No. 4-075609-00 Rev. G. TR19-1-TR19-7. Oct 2006.

31. "Evita® XL Intensive Care Ventilator. Software 6.n Instructions for Use." Dräger Medical AG & Co. 1st ed. Jul 2004. p. 8.

32. Puritan Bennett™ 840 Ventilator Pocket Guide. p. 46. Bi-level is a trademark of Covidien Puritan Bennett™. ©2008, 2011 Covidien.

33. RL Chatburn. Fundamentals of Mechanical Ventilation: A short course in the theory and application of mechanical ventilators. Mandu Press Ltd. Cleveland Height, OH; 2003.

34. Integrating the Healthcare Enterprise® IHE Patient Care Device (PCD) Technical Framework Volume 1 (PCD TF-1): Integration Profiles. Revision 3.0 – Final Text; Oct 11, 2013. 2013: IHE International, Inc. p. 17-18.

35. Integrating the Healthcare Enterprise® IHE Patient Care Device (PCD) Technical framework Volume 2 (PCDTF-2): Transactions. Revision 3.0 – Final Text; Oct 11, 2013. 2013: IHE International, Inc. pp. 33, 34, 35, 69, 120.

36. D Tandet. Focus on: advances in smart pump interoperability. 24x7 Mag. http://www.24x7mag. com/2014/03/advances-in-smart-pump-interoperability/. Accessed Mar 4, 2014.

37. AAMI White Paper 2012: Medical Device Interoperability: A Safer Path Forward. Priority Issues from the AAMI-FDA Interoperability Summit. © 2012 AAMI. p. 12-13.

38. JM Rodriques, Kumar A, Bousquet C, Trombert B Using the CEN/ISO Standard for Categorical Structure to Harmonise the Development of WHO International Terminologies. Medical Informatics in a United and Healthy Europe. KP Adlassnig, et al. (eds.) IOS Press; 2009. p. 255.

39. http://www.nlm.nih.gov/research/umls/Snomed/snomed_main.html. Accessed Dec 2014.

40. Adapted from R Richards, Rafael, JR Zaleski, S Peesapati. Liberating medical device data for clinical research: An architecture for semantic and temporal harmonization. 2nd Annual IEEE-AMA Conference. Boston, MA; Oct 16, 2011.

41. http://wiki.ihe.net/index.php?title=Consistent_Time. Accessed Feb 2015.

42. M McNickle. 5 reasons medical device data is vital to the success of EHRs. Healthcare IT News. Jan 5, 2012.

43. V Kelly. U.S. Federal Government recognizes IEEE 11073™ Standards for medical device communication: twelve IEEE standards recommended by the Food and Drug Administration for supporting medical-device interoperability and cyber security. IEEE Standards Association. http://standards.ieee.org/news/2013/ieee_11073_medical-device_communication.html. Accessed Nov 12, 2013.

44. http://www.hl7.org/about/index.cfm?ref=nav. Accessed Dec 2014.

45. Vivian Kelly, "U.S. Federal Government Recognizes IEEE 11073™ Standards for Medical-Device Communication." IEEE Standards Association. Nov 12, 2013.

46. M Clarke. Developing a Standard for Personal Health Devices based on 11073. eHealth Beyond the Horizon—Get It There. K Andersen, et al. (eds.). IOS Press. Organizing Committee of MIE; 2008.

47. http://www.hl7.org. Accessed Dec 2014. http://www.hl7.org. Accessed Dec 2014.

48. http://www.hl7.org/implement/standards/product_brief.cfm?product_id=185. Accessed Feb 2015

49. Health Level Seven. Version 2.6. Final Standard. p. 7-11. Oct 2007.

50. Intellivue Information Center HL7 Parameter Data Interface Programmer's Guide. Philips. Part Number 4535 641 03281. USA; Jan 2009. p. 30.

51. Health Level Seven. Version 2.6. Final Standard. p. 7-60. Oct 2007.

52. Health Level Seven. Version 2.6. Chapter 3: Patient Administration. Oct 2007. p. 3-1-3-2.

53. http://www.hl7.org/implement/standards/fhir/. Accessed Dec 2014.

54. http://wiki.ihe.net/index.php?title=Main_Page. Accessed Dec 2014.

55. http://www.ihe.net/technical_frameworks/#pcd. Accessed Dec 2014.

56. Integrating the Healthcare Enterprise IHE Patient Care Device Technical Framework. Volume 1 PCD TF-1: Integration Profiles. Revision 3.0 – Final Text. Oct 11, 2013. p. 7. IHE International, Inc.

57. Ibid. p.10.

58. Ibid. p.11.

59. IHE Patient Care Device Technical Framework—Volume 2; PCD TF-2: Transactions. Revision 3.0 – Final Text. Oct 11, 2013. P. 10. IHE International, Inc.

60. Ibid. p.13.

61. Ibid p. 94.

62. Health Level Seven. Version 2.6. 2007. p. 7-39.

63. IHE Patient Care Device Technical Framework—Volume 2; Revision 1.2. IHE International, Inc., Sept30, 2010. P. 55.

64. IHE Patient Care Device Technical Framework—Volume 2; PCD TF-2: Transactions. Revision 3.0 – Final Text. Oct 11, 2013. p. 64. IHE International, Inc.

65. http://www.pchalliance.org/about-pcha. Accessed Feb 2015.

66. http://www.aami.org/news/2013/020613_AAMI_Seeks_Volunteers.html. Accessed Dec 2014.

67. AAMI White Paper 2012: Medical Device Interoperability. © 2012 Association for the Advancement of Medical Instrumentation in AAMI MDI/ 2012-03-30. Association for the Advancement of Medical Instrumentation 4301 N. Fairfax Drive, Suite 301 Arlington, VA 22203-1633 www.aami.org. p. 23.

68. National Heart, Lung, and Blood Institute. How is a heart attack diagnosed? http://www.nhlbi.nih.gov/health/health-topics/topics/heartattack/diagnosis.html. Accessed Dec 2014.

69. Intellivue Information Center HL7 Parameter Data Interface Programmer's Guide. Part Number 4535 641 03281. U.S.A.; Jan 2009. p. 2-17.

70. A Rea-Neto, A, Youssef NC, Tuche F, et al. Diagnosis of ventilator-associated pneumonia: a systematic review of the literature. Crit Care. 2008,12:R56.

71. AR Mato, Fuchs BD, Heitjan DF, et al. Utility of the systemic inflammatory response syndrome (SIRS) criteria in predicting the onset of septic shock in hospitalized patients with hematologic malignancies. Cancer Biol Ther. 2009;8:12,1095-1100.

72. KD Fairchild, MT O'Shea. Heart Rate Characteristics: Physiomarkers for Detection of Late-Onset Neonatal Sepsis. Clin. Perinatol. 2010; 37(3):581-598.

73. Mato, Anthony R. et al. Utility of the systemic inflammatory response syndrome (SIRS) criteria in predicting the onset of septic shock in hospitalized patients with hematologic malignancies. Cancer Biology & Therapy 8:12, 1095-1100; Jun 15, 2009.

74. Patient Identification. Patient Safety Solutions. Volume 1. Solution 2. May 2007.

75. MJ Gozdan. Patient safety: using technology to reduce medication errors. Nursing. 2009;39,6:57-58.

76. John R. Zaleski, Integrating Device Data into the Electronic Medical Record: A Developer's Guide to Design and a Practitioner's Guide to Application. Publicis Publishing, Erlangen. 2009. p. 122.

77. Medical Device Data Systems. http://www.fda.gov/MedicalDevices/ProductsandMedicalProcedures/GeneralHospitalDevicesandSupplies/MedicalDeviceDataSystems/default.htm. Accessed Dec 2014.

78. Identifying an MDDS. http://www.fda.gov/MedicalDevices/ProductsandMedicalProcedures/GeneralHospitalDevicesandSupplies/MedicalDeviceDataSystems/ucm251906.htm. Accessed Dec 2014.

79. FDA finalizes regulation for certain software, hardware used with medical devices. FDA News Release. Feb 14, 2011.

80. Federal Register. Volume 76, No. 31 / Feb 15, 2011. Rules and Regulations; pp. 8637-8649.

81. N Otto. FDA cuts its oversight of medical device data systems. MED Device Online. Accessed Jun 25, 2014.

82. FDA Easing Oversight of Medical Device Data Systems, mHealth. iHealthbeat, Monday Feb 9, 2015.

83. Premarket Notification (510k). http://www.fda.gov/MedicalDevices/DeviceRegulationandGuidance/HowtoMarketYourDevice/PremarketSubmissions/PremarketNotification510k. Accessed Dec 2014.

84. JR Zaleski. Integrating Medical Device Data into the Electronic Medical Record: A Developer's Guide to Design and a Practitioner's Guide to Application. Publicis Publishing, Erlangen. 2009. p. 196-208.

85. Ibid. p. 207-208.

86. Ibid. p. 208.

87. http://www.fda.gov/medicaldevices/productsandmedicalprocedures/generalhospitaldevicesandsupplies/medicaldevicedatasystems/ucm251897.htm. Accessed Feb 2015.

88. ISO 14971:2007. Medical Devices—Application of Risk Management to Medical Devices. (Geneva: International Organization for Standardization, 2007).

89. N Youssef, WA Hyman. Analysis of risk: are current methods theoretically sound? Medical Device and Diagnostic Industry. 2009;3,10:38–46.

90. Risk analysis: beyond probability and severity. Medical Device and Diagnostic Industry. http://www.mddionline.com/article/risk-analysis-beyond-probability-and-severity. Published Aug 5, 2010. Accessed Feb, 2015.

91. National Electrical Manufacturers Association, MDS2. Rosslyn, Virginia 22209. www.nema.org. Accessed Dec 2014.

92. Ibid. p. 1.

93. http://www.iso.org/iso/catalogue_detail.htm?csnumber=44863. Accessed Feb 2015.

94. http://www.tutorialspoint.com/sdlc/sdlc_v_model.htm. Accessed Dec 2014.

95. R Kay. QuickStudy: system development life cycle. ComputerWorld. May 14, 2002. http://www.computerworld.com/s/article/71151/System_Development_Life_Cycle. Accessed Dec 2014.

96. M Habib. Agile software development methodologies and how to apply them. Code Project. Dec 30, 2013. http://www.codeproject.com/Articles/604417/Agile-software-development-methodologies-and-how-to Accessed Feb 2015.

97. Project Management Institute http://www.pmi.org/Certification/New-PMI-Agile-Certification/PMI-Agile-Toolbox.aspx Accessed Feb 2015.

Index